AST TOUR

5

TSUKUMIZU

GIRLS' LAST TOUR

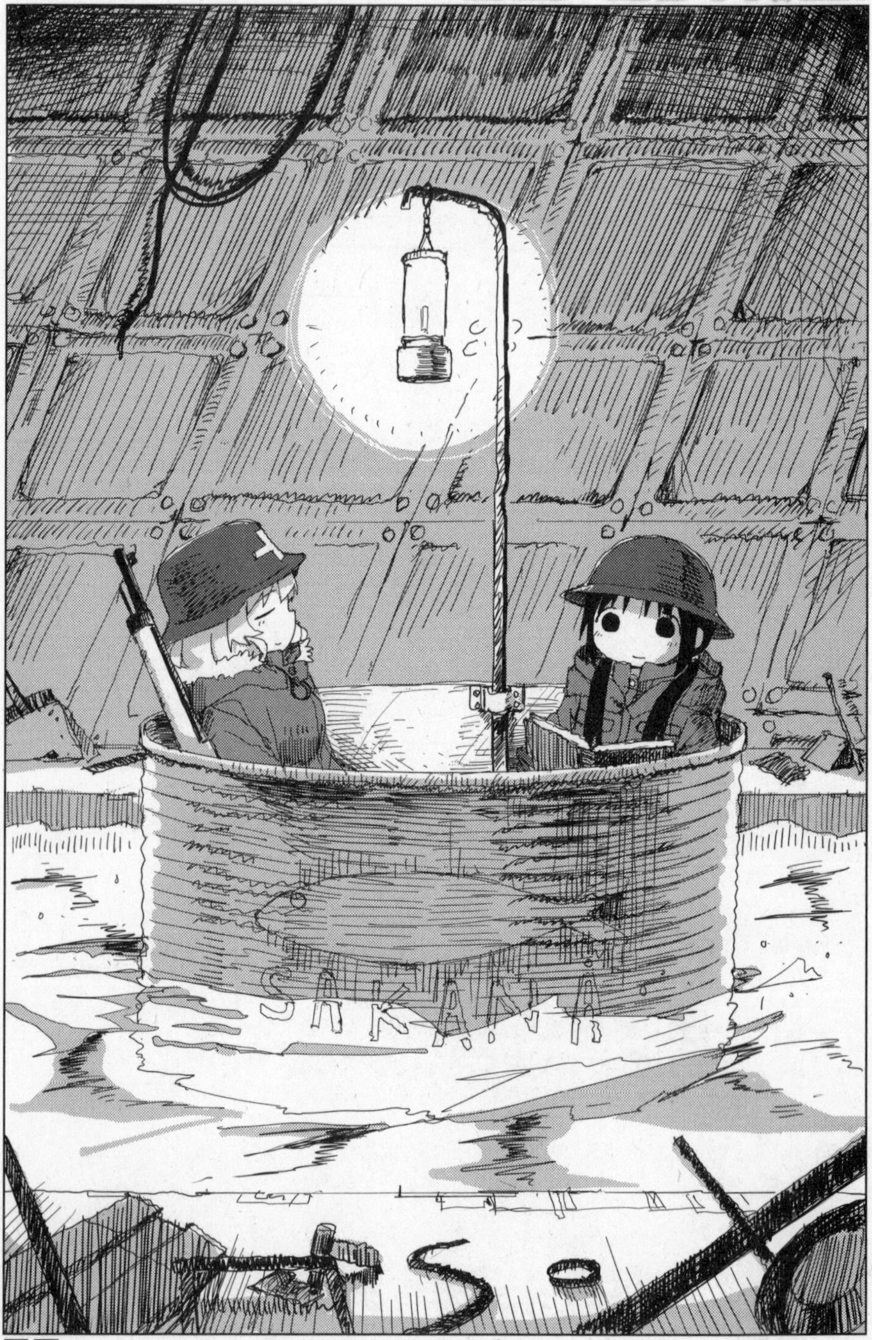
SAKANA

33 WATERWAY

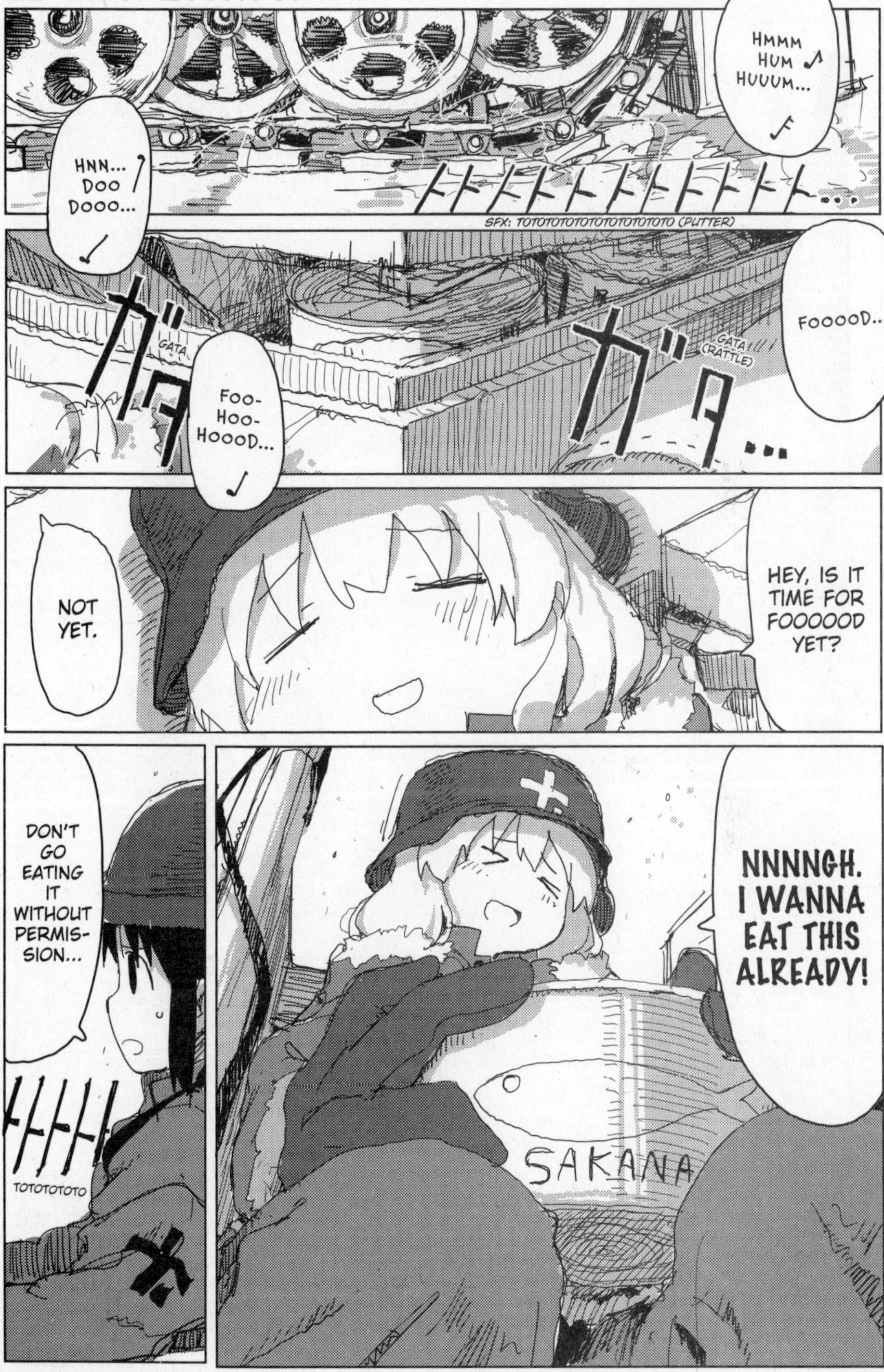
HMMM HUM HUUUM...
HNN... DOO DOOO...
SFX: TOTOTOTOTOTOTOTOTOTOTOTO (PUTTER)
FOOOOD...
GATA (RATTLE)
FOO-HOO-HOOOD...
GATA
HEY, IS IT TIME FOR FOOOOOD YET?
NOT YET.
NNNNGH. I WANNA EAT THIS ALREADY!
SAKANA
DON'T GO EATING IT WITHOUT PERMIS-SION...
TOTOTOTOTO

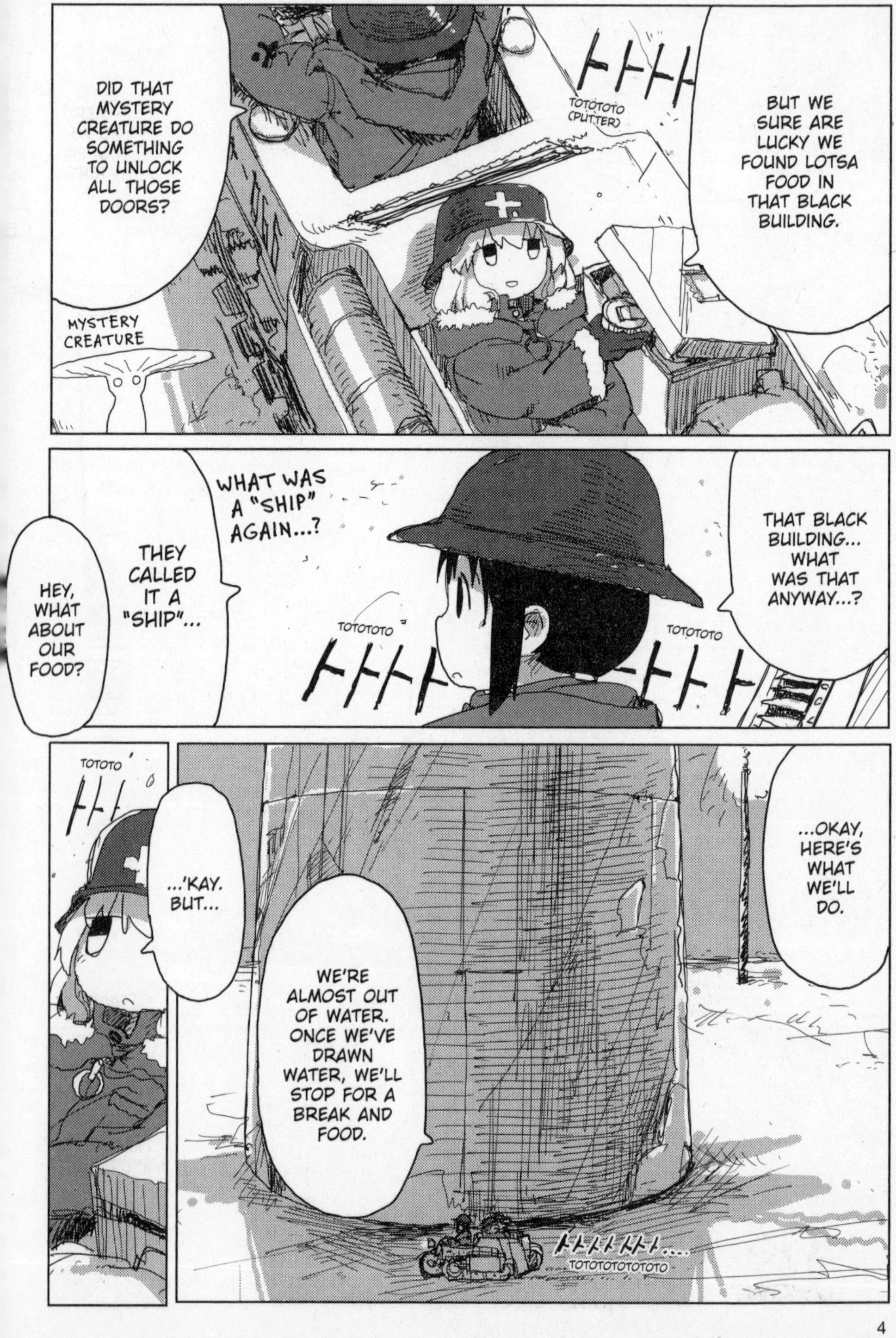
BUT WE SURE ARE LUCKY WE FOUND LOTSA FOOD IN THAT BLACK BUILDING.
TOTOTOTO (PUTTER)
DID THAT MYSTERY CREATURE DO SOMETHING TO UNLOCK ALL THOSE DOORS?
MYSTERY CREATURE
THAT BLACK BUILDING... WHAT WAS THAT ANYWAY...?
TOTOTOTO
WHAT WAS A "SHIP" AGAIN...?
THEY CALLED IT A "SHIP"...
TOTOTOTO
HEY, WHAT ABOUT OUR FOOD?
...OKAY, HERE'S WHAT WE'LL DO.
WE'RE ALMOST OUT OF WATER. ONCE WE'VE DRAWN WATER, WE'LL STOP FOR A BREAK AND FOOD.
TOTOTOTOTOTOTO
TOTOTO
...'KAY. BUT...

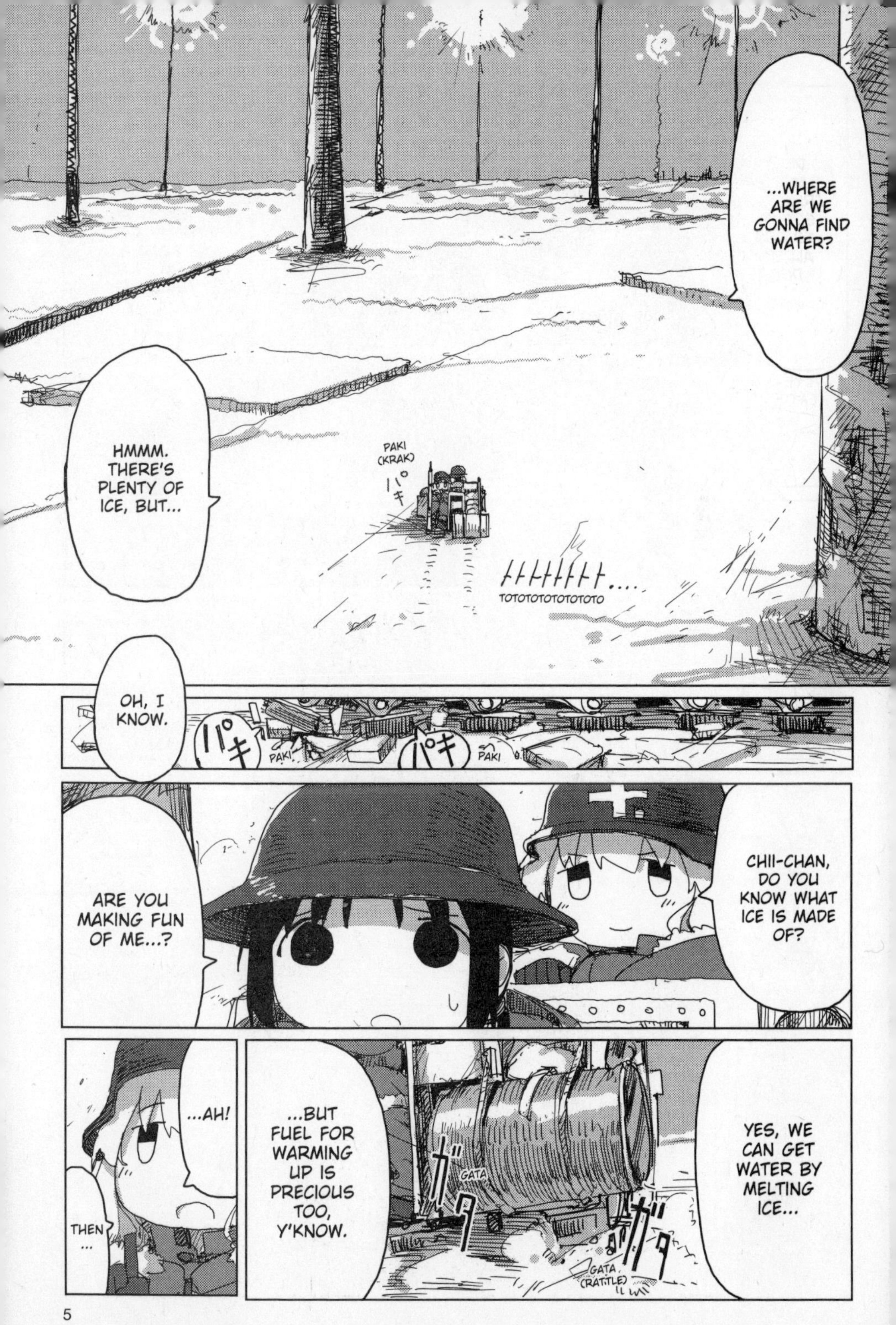
...WHERE ARE WE GONNA FIND WATER?
HMMM. THERE'S PLENTY OF ICE, BUT...
PAKI (KRAK)
パキ
TOTOTOTOTOTOTOTO
OH, I KNOW.
パキ
PAKI
パキ
PAKI
CHII-CHAN, DO YOU KNOW WHAT ICE IS MADE OF?
ARE YOU MAKING FUN OF ME...?
YES, WE CAN GET WATER BY MELTING ICE...
ガタ
GATA (CRATTLE)
ガタ
GATA
...BUT FUEL FOR WARMING UP IS PRECIOUS TOO, Y'KNOW.
...AH!
THEN ...

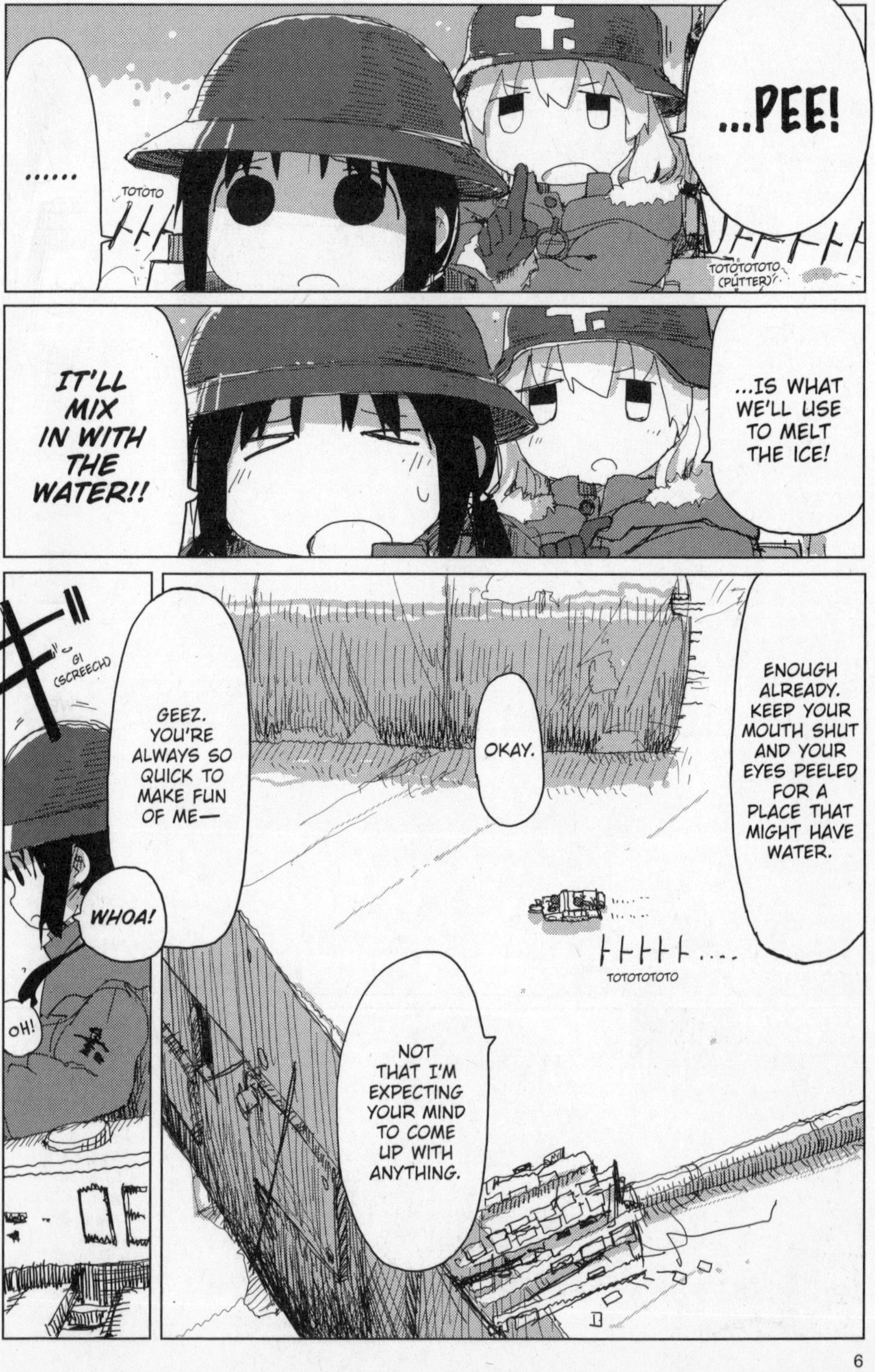
...PEE!
TOTOTOTOTO (PUTTER)
......
TOTOTO
...IS WHAT WE'LL USE TO MELT THE ICE!
IT'LL MIX IN WITH THE WATER!!
ENOUGH ALREADY. KEEP YOUR MOUTH SHUT AND YOUR EYES PEELED FOR A PLACE THAT MIGHT HAVE WATER.
OKAY.
GEEZ. YOU'RE ALWAYS SO QUICK TO MAKE FUN OF ME—
TOTOTOTOTO
NOT THAT I'M EXPECTING YOUR MIND TO COME UP WITH ANYTHING.
GI (SCREECH)
WHOA!
OH!

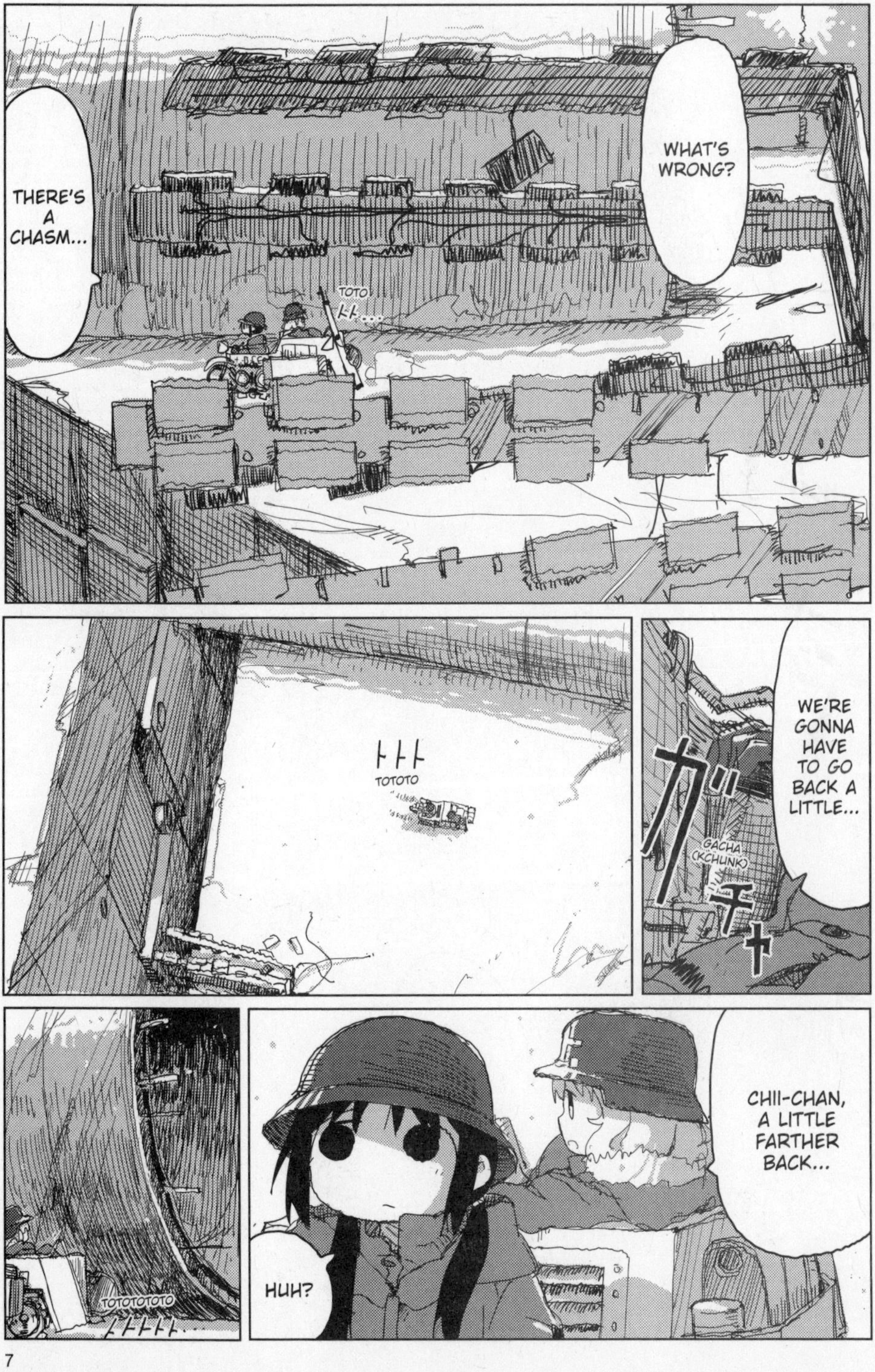
WHAT'S WRONG?
TOTO
ドド…
THERE'S A CHASM...
WE'RE GONNA HAVE TO GO BACK A LITTLE...
ガチャ
GACHA (KCHUNK)
トトト
TOTOTO
CHII-CHAN, A LITTLE FARTHER BACK...
HUH?
TOTOTOTOTO
トトトトト…

COULDN'T WE GO THROUGH THAT TO GET ACROSS?

LOOKS LIKE WE COULD.

TOTOTO
(PUTTER)
トトト...

THERE'S A LITTLE BUMP, BUT IT'S DOABLE...

ガッ

GATTA
(KRRK)

タ

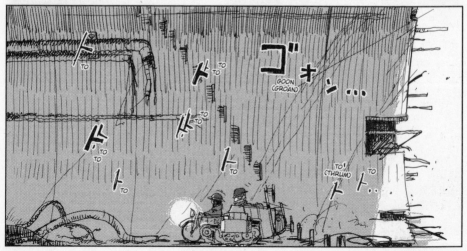

ト
TO

ト
TO
TO

ゴォ゛ン...
GOON
(GROAN)

ト
TO
TO

ト
TO
TO

ト
TO

ト
TO

ト
TO'!
(THRUM)

ト...
TO

8

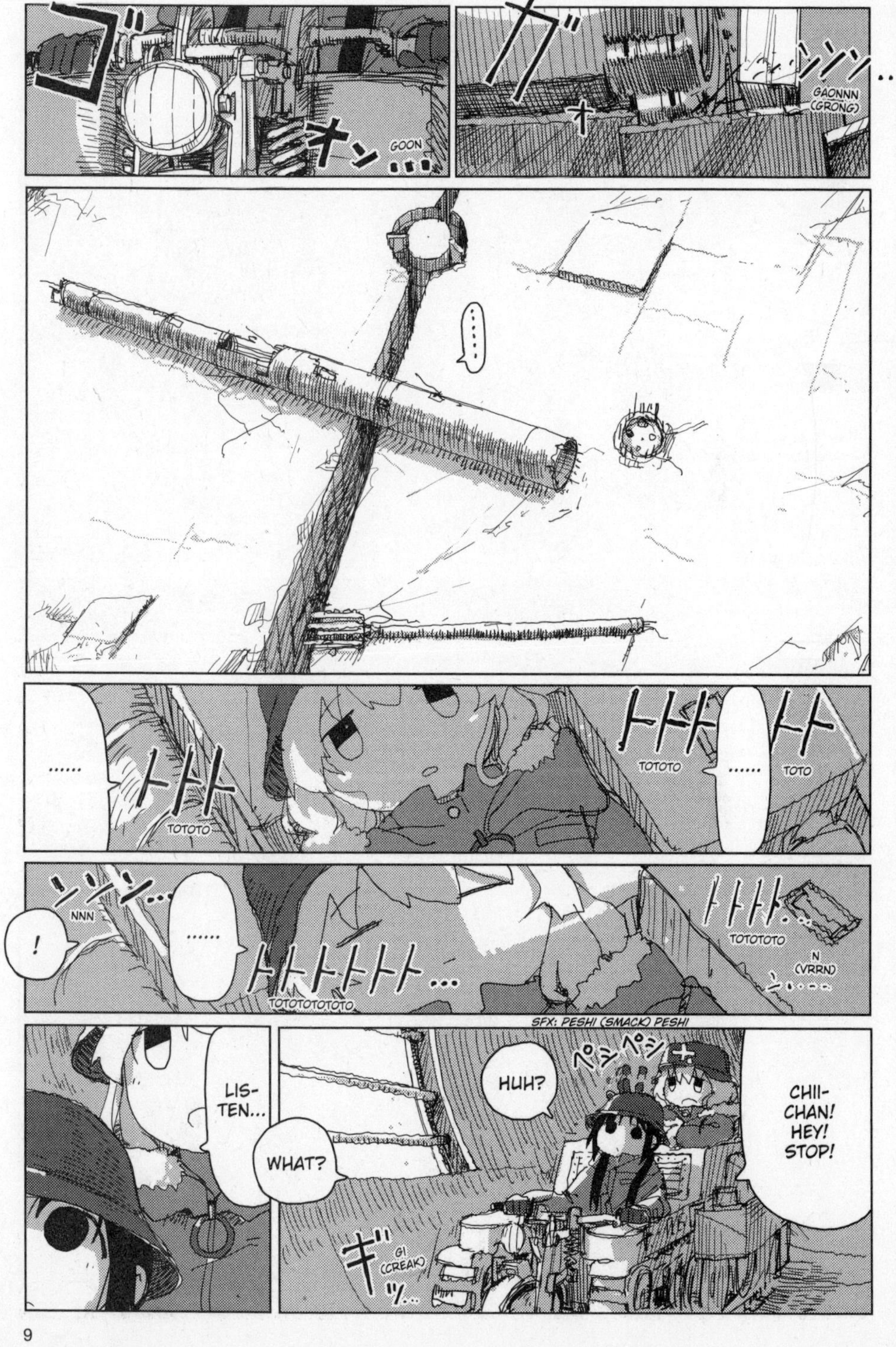
GAONNN (GRONG)
GOON
......
TOTO
......
TOTOTO
......
TOTOTO
N (VRRN)
TOTOTOTO
TOTOTOTOTOTO
......
NNN
!
SFX: PESHI (SMACK) PESHI
CHII-CHAN! HEY! STOP!
HUH?
WHAT?
GI (CREAK)
LIS-TEN...

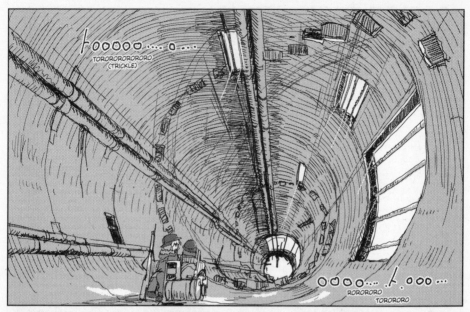

トoooo....。.... TORORORORORORO (TRICKLE)

oooo....卜ooo.... RORORORO TORORORO

IT'S COMING FROM BELOW.

AH.

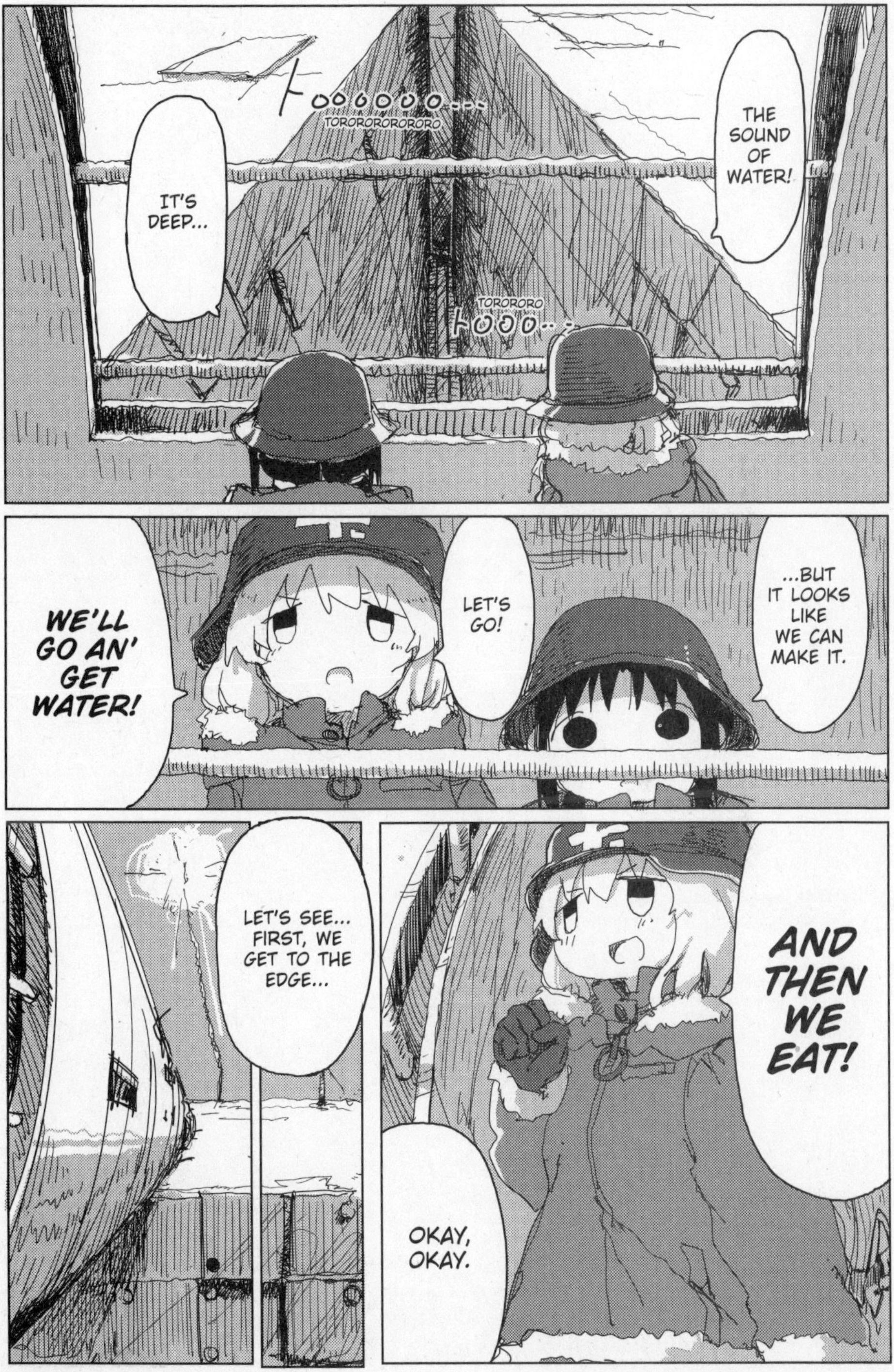
THE SOUND OF WATER!
TORORORORORORO
IT'S DEEP...
TORORORO
...BUT IT LOOKS LIKE WE CAN MAKE IT.
LET'S GO!
WE'LL GO AN' GET WATER!
AND THEN WE EAT!
OKAY, OKAY.
LET'S SEE... FIRST, WE GET TO THE EDGE...

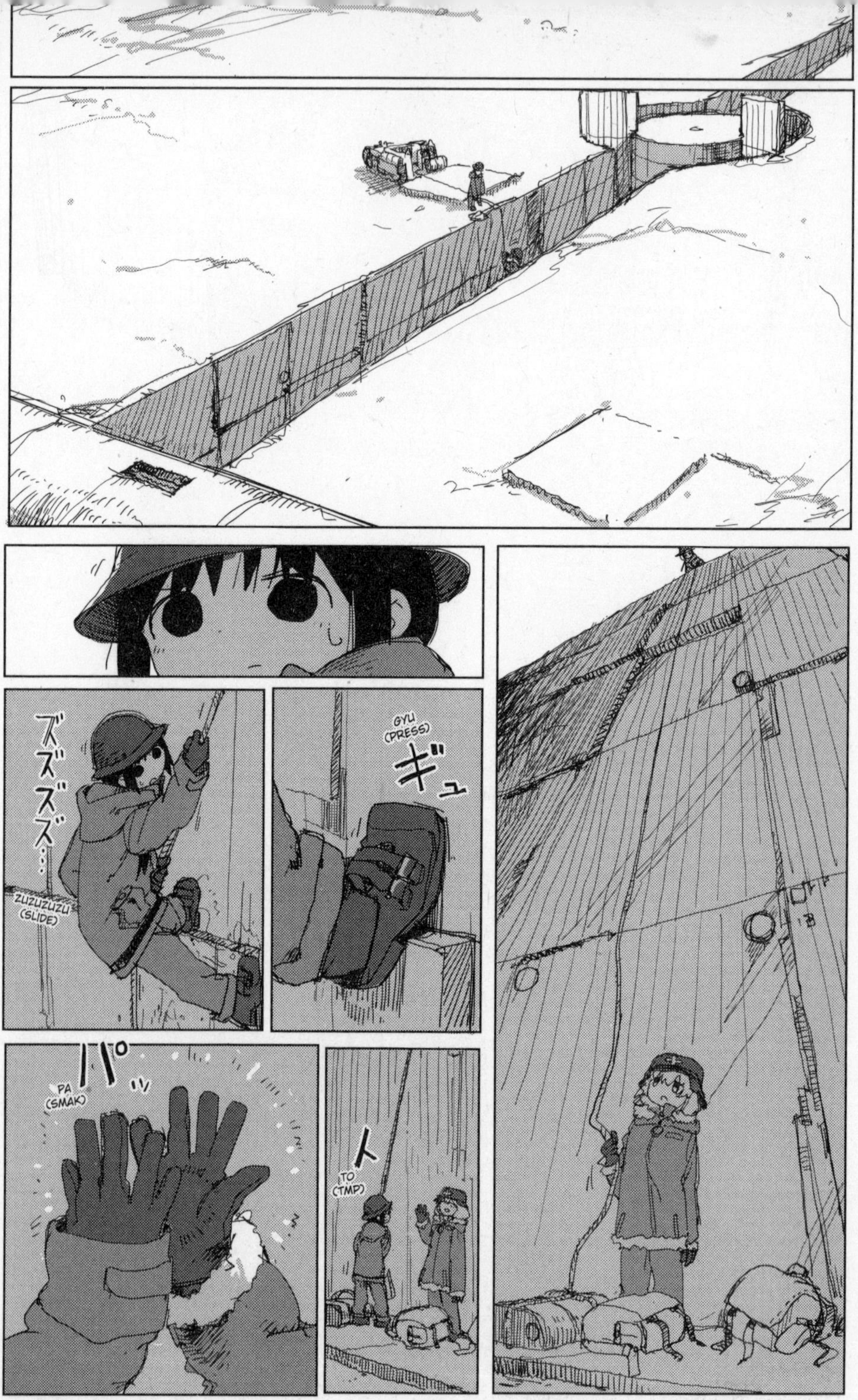
ギュ
GYU (PRESS)
ズズズズ…
ZUZUZUZU (SLIDE)
ト
TO (TMP)
パッ
PA (SMAK)

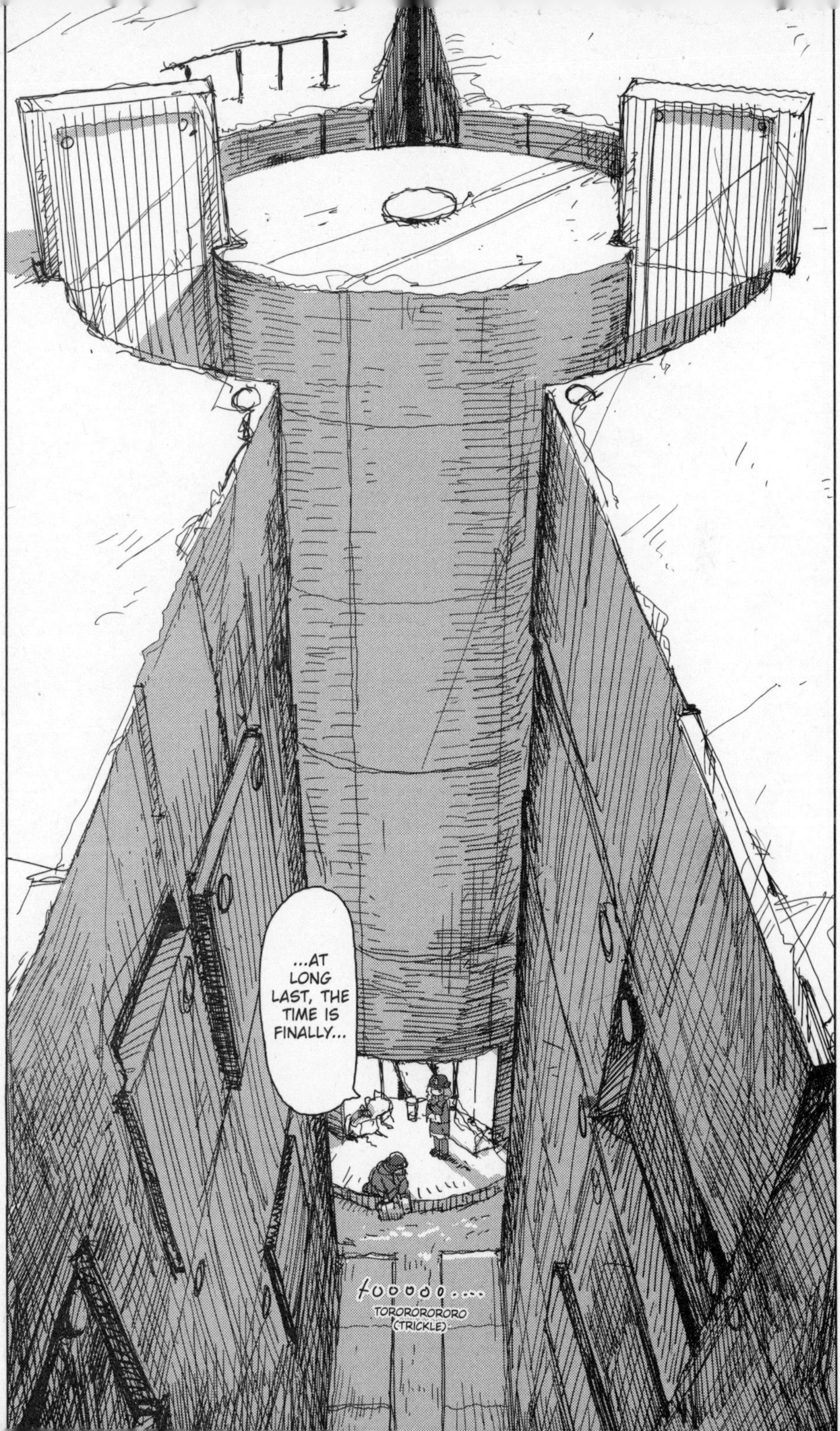
...AT LONG LAST, THE TIME IS FINALLY...
TOROROROROROR (TRICKLE)

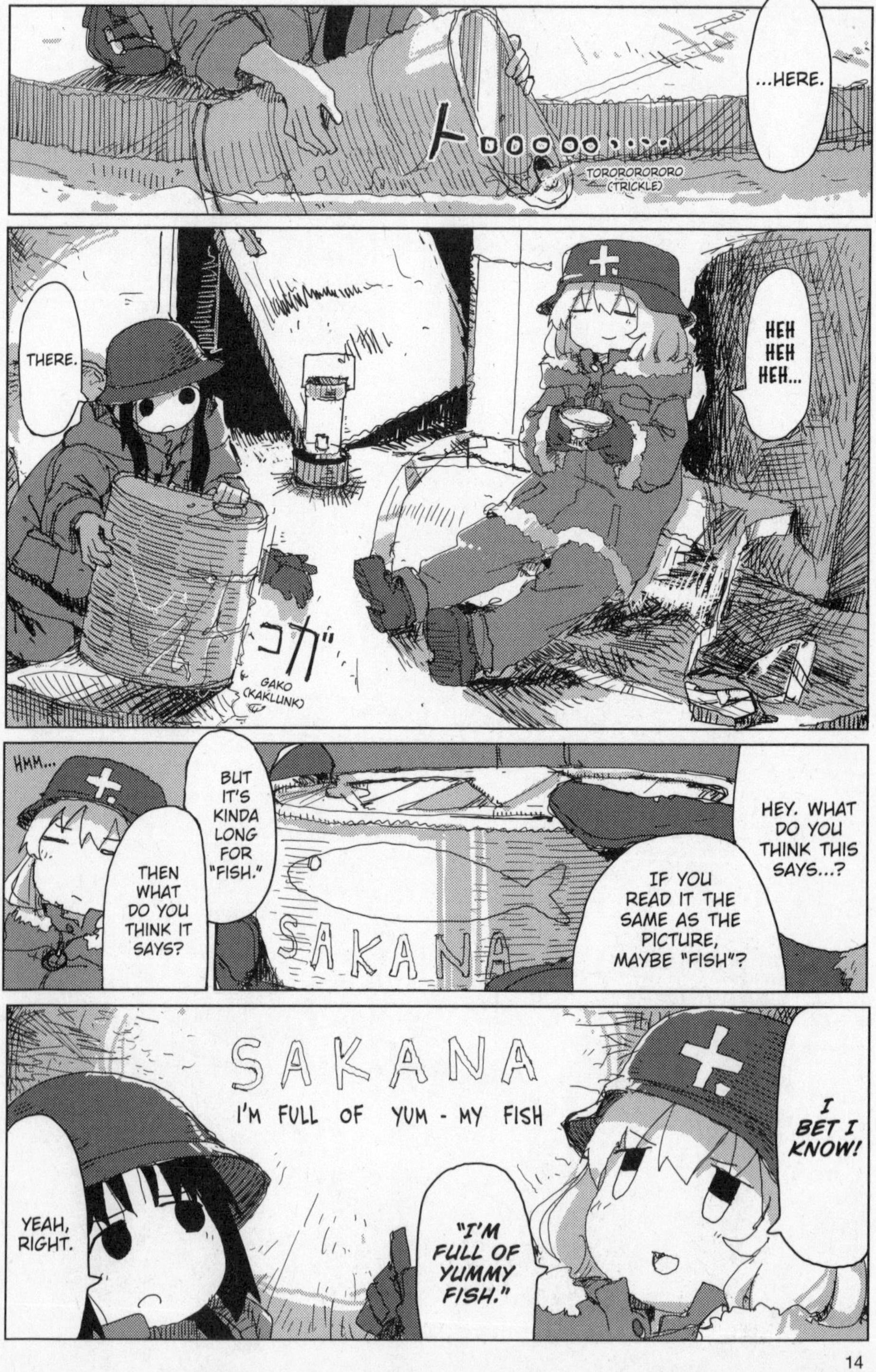
...HERE.
TORORORORORO (TRICKLE)
HEH HEH HEH...
THERE.
GAKO (KAKLUNK)
HEY. WHAT DO YOU THINK THIS SAYS...?
IF YOU READ IT THE SAME AS THE PICTURE, MAYBE "FISH"?
SAKANA
BUT IT'S KINDA LONG FOR "FISH."
THEN WHAT DO YOU THINK IT SAYS?
HMM...
I BET I KNOW!
SAKANA
I'M FULL OF YUM - MY FISH
"I'M FULL OF YUMMY FISH."
YEAH, RIGHT.

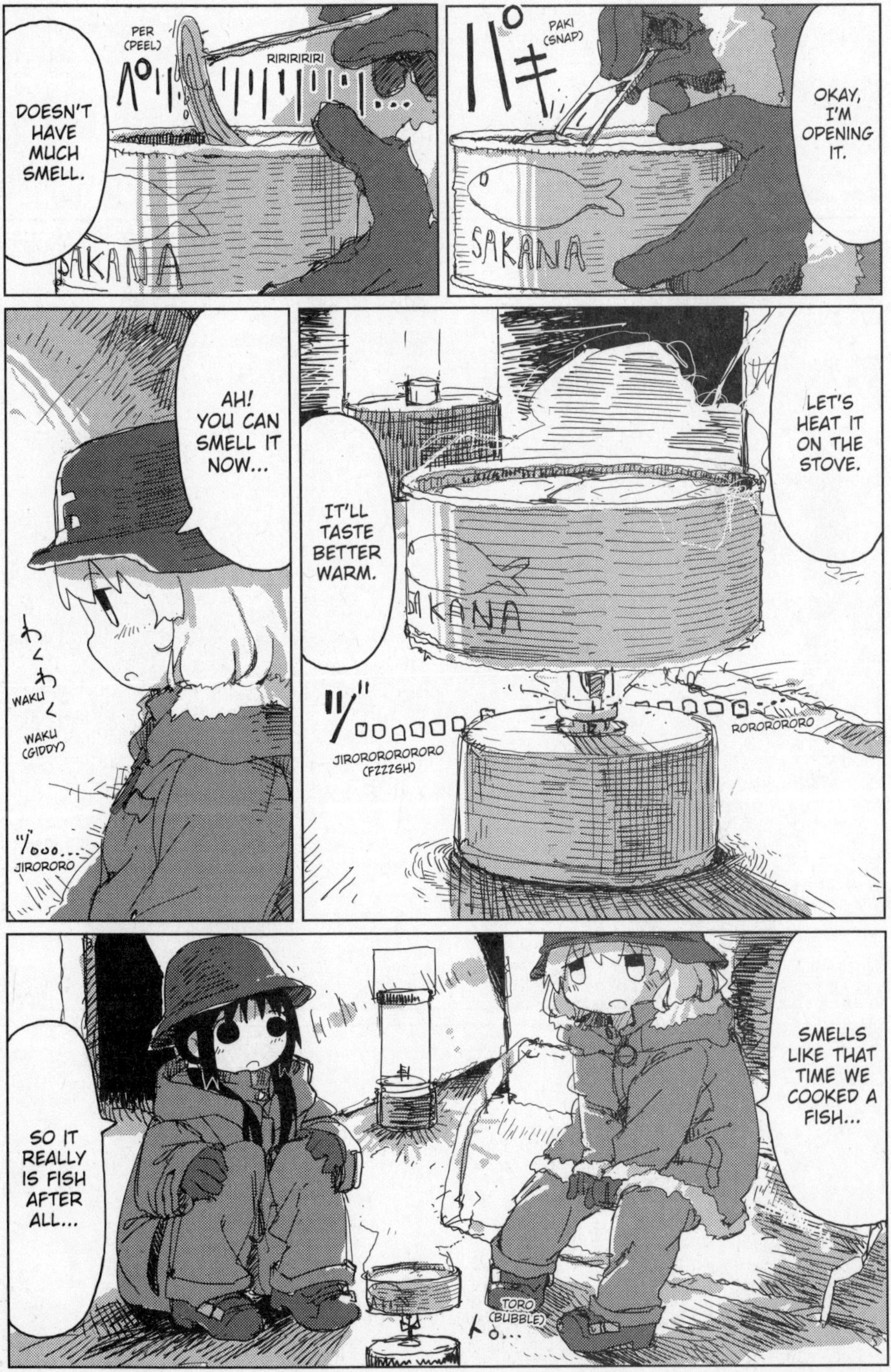

OKAY, I'M OPENING IT.
パキ
PAKI (SNAP)
ペリ
PER (PEEL)
RIRIRIRIRI
DOESN'T HAVE MUCH SMELL.
LET'S HEAT IT ON THE STOVE.
IT'LL TASTE BETTER WARM.
RORORORORO
JIROROROROROR0 (FZZZSH)
AH! YOU CAN SMELL IT NOW...
わくわく
WAKU WAKU (GIDDY)
JIROROR0
SMELLS LIKE THAT TIME WE COOKED A FISH...
TORO (BUBBLE)
SO IT REALLY IS FISH AFTER ALL...

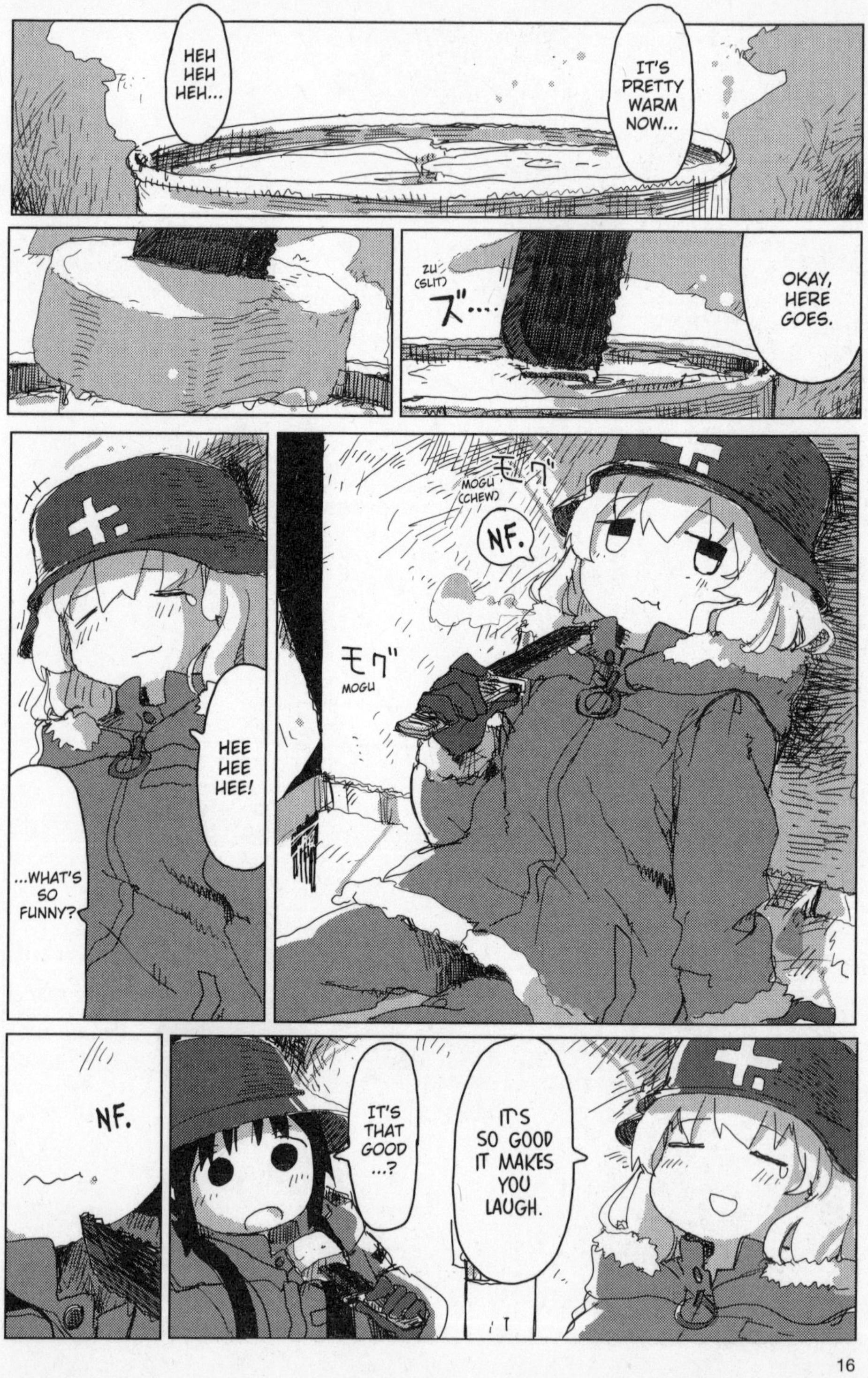
IT'S PRETTY WARM NOW...
HEH HEH HEH...
OKAY, HERE GOES.
ZU (SLIT)
ズ...
モグ
MOGU (CHEW)
NF.
モグ
MOGU
HEE HEE HEE!
...WHAT'S SO FUNNY?
IT'S SO GOOD IT MAKES YOU LAUGH.
IT'S THAT GOOD ...?
NF.

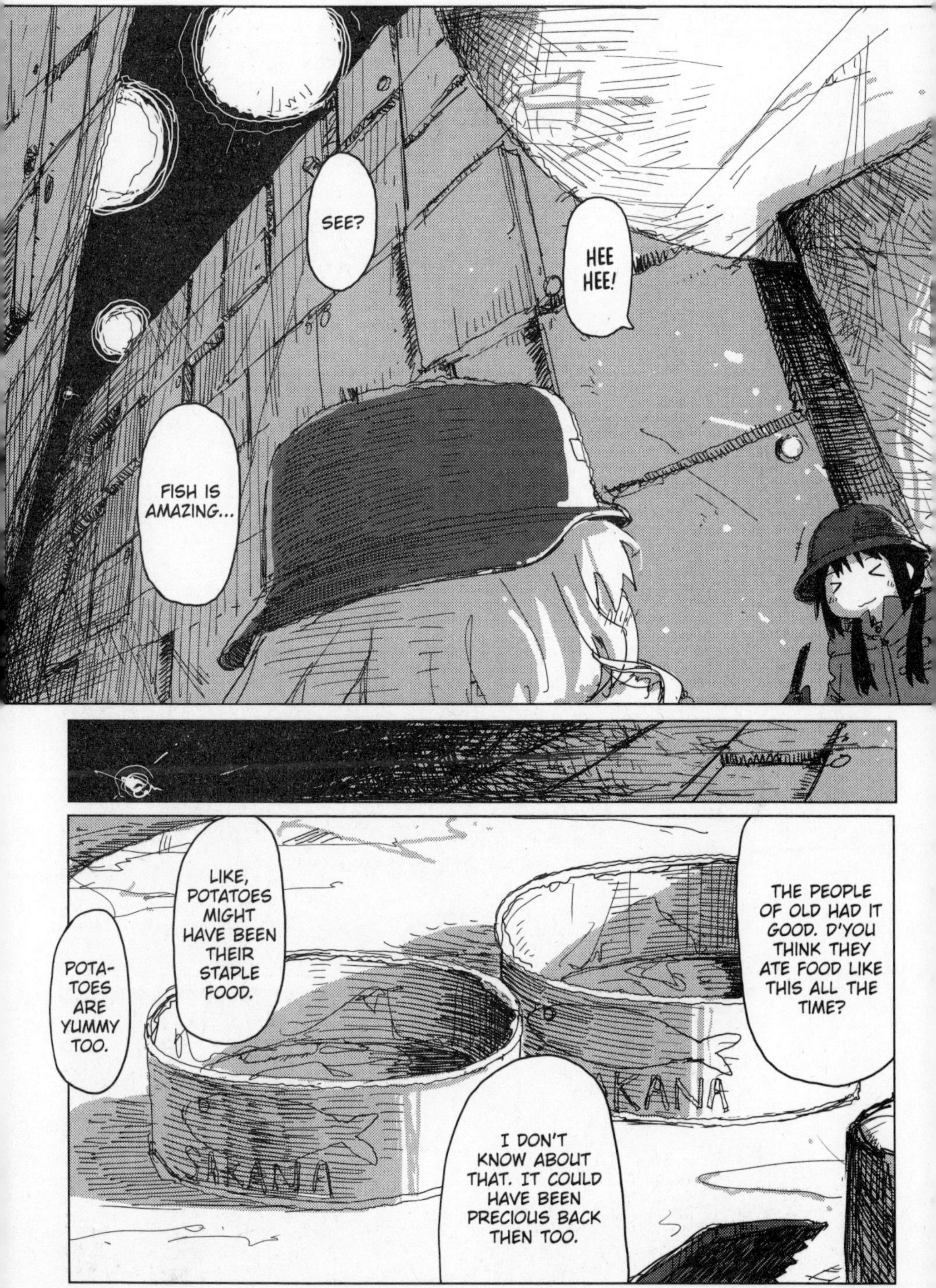

SEE?
HEE HEE!
FISH IS AMAZING...
THE PEOPLE OF OLD HAD IT GOOD. D'YOU THINK THEY ATE FOOD LIKE THIS ALL THE TIME?
KANA
I DON'T KNOW ABOUT THAT. IT COULD HAVE BEEN PRECIOUS BACK THEN TOO.
LIKE, POTATOES MIGHT HAVE BEEN THEIR STAPLE FOOD.
SAKANA
POTA-TOES ARE YUMMY TOO.

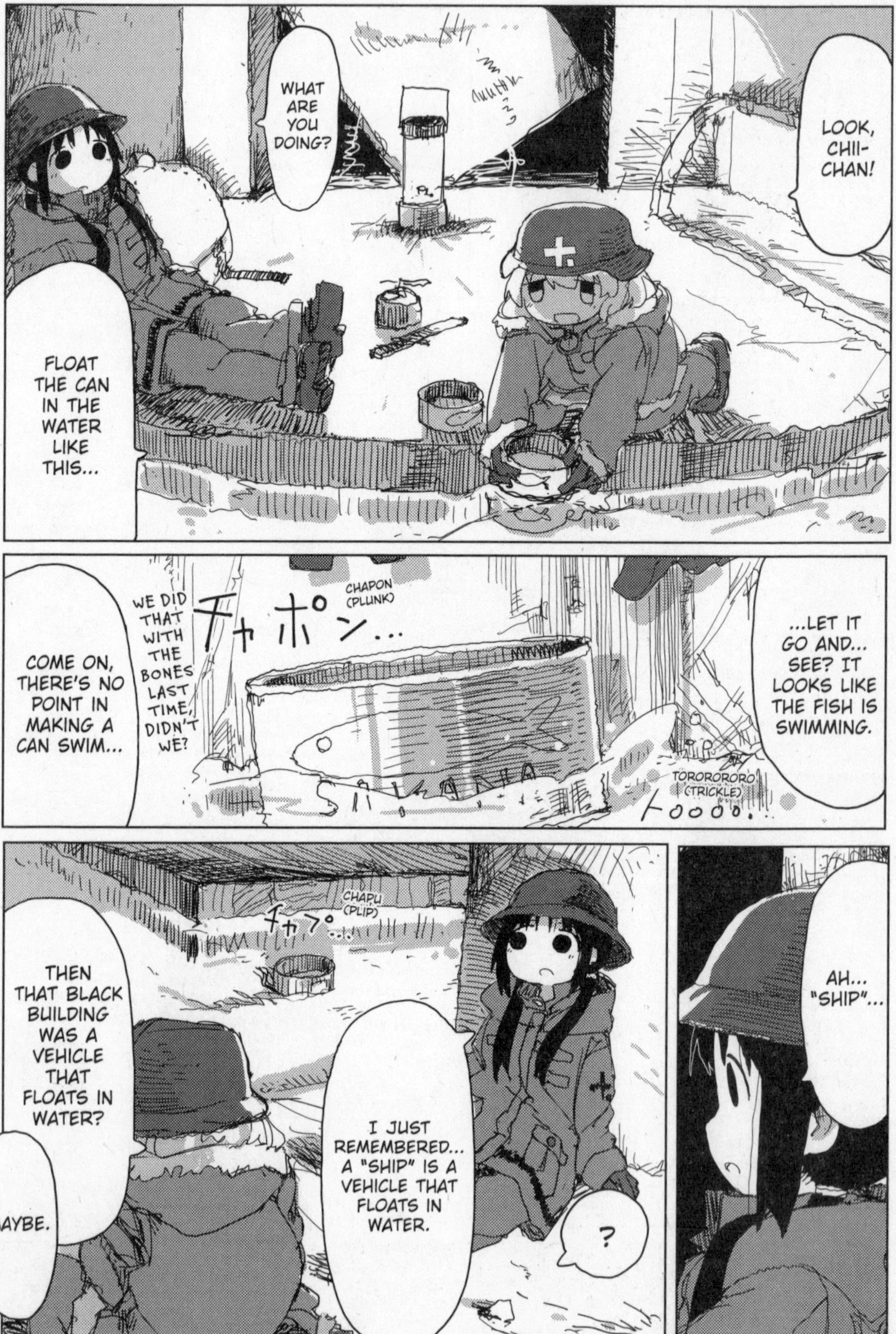

LOOK, CHII-CHAN!
WHAT ARE YOU DOING?
FLOAT THE CAN IN THE WATER LIKE THIS...
...LET IT GO AND... SEE? IT LOOKS LIKE THE FISH IS SWIMMING.
チャポン…
CHAPON (PLUNK)
WE DID THAT WITH THE BONES LAST TIME, DIDN'T WE?
TORORORORO (TRICKLE)
COME ON, THERE'S NO POINT IN MAKING A CAN SWIM...
AH... "SHIP"...
チャプ…
CHAPU (PLIP)
I JUST REMEMBERED... A "SHIP" IS A VEHICLE THAT FLOATS IN WATER.
?
THEN THAT BLACK BUILDING WAS A VEHICLE THAT FLOATS IN WATER?
MAYBE.

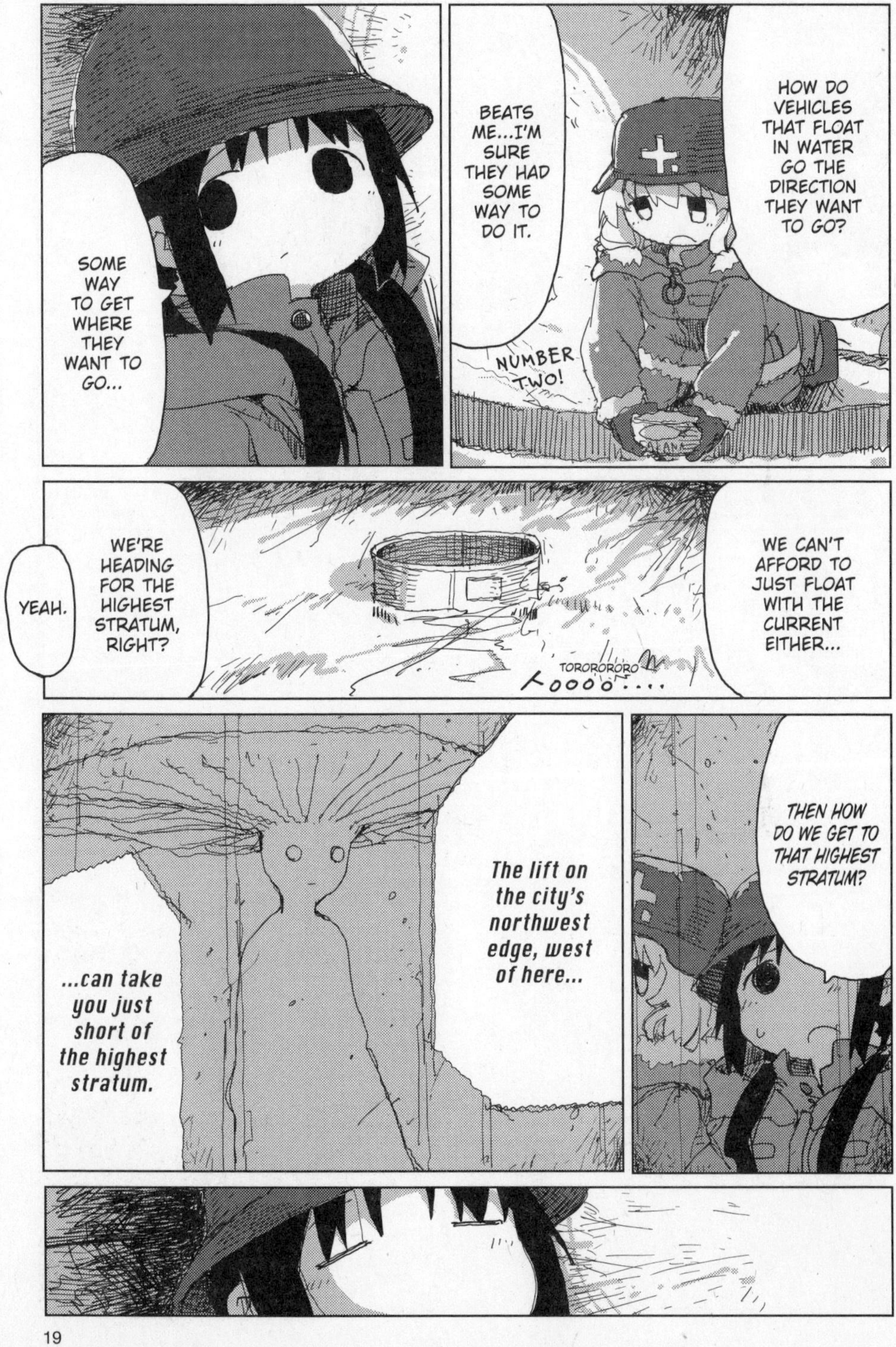
HOW DO VEHICLES THAT FLOAT IN WATER GO THE DIRECTION THEY WANT TO GO?
BEATS ME...I'M SURE THEY HAD SOME WAY TO DO IT.
NUMBER TWO!
SOME WAY TO GET WHERE THEY WANT TO GO...
WE CAN'T AFFORD TO JUST FLOAT WITH THE CURRENT EITHER...
TORORORORO
WE'RE HEADING FOR THE HIGHEST STRATUM, RIGHT?
YEAH.
THEN HOW DO WE GET TO THAT HIGHEST STRATUM?
The lift on the city's northwest edge, west of here...
...can take you just short of the highest stratum.

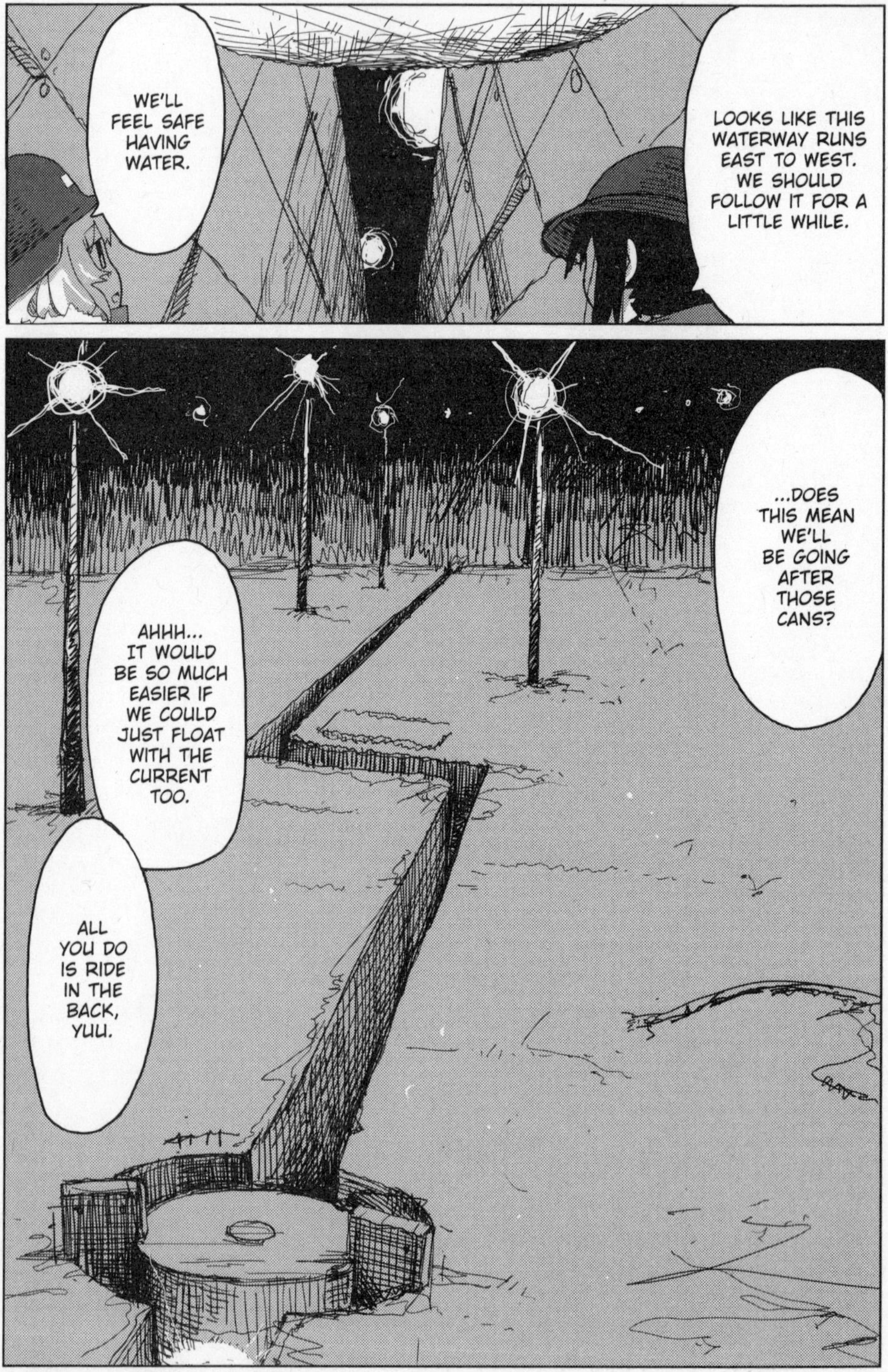
LOOKS LIKE THIS WATERWAY RUNS EAST TO WEST. WE SHOULD FOLLOW IT FOR A LITTLE WHILE.
WE'LL FEEL SAFE HAVING WATER.
...DOES THIS MEAN WE'LL BE GOING AFTER THOSE CANS?
AHHH... IT WOULD BE SO MUCH EASIER IF WE COULD JUST FLOAT WITH THE CURRENT TOO.
ALL YOU DO IS RIDE IN THE BACK, YUU.

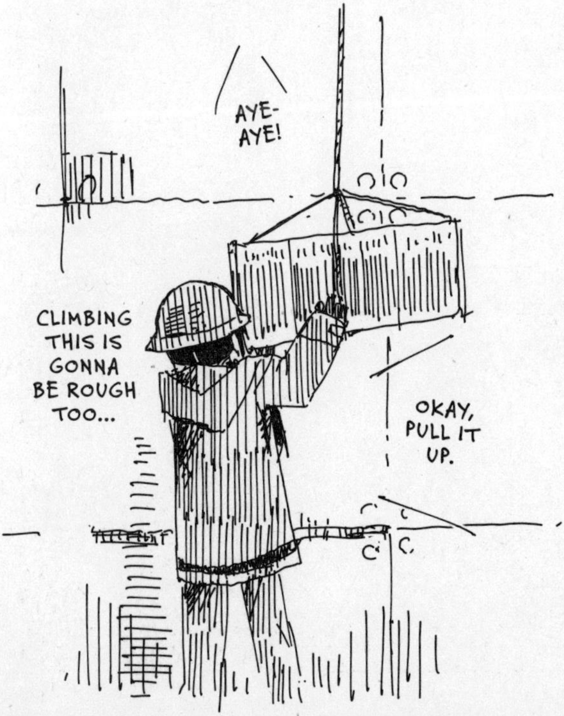
OKAY, PULL IT UP.
AYE-AYE!
CLIMBING THIS IS GONNA BE ROUGH TOO...

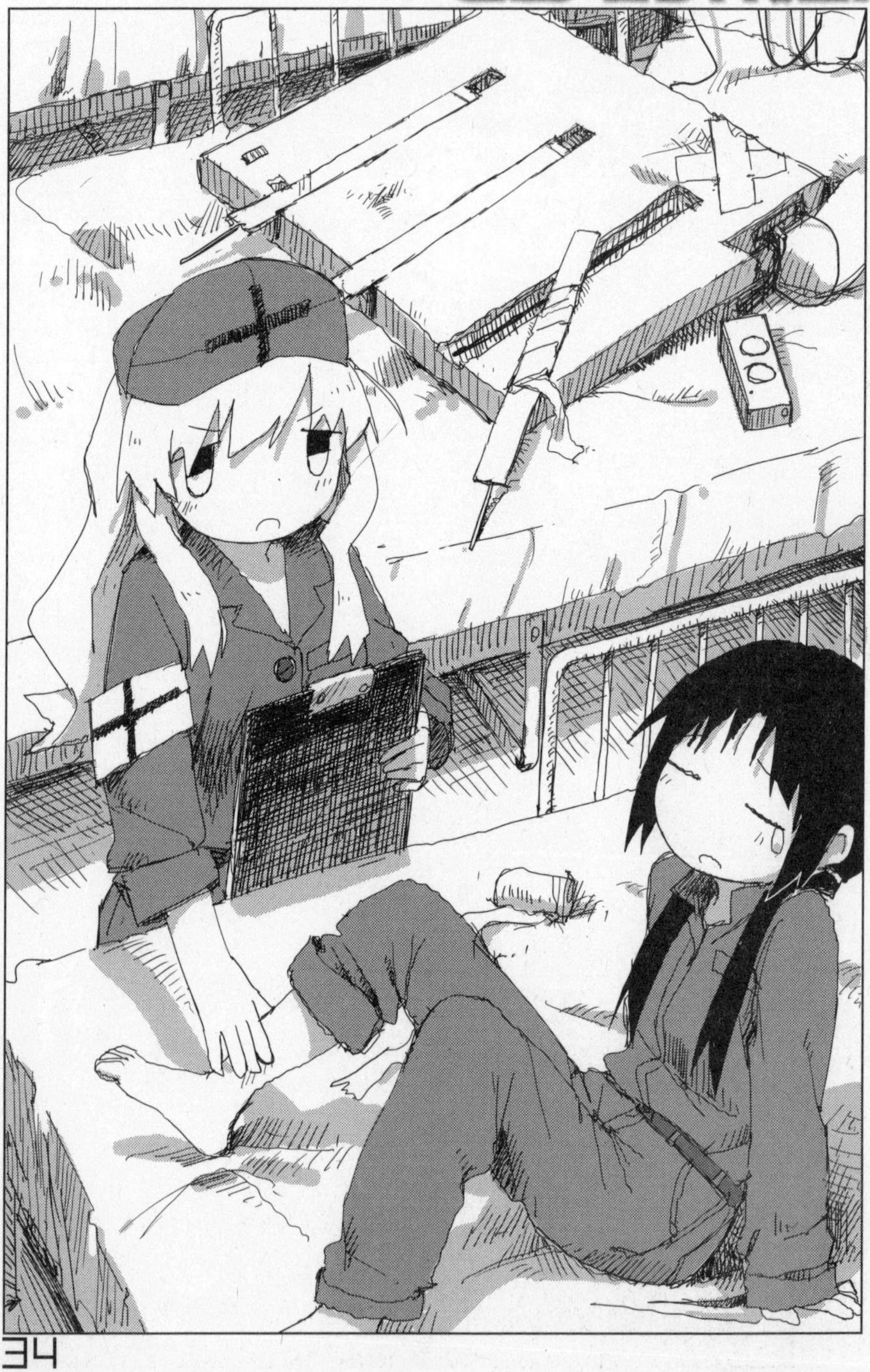

34 INJURY

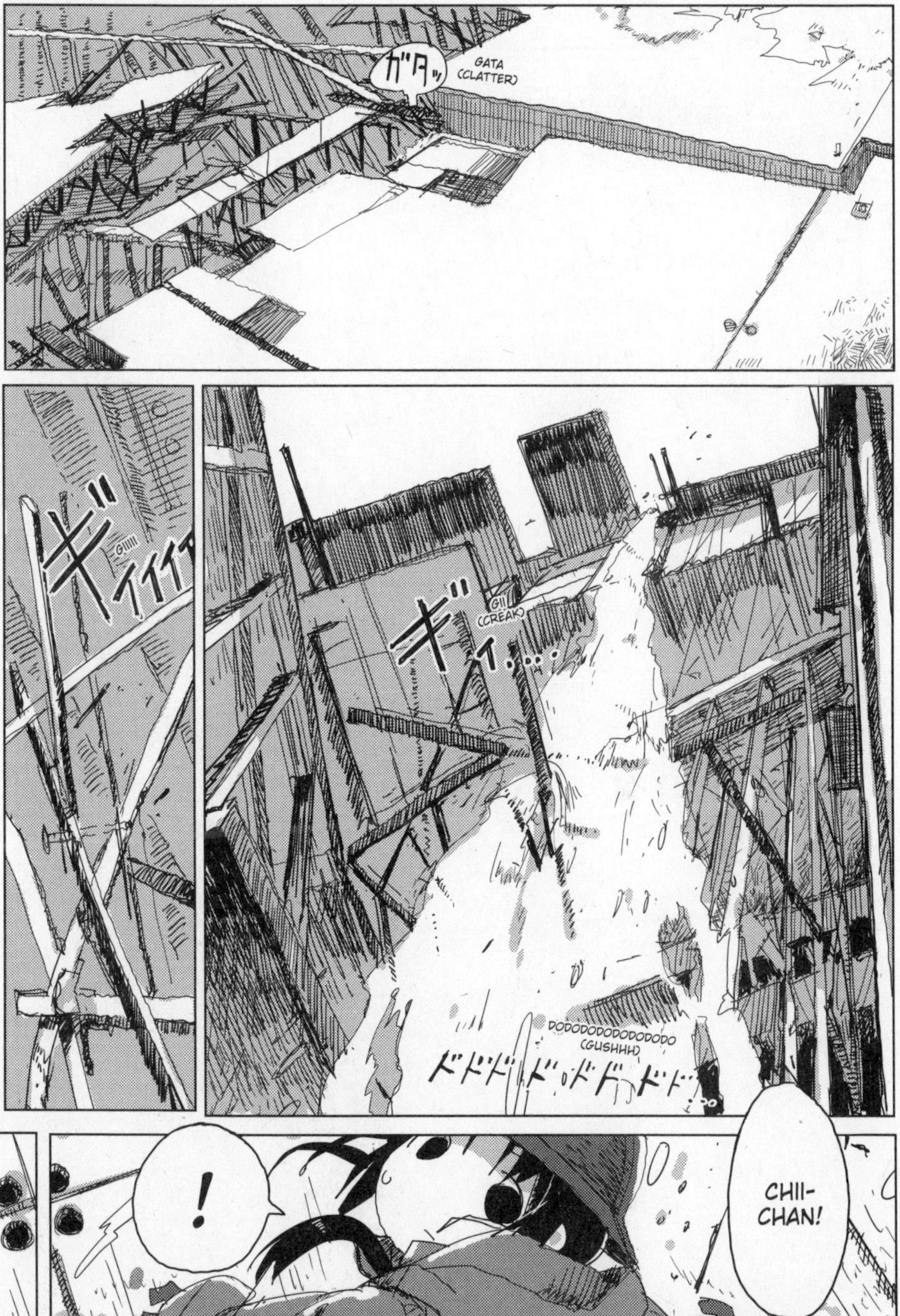
ガタッ
GATA
(CLATTER)
ギイ…
GII
(CREAK)
DODODODODODODODO
(GUSHHH)
GIIII
CHII-CHAN!
!

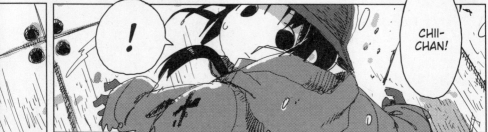

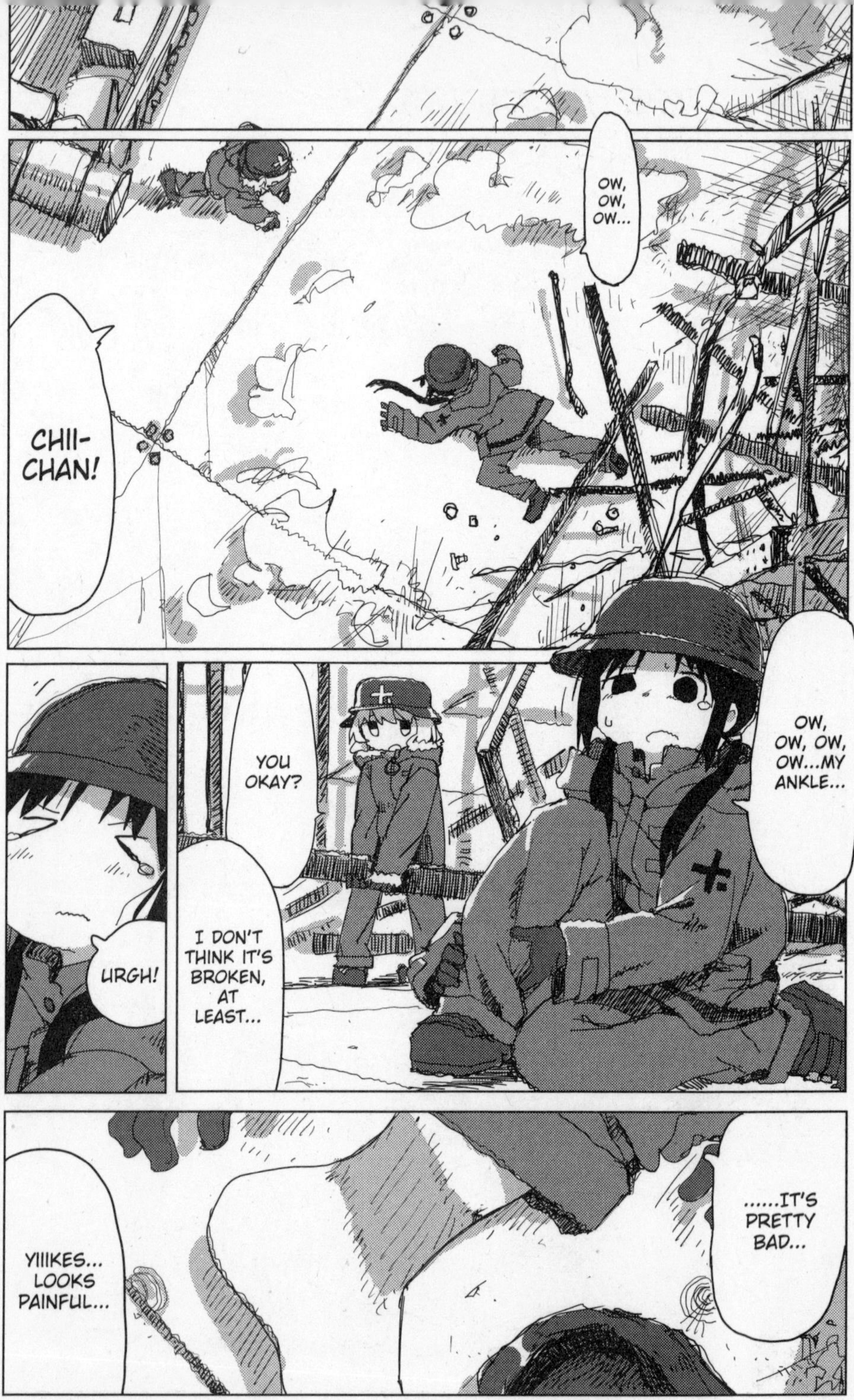
OW, OW, OW...
CHII-CHAN!
OW, OW, OW, OW...MY ANKLE...
YOU OKAY?
I DON'T THINK IT'S BROKEN, AT LEAST...
URGH!
......IT'S PRETTY BAD...
YIIIKES... LOOKS PAINFUL...

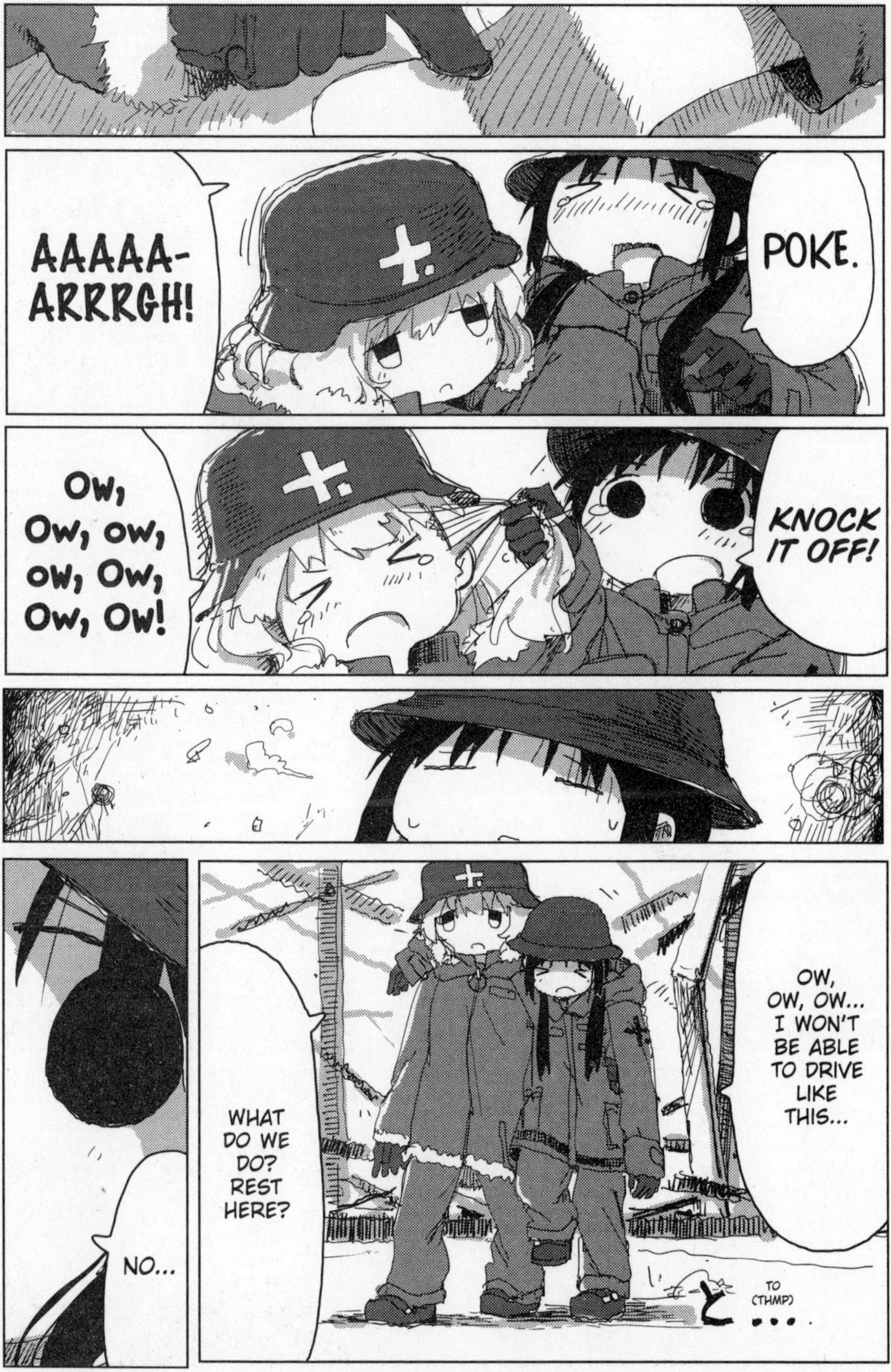
POKE.
AAAAA-ARRRGH!
KNOCK IT OFF!
Ow, Ow, ow, ow, Ow, Ow, Ow!
OW, OW, OW... I WON'T BE ABLE TO DRIVE LIKE THIS...
TO (THMP)
WHAT DO WE DO? REST HERE?
NO...

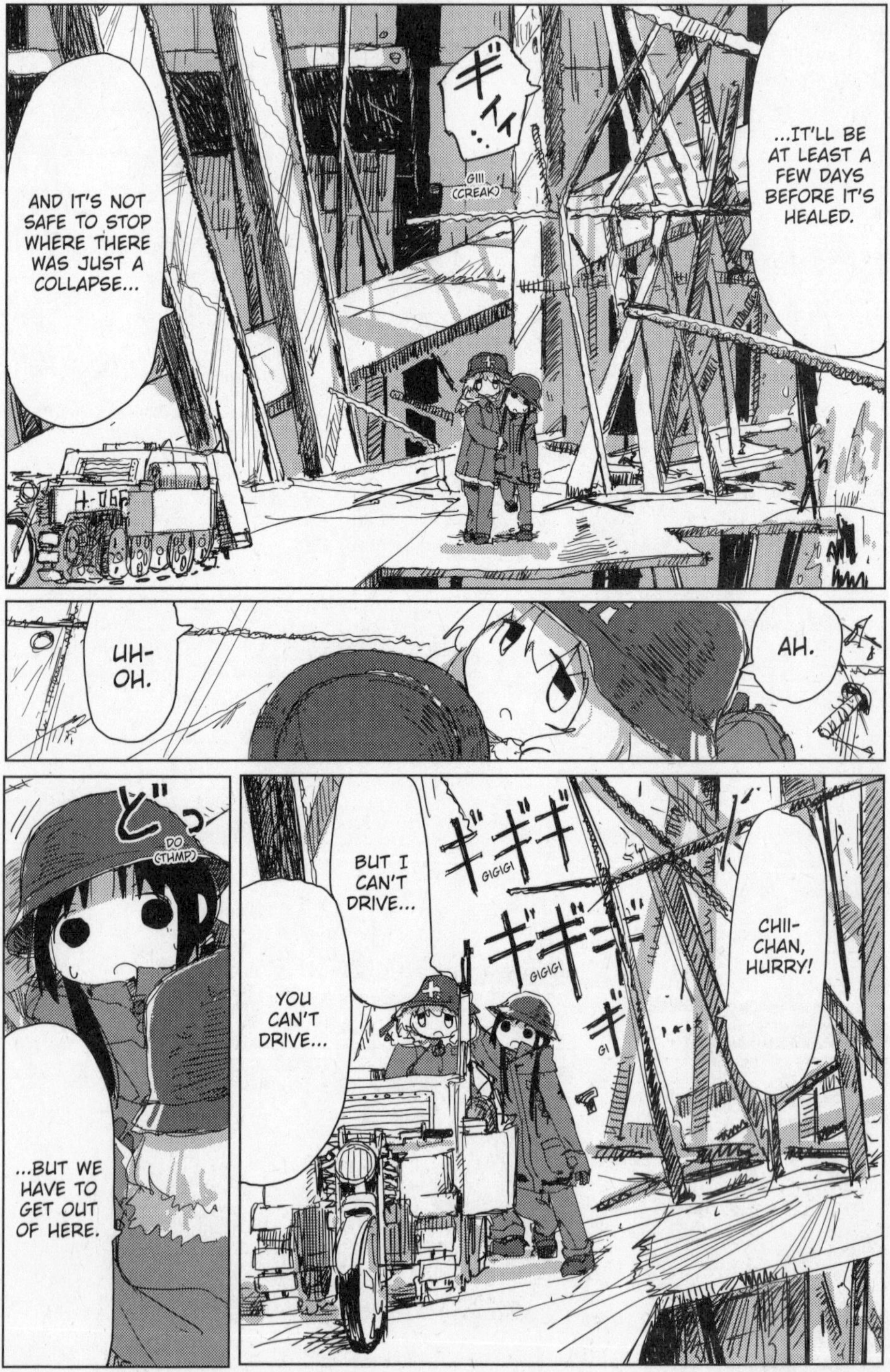
...IT'LL BE AT LEAST A FEW DAYS BEFORE IT'S HEALED.
ギィィ…
GIII (CREAK)
AND IT'S NOT SAFE TO STOP WHERE THERE WAS JUST A COLLAPSE...
AH.
UH-OH.
CHII-CHAN, HURRY!
ギギギ
GIGIGI
ギギギ
GIGIGI
ギ
GI
BUT I CAN'T DRIVE...
YOU CAN'T DRIVE...
どっ
DO (THMP)
...BUT WE HAVE TO GET OUT OF HERE.

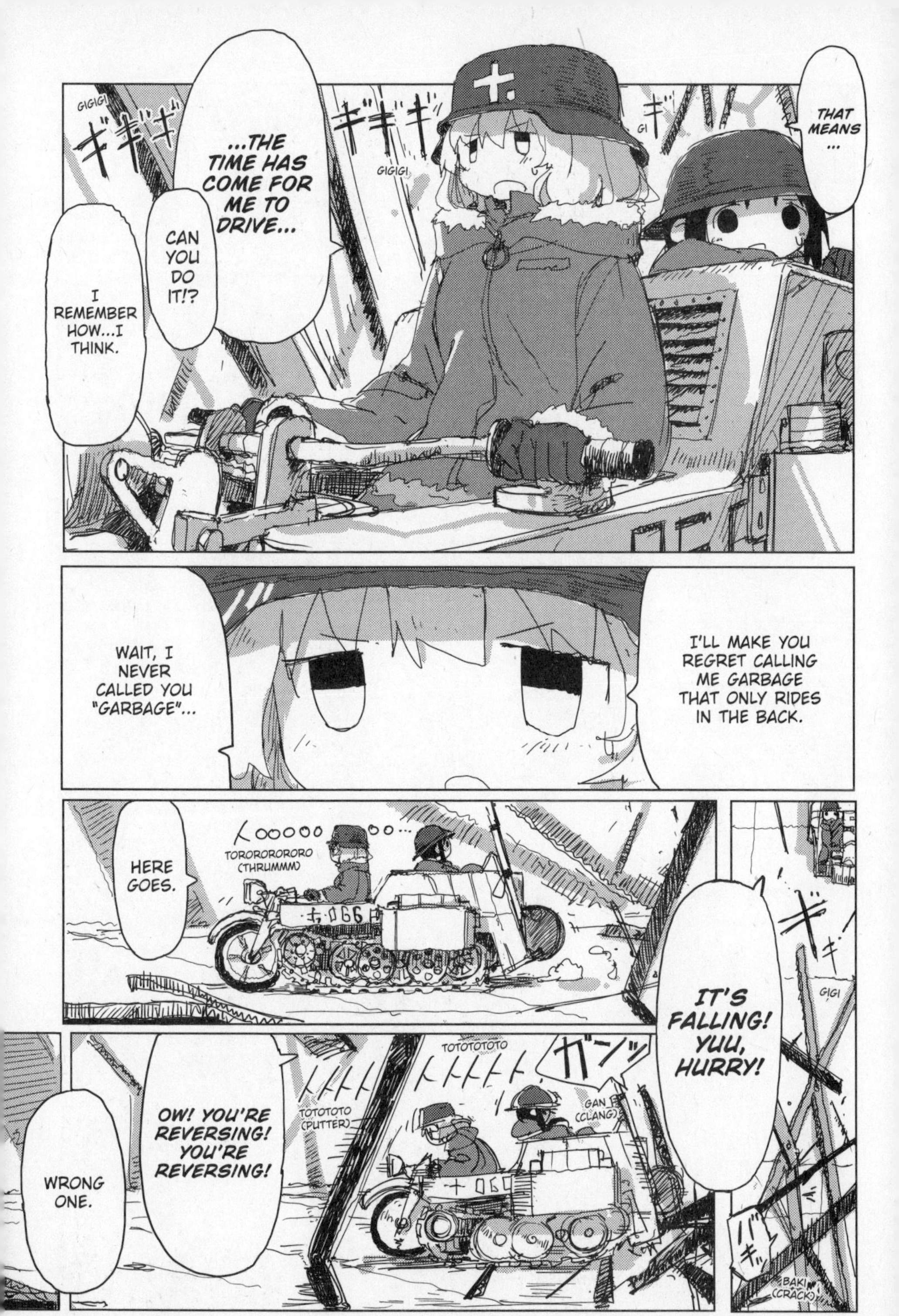
THAT MEANS ...
GI
ギ
GIGIGI
ギギギ
...THE TIME HAS COME FOR ME TO DRIVE...
CAN YOU DO IT!?
I REMEMBER HOW...I THINK.
GIGIGI
ギギギ
I'LL MAKE YOU REGRET CALLING ME GARBAGE THAT ONLY RIDES IN THE BACK.
WAIT, I NEVER CALLED YOU "GARBAGE"...
IT'S FALLING! YUU, HURRY!
GIGI
BAKI (CRACK)
TOROROROROROR (THRUMMM)
HERE GOES.
GAN (CLANG)
ガンッ
TOTOTOTOTO
トトトトト
TOTOTOTO (PUTTER)
OW! YOU'RE REVERSING! YOU'RE REVERSING!
WRONG ONE.

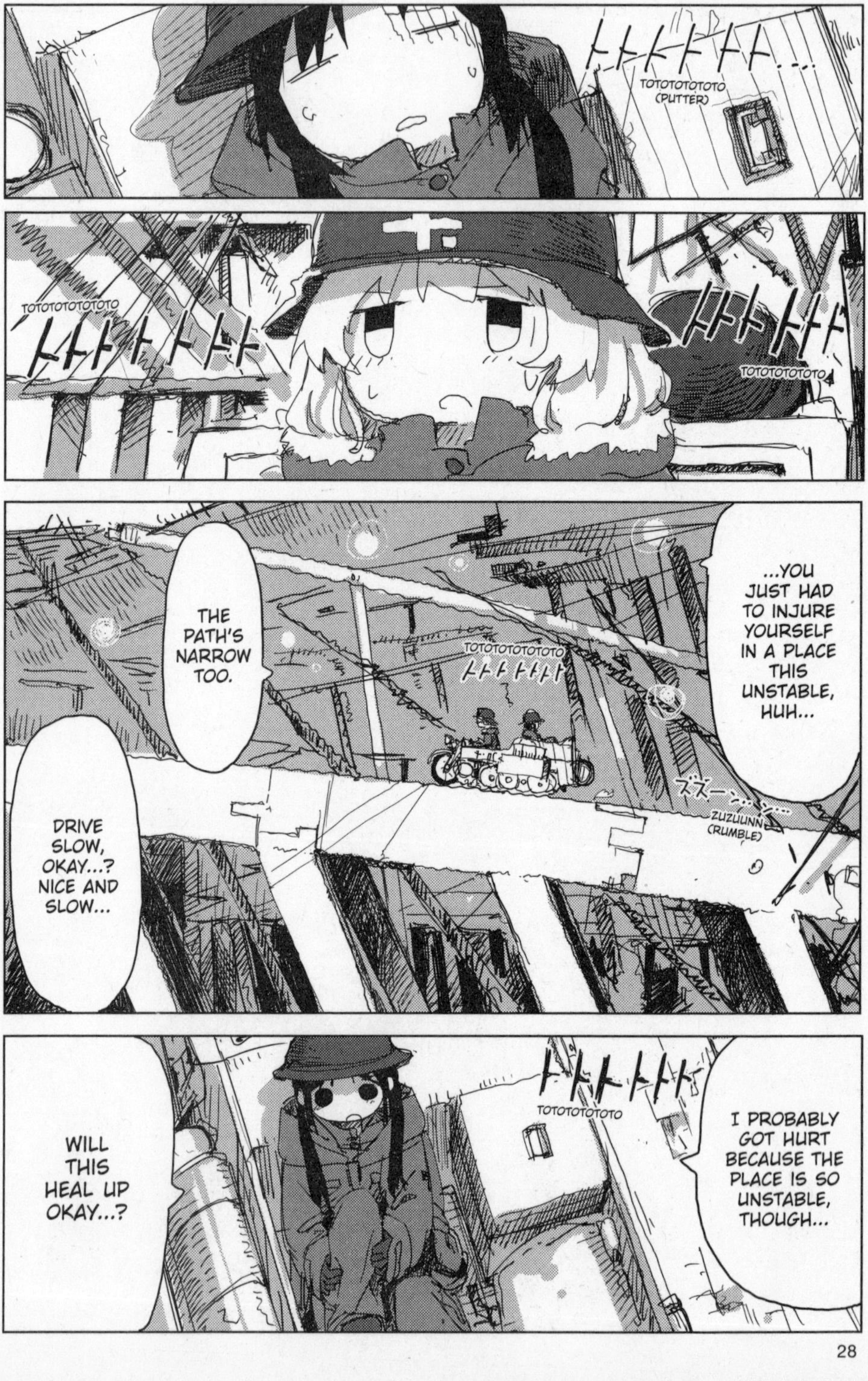
TOTOTOTOTOTO
(PUTTER)
TOTOTOTOTOTO
TOTOTOTOTOTOTO
...YOU JUST HAD TO INJURE YOURSELF IN A PLACE THIS UNSTABLE, HUH...
THE PATH'S NARROW TOO.
TOTOTOTOTOTOTO
ZUZUUNN
(RUMBLE)
DRIVE SLOW, OKAY...? NICE AND SLOW...
I PROBABLY GOT HURT BECAUSE THE PLACE IS SO UNSTABLE, THOUGH...
TOTOTOTOTOTO
WILL THIS HEAL UP OKAY...?

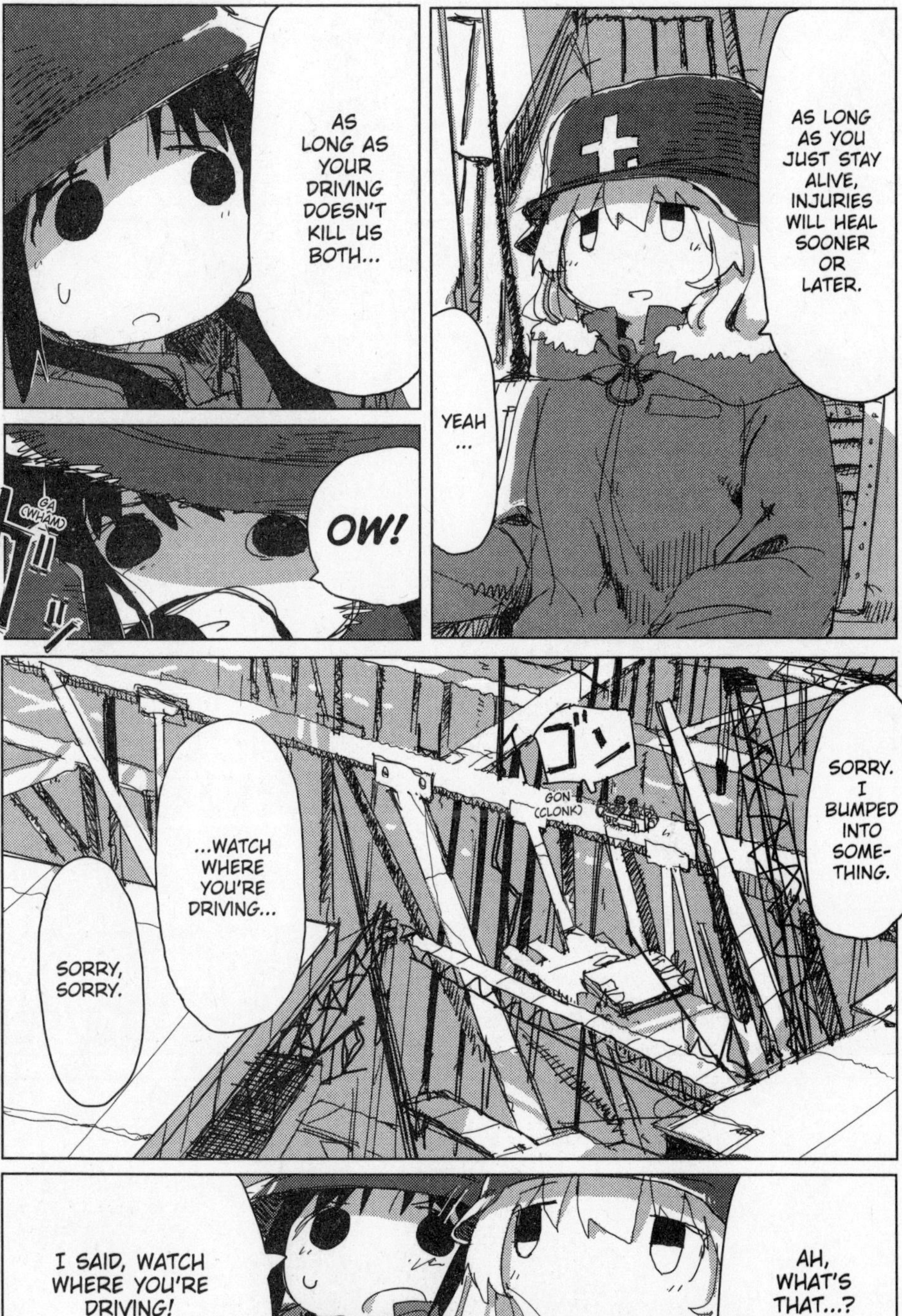
AS LONG AS YOU JUST STAY ALIVE, INJURIES WILL HEAL SOONER OR LATER.
YEAH ...
AS LONG AS YOUR DRIVING DOESN'T KILL US BOTH...
OW!
GA (WHAM)
SORRY. I BUMPED INTO SOME-THING.
GON (CLONK)
...WATCH WHERE YOU'RE DRIVING...
SORRY, SORRY.
AH, WHAT'S THAT...?
I SAID, WATCH WHERE YOU'RE DRIVING!

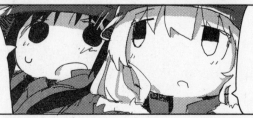

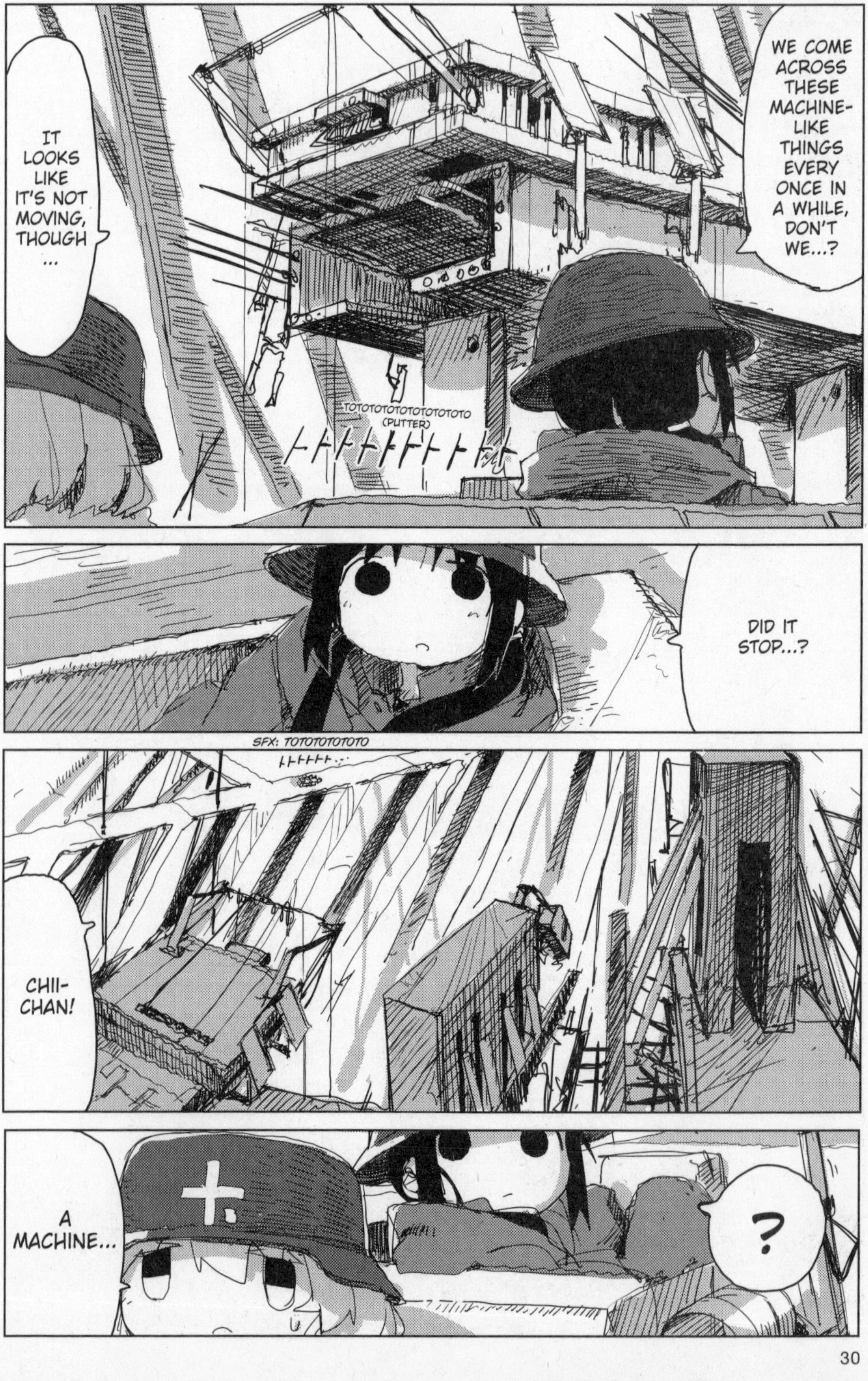
WE COME ACROSS THESE MACHINE-LIKE THINGS EVERY ONCE IN A WHILE, DON'T WE...?
IT LOOKS LIKE IT'S NOT MOVING, THOUGH ...
TOTOTOTOTOTOTOTOTOTO (PUTTER)
DID IT STOP...?
SFX: TOTOTOTOTOTO
CHII-CHAN!
?
A MACHINE...

IT'S MOVING ...

... TOWARD US.

GASHA
ガシャ…

ガシャ…
GASHA (KSHAK)

ギィ
GI (CREAK)

ギッ

WHAT ARE WE GONNA DO...?

CAN'T PASS AROUND IT...

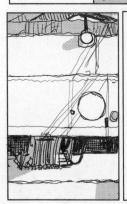

MOVE, PLEASE!

EXCUSE MEEE!

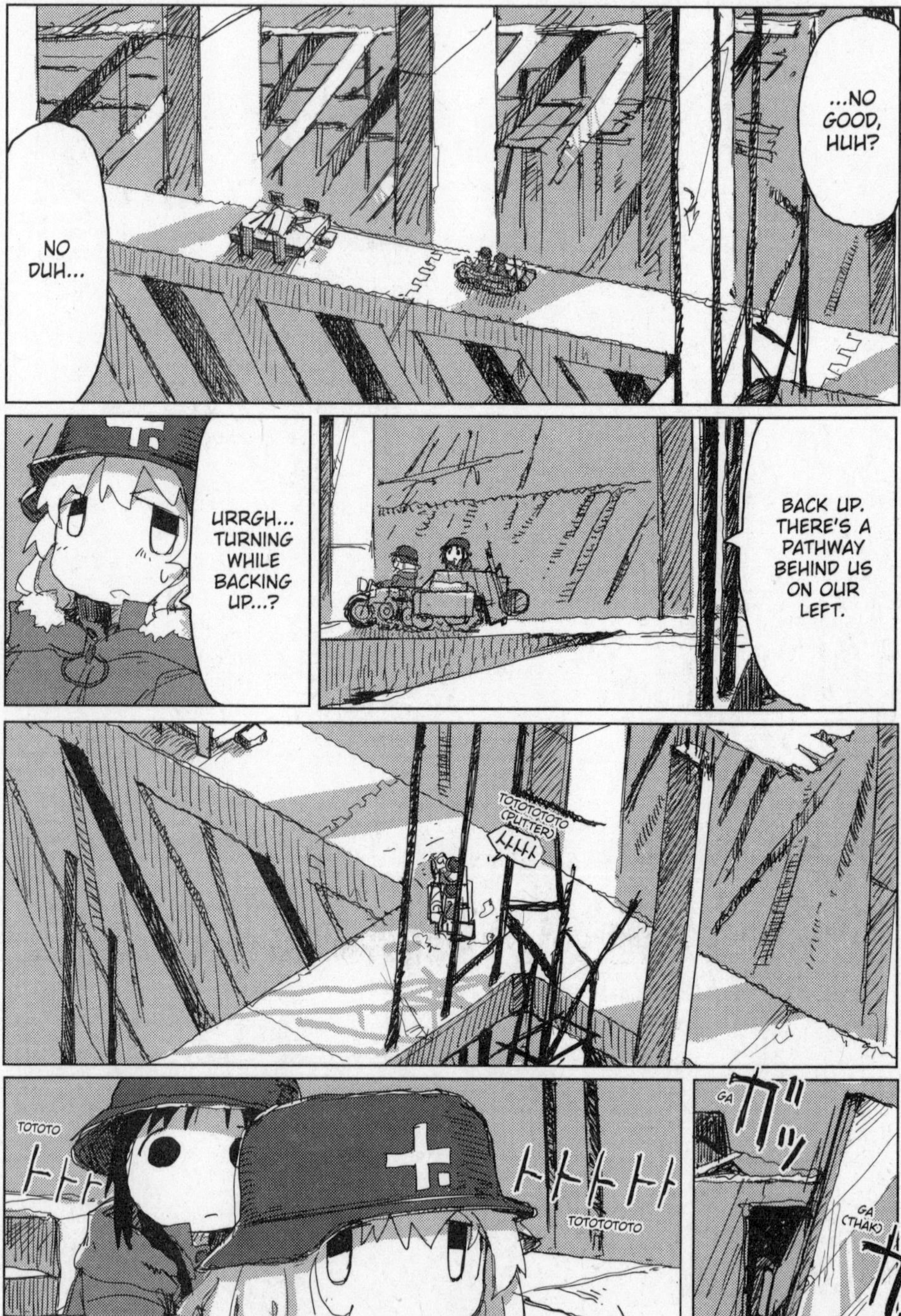
...NO GOOD, HUH?
NO DUH...
BACK UP. THERE'S A PATHWAY BEHIND US ON OUR LEFT.
URRGH... TURNING WHILE BACKING UP...?
TOTOTOTOTO (PUTTER)
GA
ガッ
GA (THAK)
ガッ
トトトトト
TOTOTOTOTO
TOTOTO
トトト

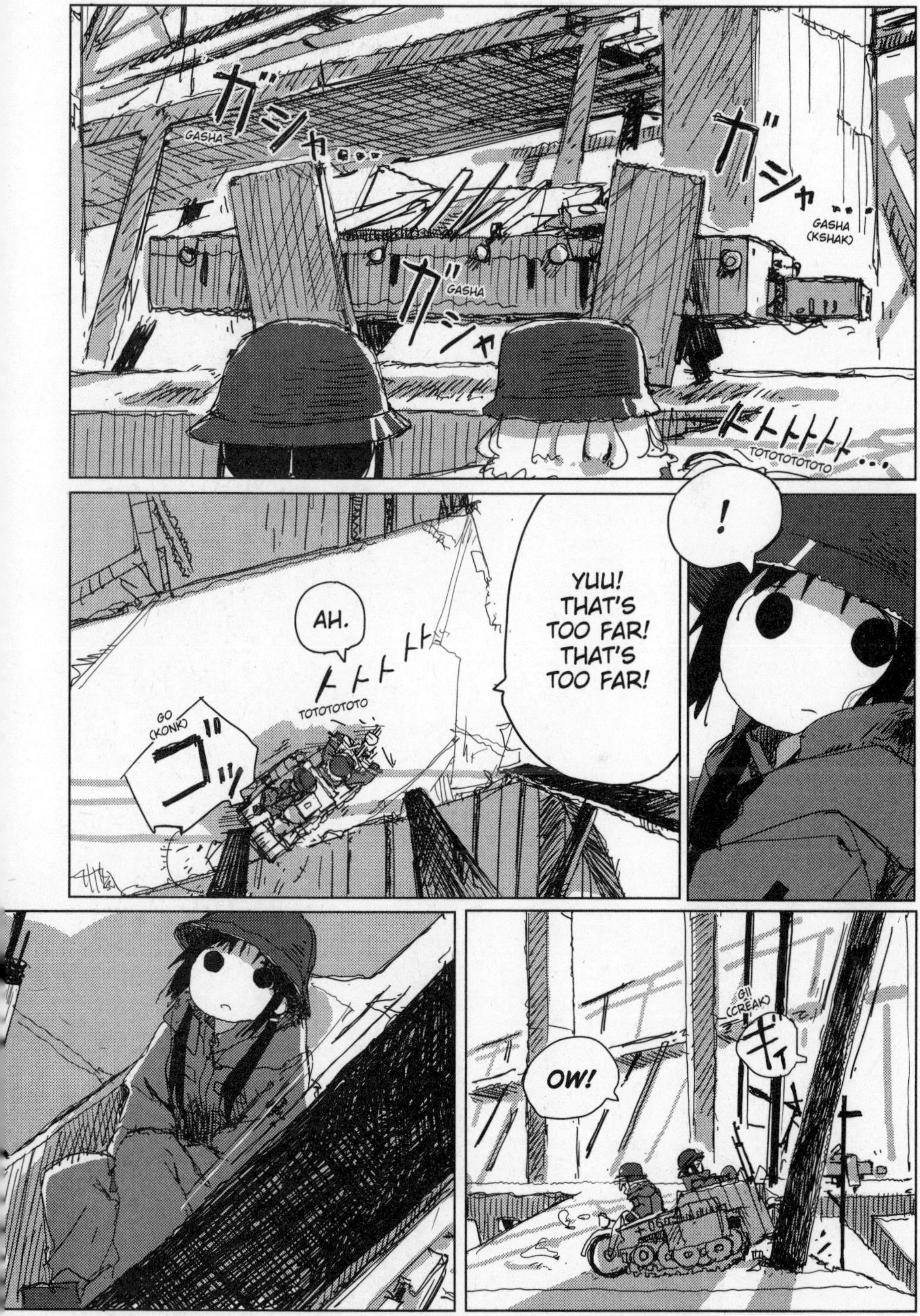
ガシャ
GASHA (KSHAK)
ガシャ
GASHA
ガシャ
GASHA
トトトトトト
TOTOTOTOTOTO...
!
YUU! THAT'S TOO FAR! THAT'S TOO FAR!
AH.
トトトト
TOTOTOTOTO
ゴッ
GO (KONK)
ギィ
GII (CREAK)
OW!

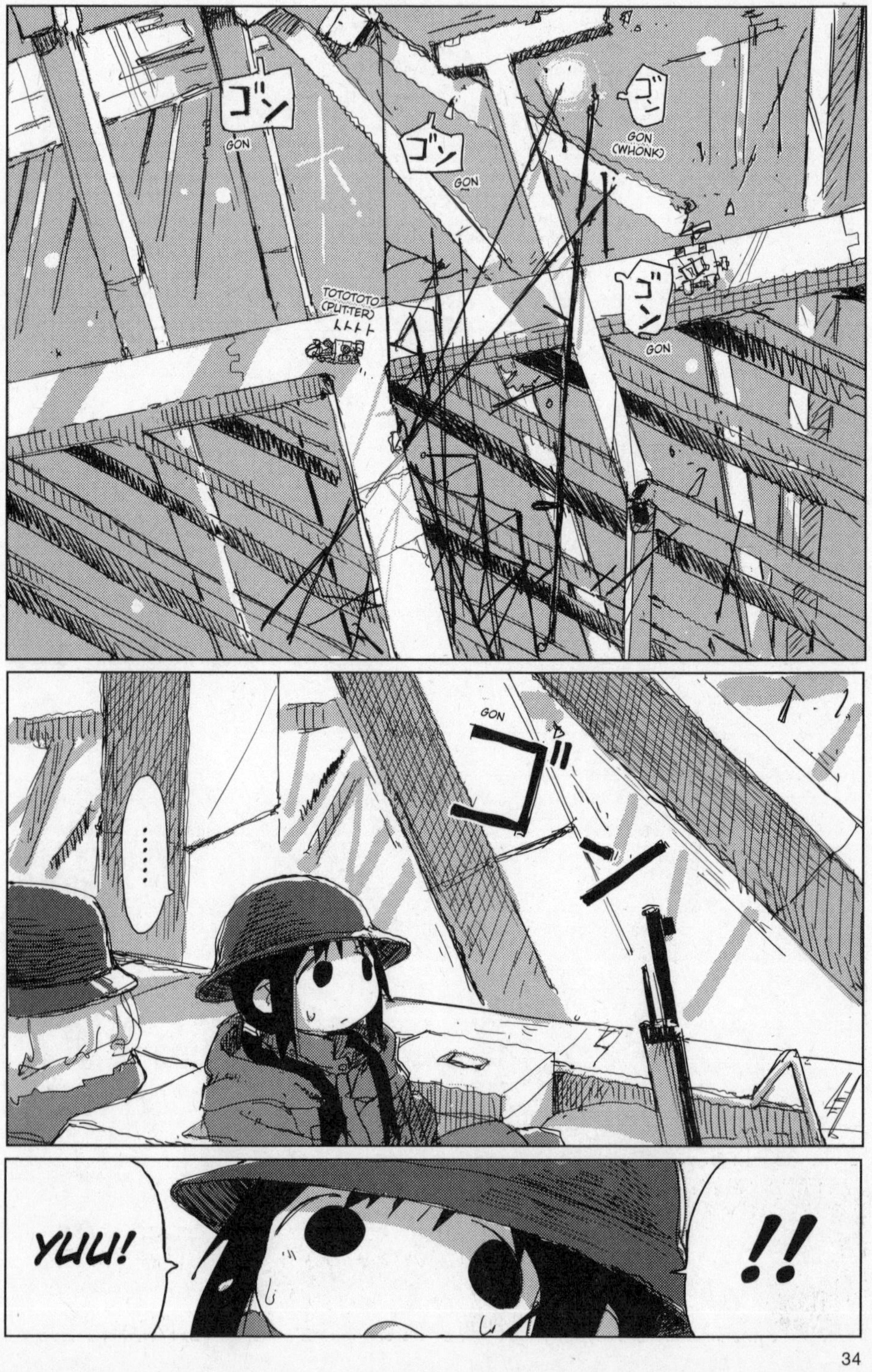
ゴン
GON
(WHONK)
ゴン
GON
ゴン
GON
ゴン
GON
TOTOTOTO
(PUTTER)
トトトト
GON
ゴン
……
!!
YUU!

GON
GON
GON
TOTOTOTOTOTOTO
STOP! BRAKE! BRAKE!
HEY!

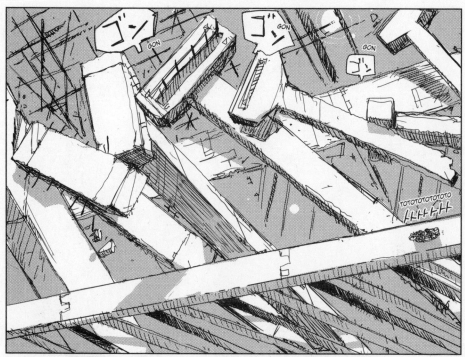

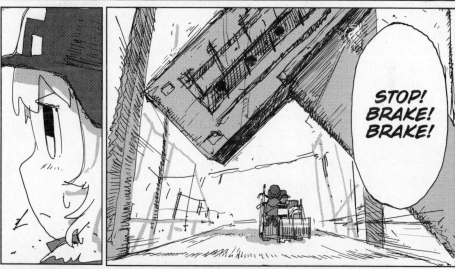

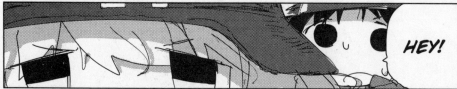

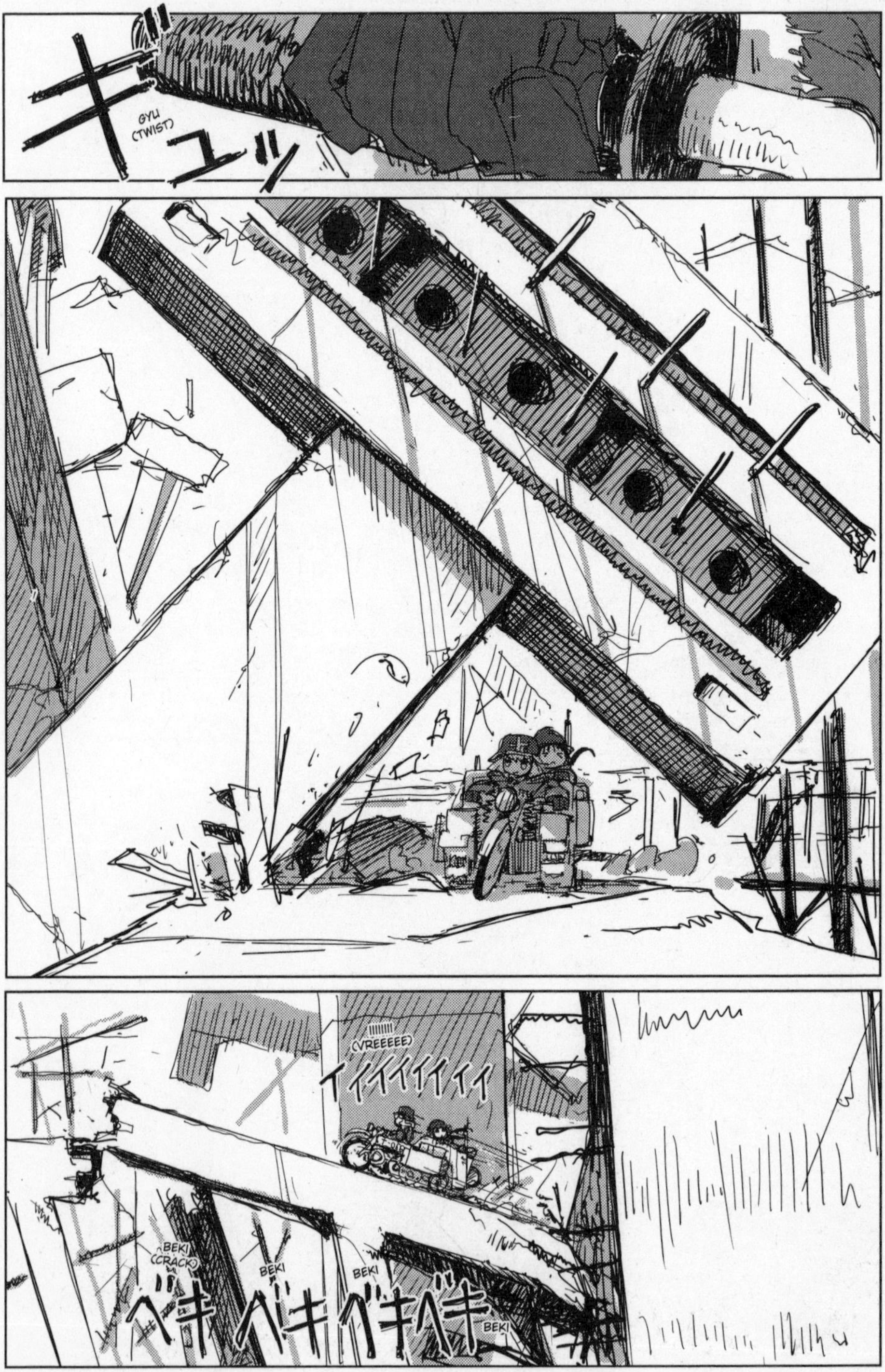
ギュッ
GYU (TWIST)
イイイイイイイ
(VREEEEE)
ベキベキベキベキ
BEKI (CRACK)
BEKI
BEKI
BEKI

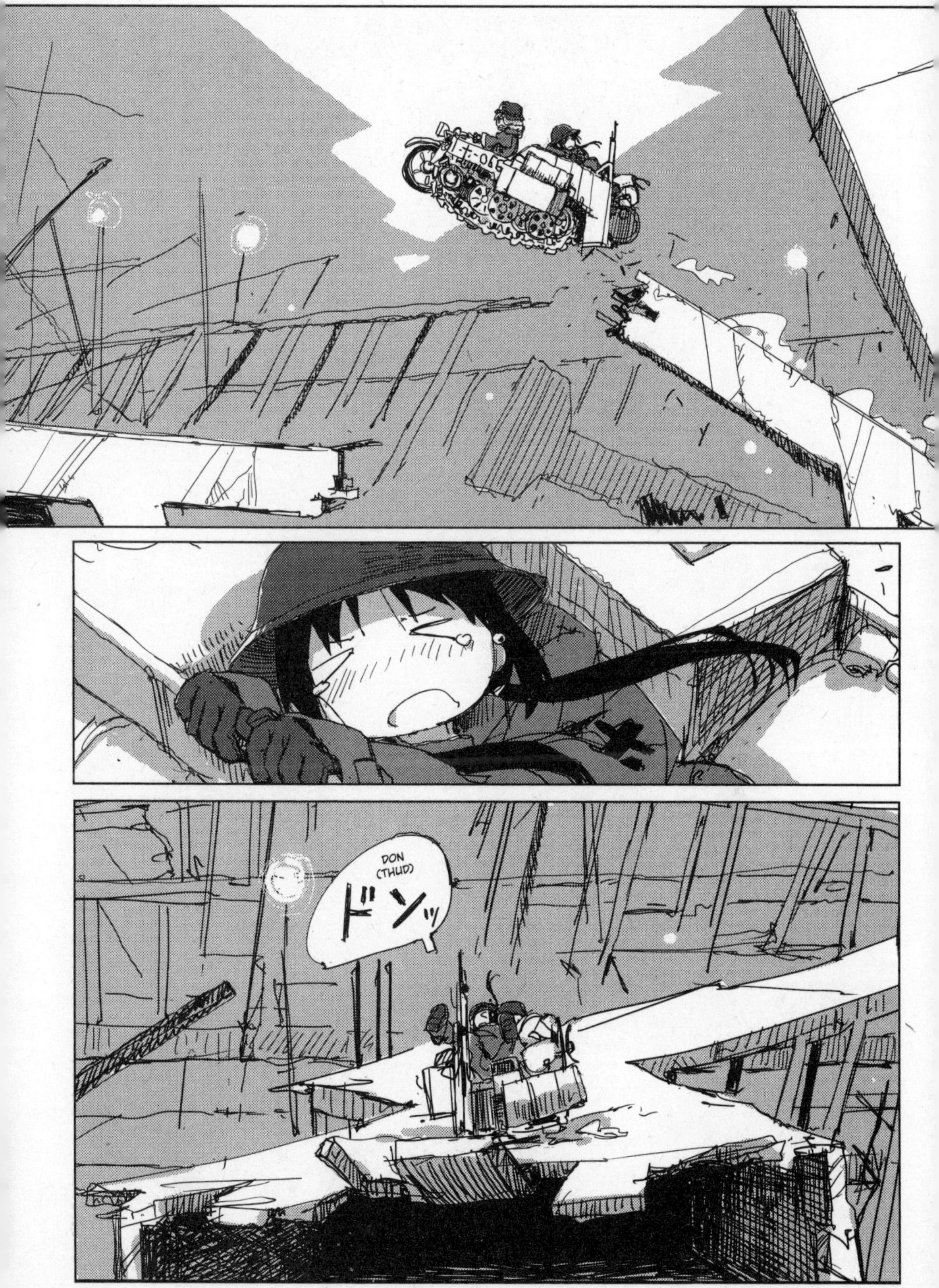
DON (THUD)
ドンッ

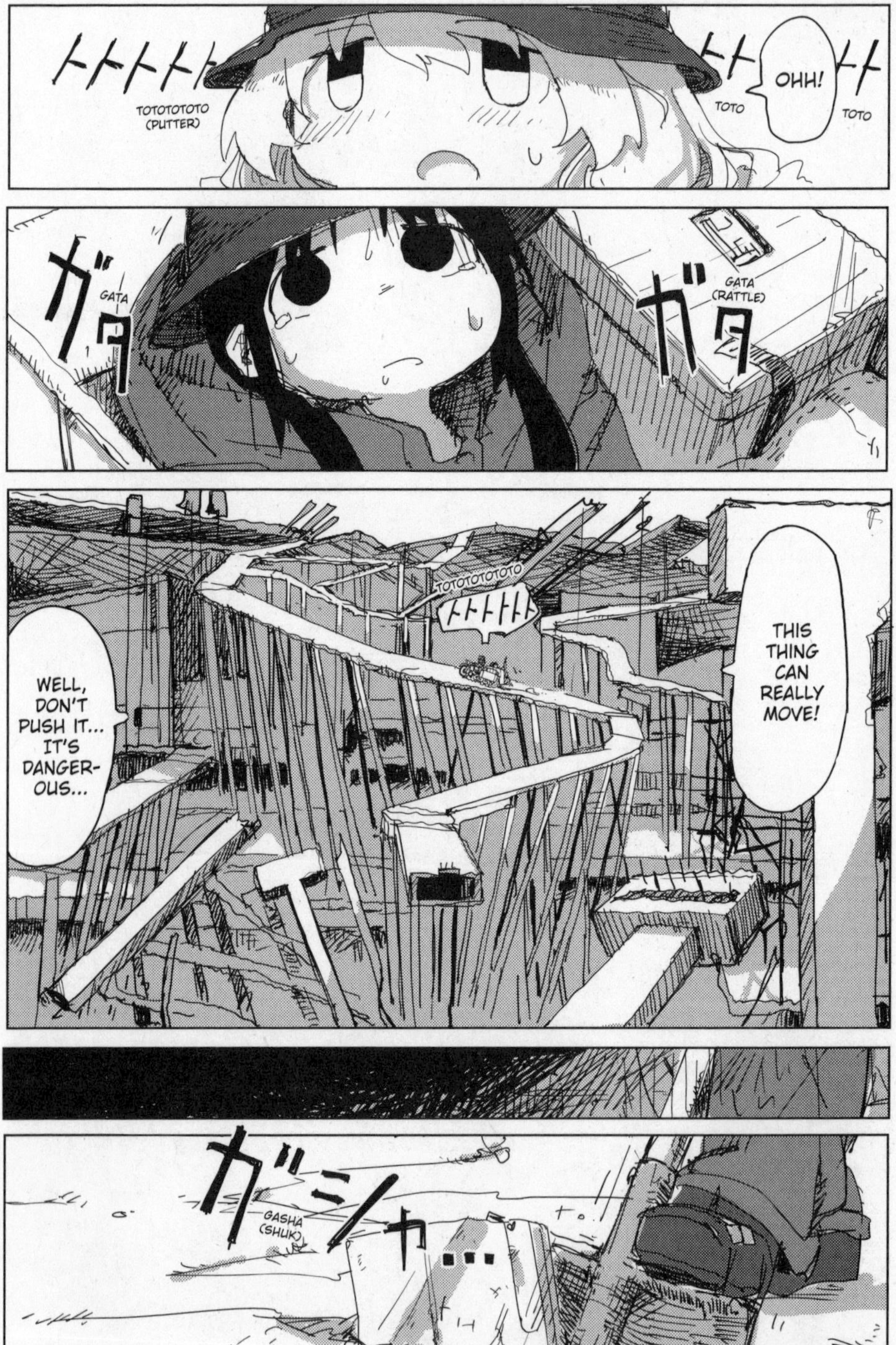

OHH!
TOTO
TOTO
TOTOTOTOTO (PUTTER)
GATA (RATTLE)
GATA
THIS THING CAN REALLY MOVE!
TOTOTOTOTOTO
WELL, DON'T PUSH IT... IT'S DANGER-OUS...
GASHA (SHUK)

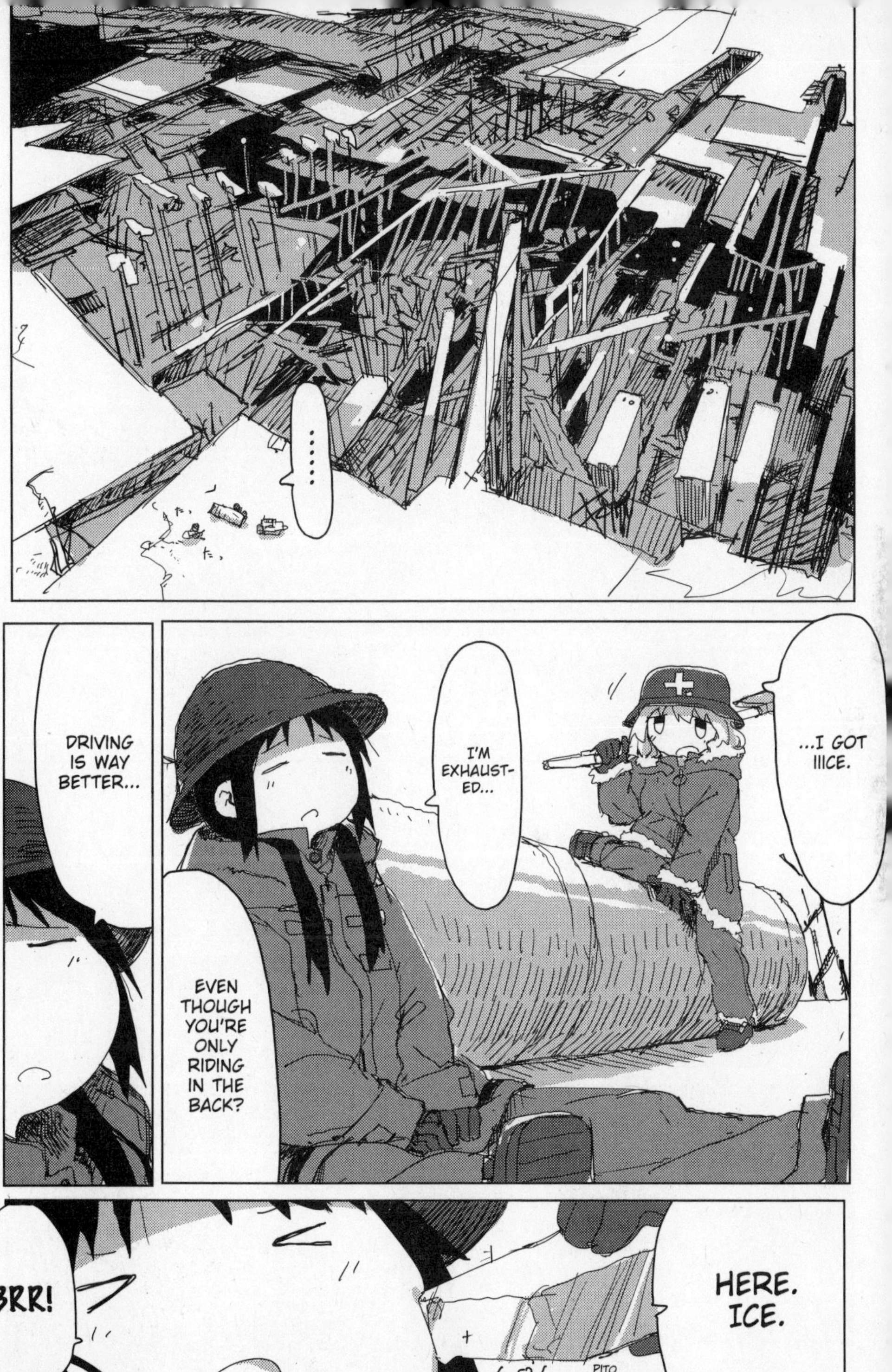
......
...I GOT IIICE.
I'M EXHAUST-ED...
EVEN THOUGH YOU'RE ONLY RIDING IN THE BACK?
DRIVING IS WAY BETTER...
HERE. ICE.
PITO (PRESS)
BRR!

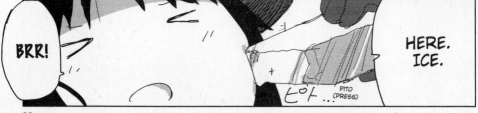

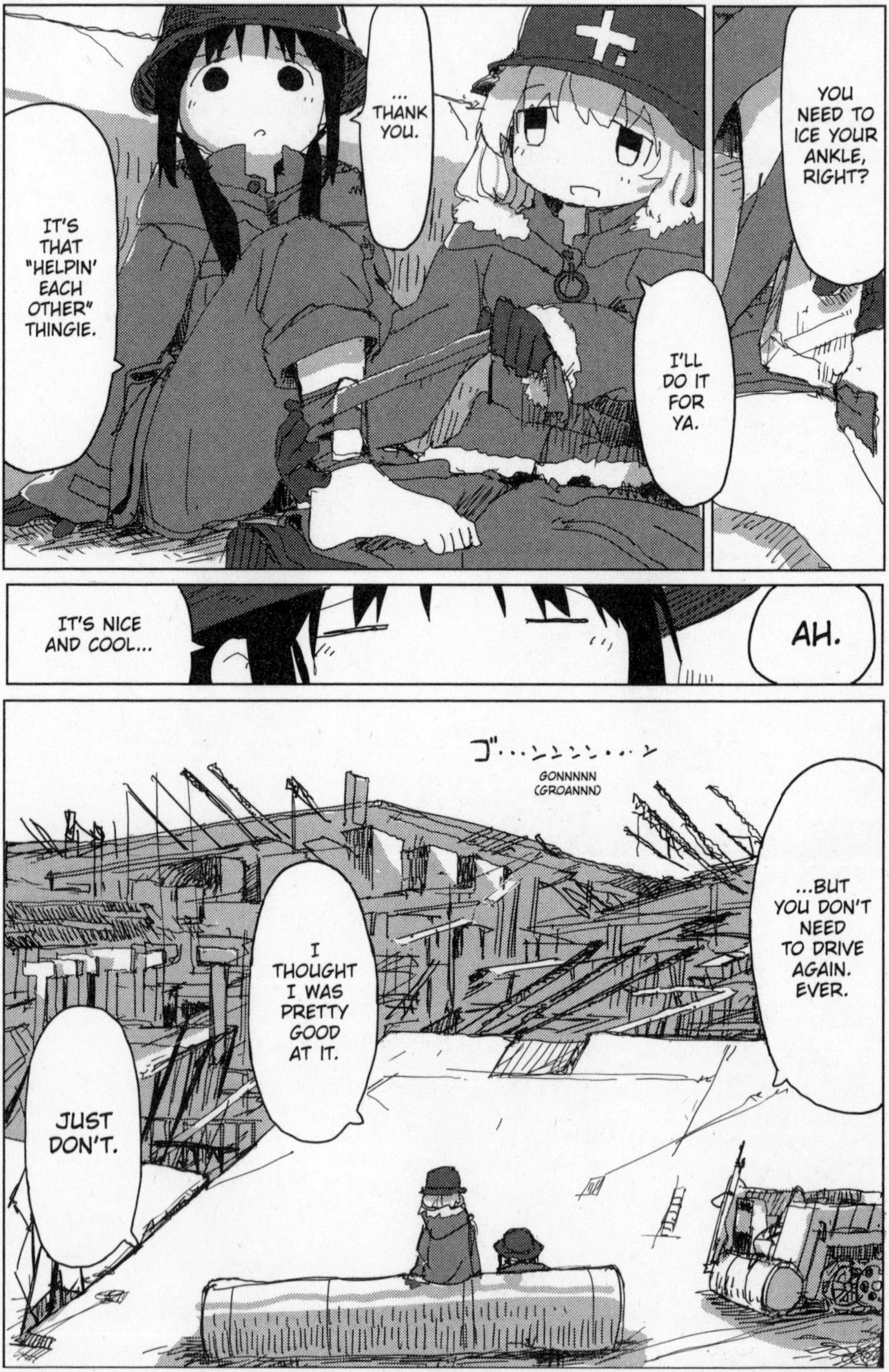
YOU NEED TO ICE YOUR ANKLE, RIGHT?
I'LL DO IT FOR YA.
... THANK YOU.
IT'S THAT "HELPIN' EACH OTHER" THINGIE.
AH.
IT'S NICE AND COOL...
ゴ…ンンンン…ン
GONNNNN (GROANNN)
...BUT YOU DON'T NEED TO DRIVE AGAIN. EVER.
I THOUGHT I WAS PRETTY GOOD AT IT.
JUST DON'T.

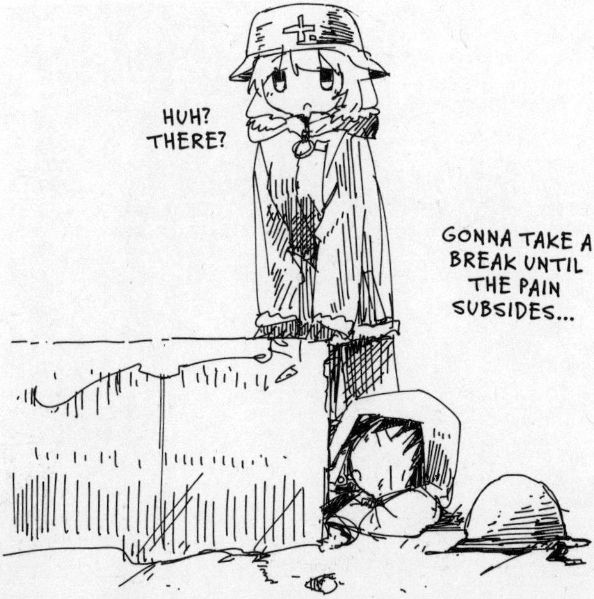
GONNA TAKE A BREAK UNTIL THE PAIN SUBSIDES...
HUH? THERE?

GIRLS' LAST TOUR

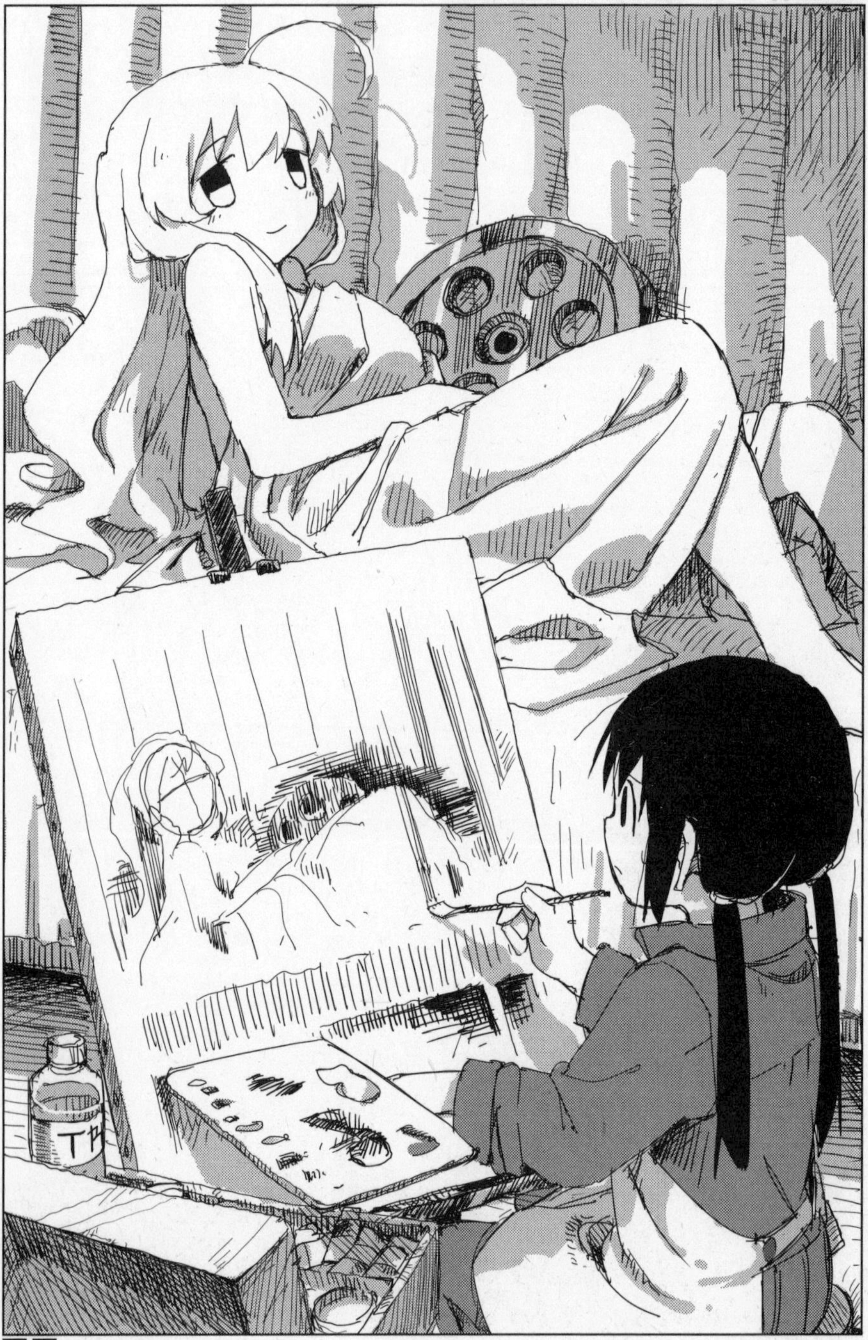

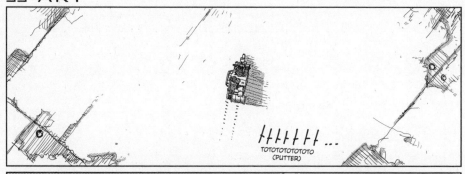

†††††† ...
TOTOTOTOTOTOTO
(PUTTER)

DO YOU SEE THAT?

...YEAH.

CHII-CHAN.

TOTOTOTOTO
(PUTTER)

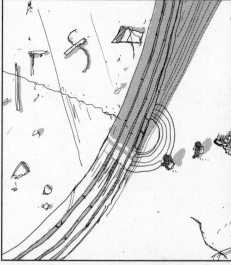

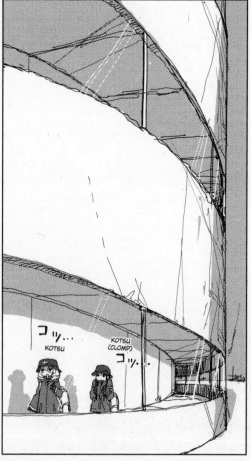

コツ…
KOTSU

KOTSU
(CLOMP)
コツ…

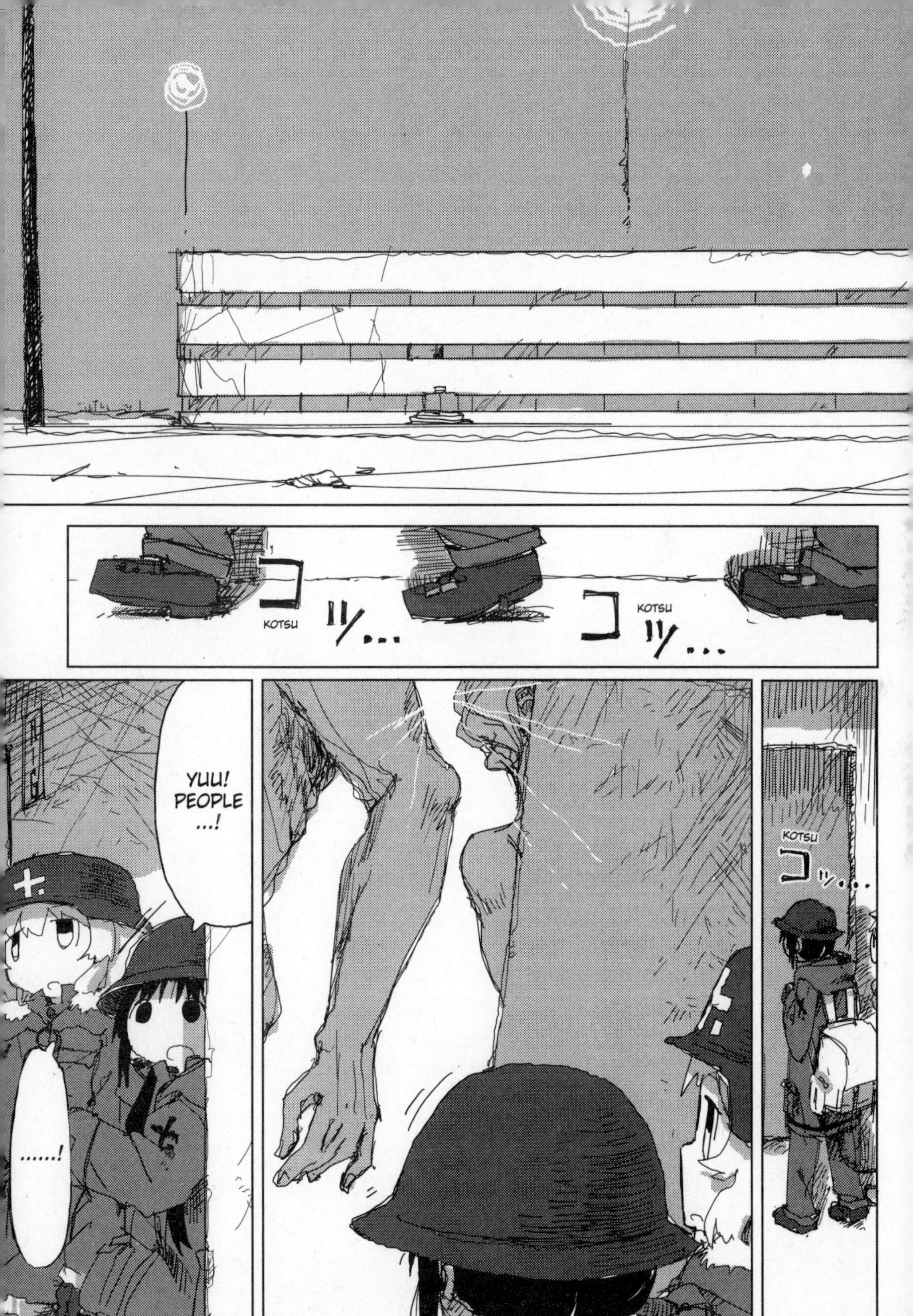

コッ...
KOTSU
コッ...
KOTSU
コッ...
KOTSU
YUU! PEOPLE ...!
......!

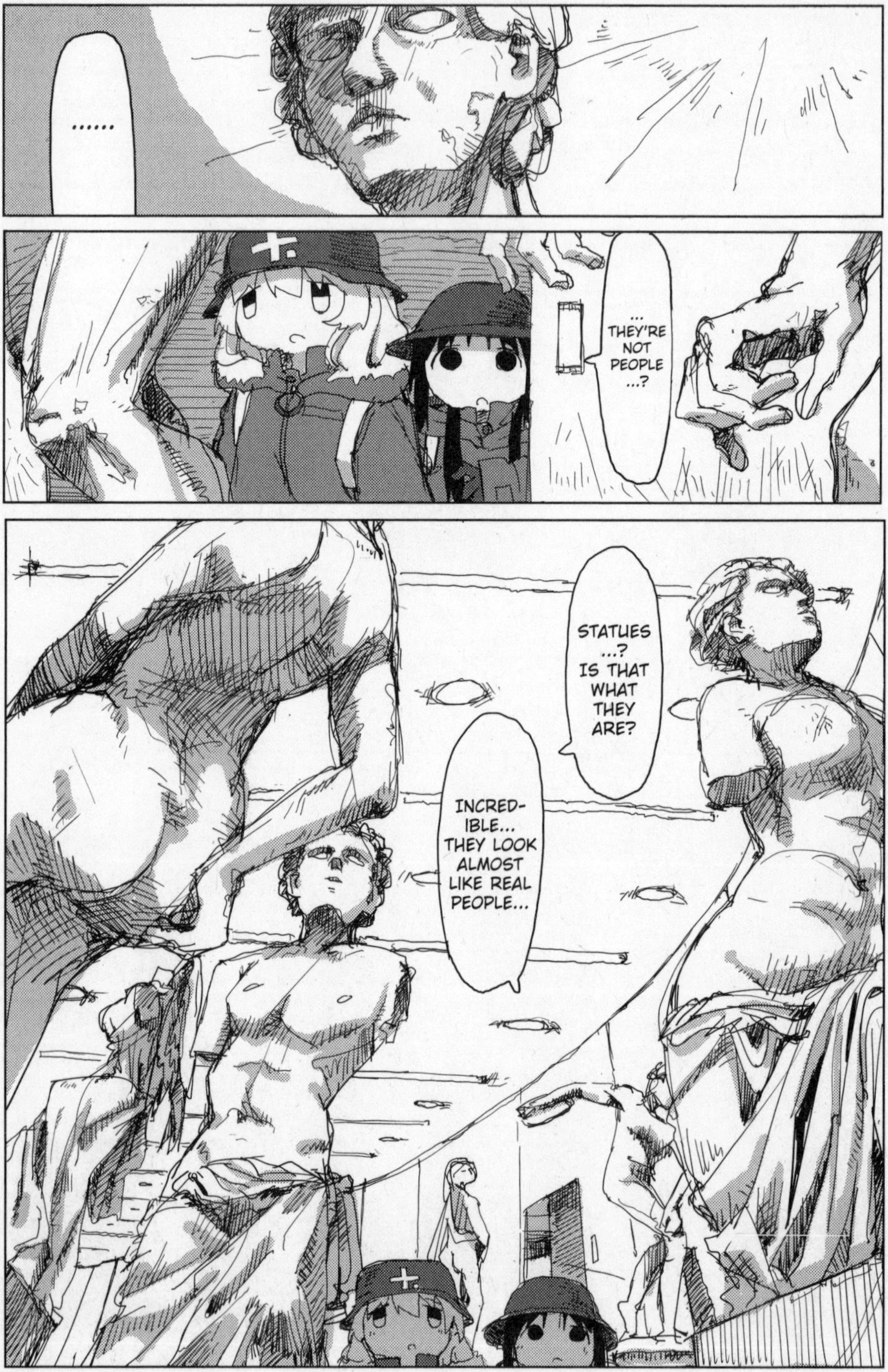
......
... THEY'RE NOT PEOPLE ...?
STATUES ...? IS THAT WHAT THEY ARE?
INCRED-IBLE... THEY LOOK ALMOST LIKE REAL PEOPLE...

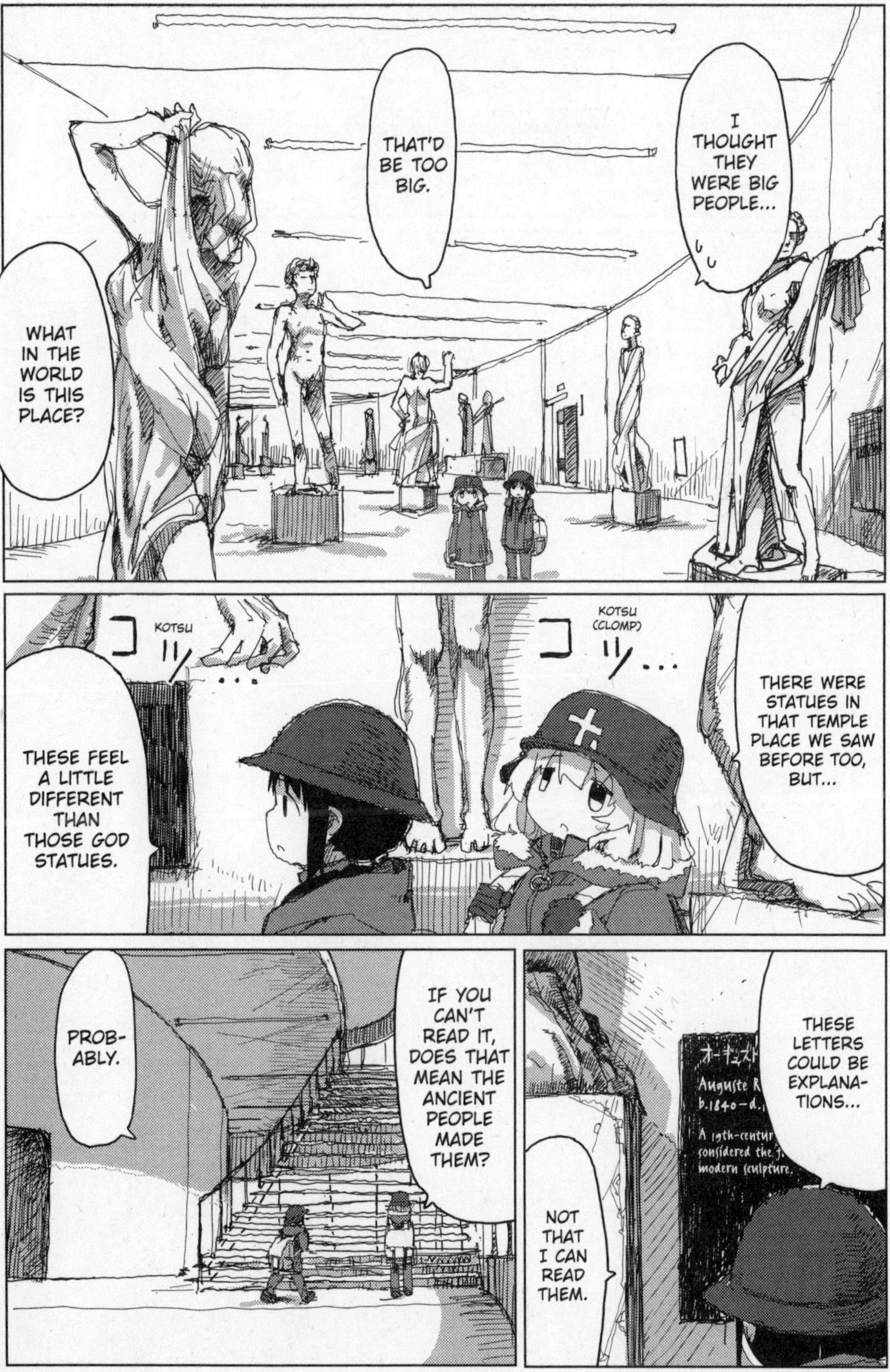

I THOUGHT THEY WERE BIG PEOPLE...
THAT'D BE TOO BIG.
WHAT IN THE WORLD IS THIS PLACE?
コツ...
KOTSU (CLOMP)
THERE WERE STATUES IN THAT TEMPLE PLACE WE SAW BEFORE TOO, BUT...
コツ...
KOTSU
THESE FEEL A LITTLE DIFFERENT THAN THOSE GOD STATUES.
THESE LETTERS COULD BE EXPLANATIONS...
Auguste R
b.1840–d.
A 19th-century
considered the f
modern sculpture.
NOT THAT I CAN READ THEM.
IF YOU CAN'T READ IT, DOES THAT MEAN THE ANCIENT PEOPLE MADE THEM?
PROB-ABLY.

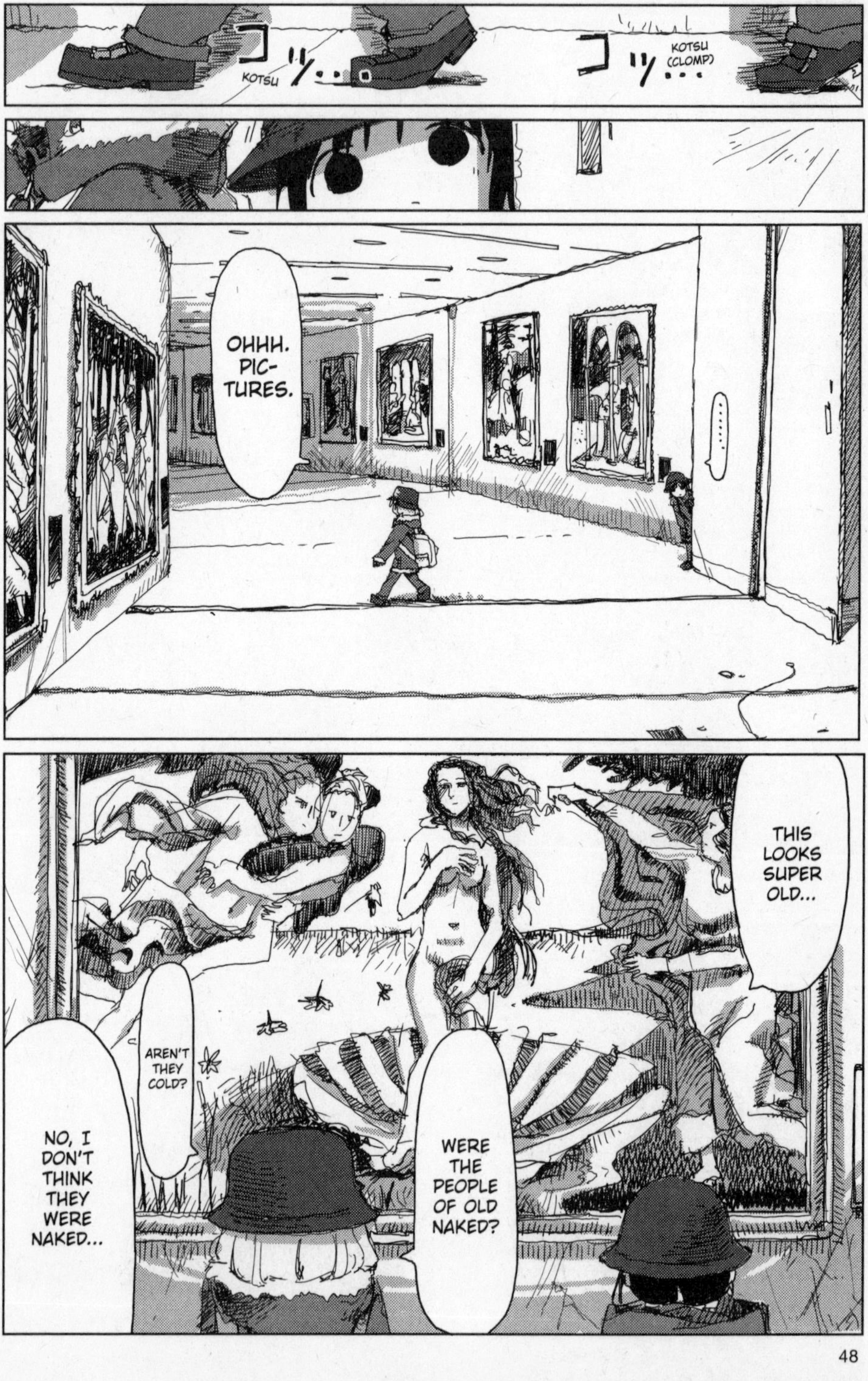
コッ…
KOTSU (CLOMP)
コッ…
KOTSU
OHHH. PIC-TURES.
......
THIS LOOKS SUPER OLD...
WERE THE PEOPLE OF OLD NAKED?
AREN'T THEY COLD?
NO, I DON'T THINK THEY WERE NAKED...

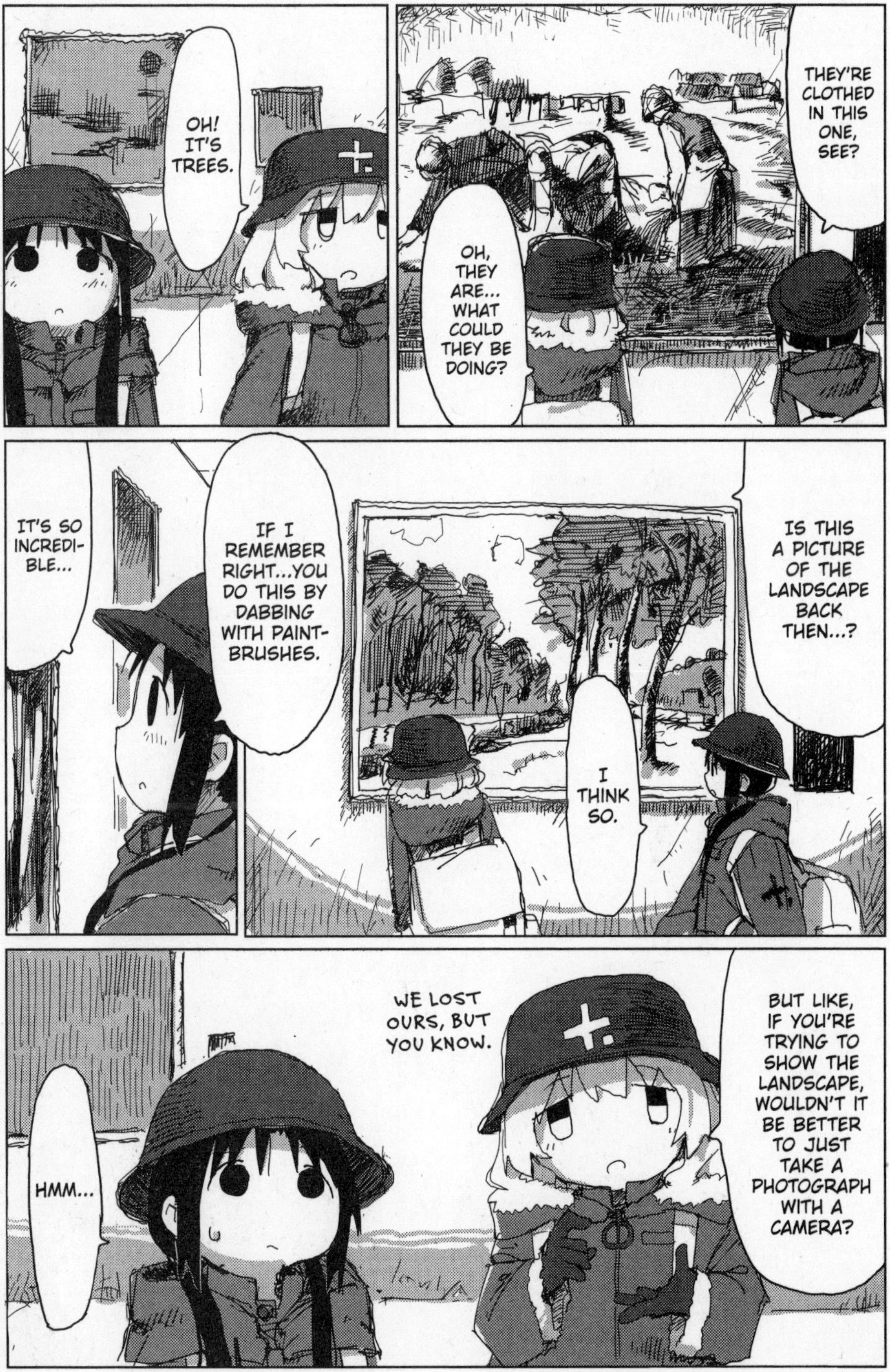
THEY'RE CLOTHED IN THIS ONE, SEE?
OH, THEY ARE... WHAT COULD THEY BE DOING?
OH! IT'S TREES.
IS THIS A PICTURE OF THE LANDSCAPE BACK THEN...?
I THINK SO.
IF I REMEMBER RIGHT...YOU DO THIS BY DABBING WITH PAINT-BRUSHES.
IT'S SO INCREDI-BLE...
BUT LIKE, IF YOU'RE TRYING TO SHOW THE LANDSCAPE, WOULDN'T IT BE BETTER TO JUST TAKE A PHOTOGRAPH WITH A CAMERA?
WE LOST OURS, BUT YOU KNOW.
HMM...

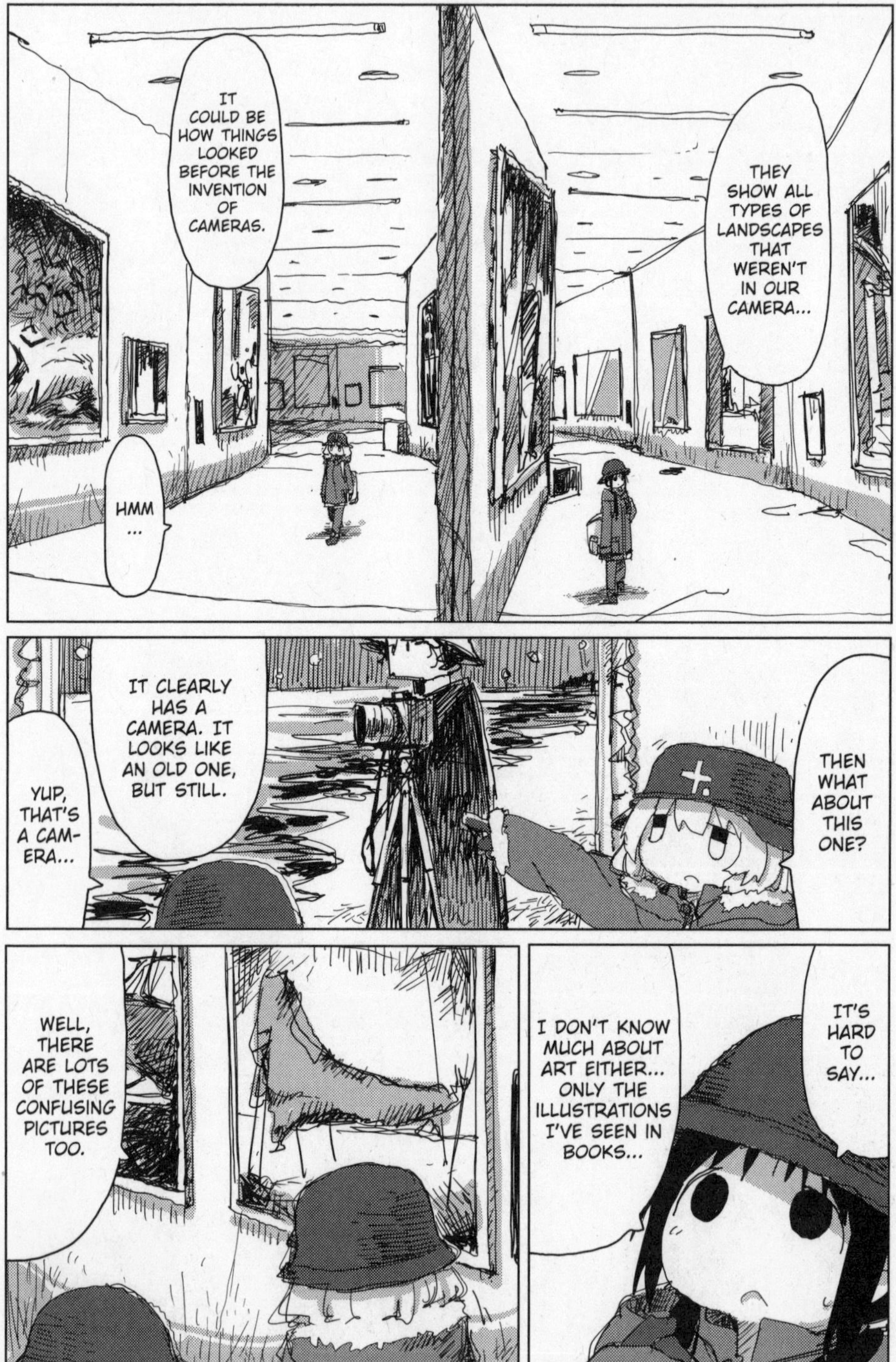
THEY SHOW ALL TYPES OF LANDSCAPES THAT WEREN'T IN OUR CAMERA...
IT COULD BE HOW THINGS LOOKED BEFORE THE INVENTION OF CAMERAS.
HMM...
THEN WHAT ABOUT THIS ONE?
IT CLEARLY HAS A CAMERA. IT LOOKS LIKE AN OLD ONE, BUT STILL.
YUP, THAT'S A CAMERA...
IT'S HARD TO SAY...
I DON'T KNOW MUCH ABOUT ART EITHER... ONLY THE ILLUSTRATIONS I'VE SEEN IN BOOKS...
WELL, THERE ARE LOTS OF THESE CONFUSING PICTURES TOO.

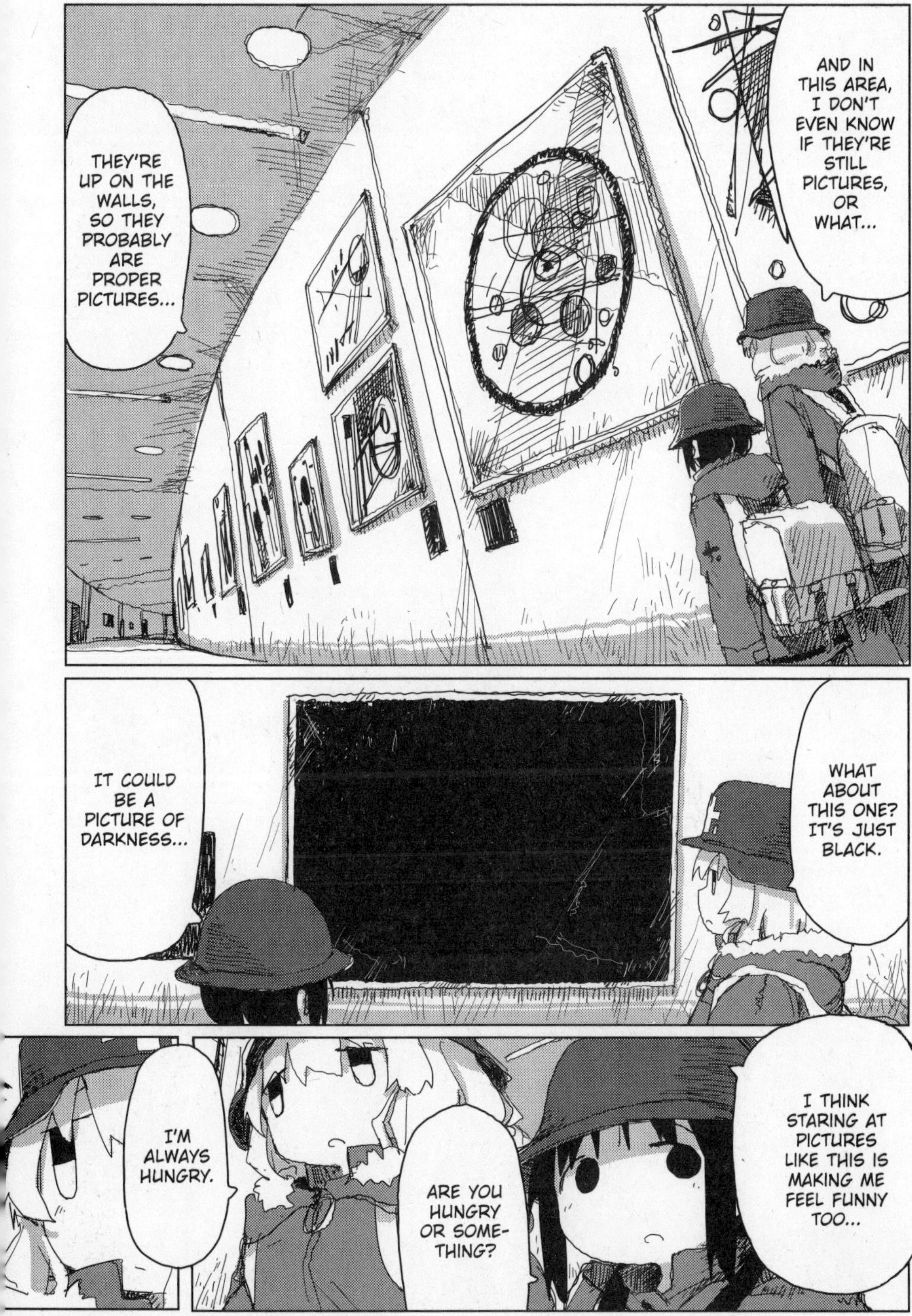
AND IN THIS AREA, I DON'T EVEN KNOW IF THEY'RE STILL PICTURES, OR WHAT...
THEY'RE UP ON THE WALLS, SO THEY PROBABLY ARE PROPER PICTURES...
WHAT ABOUT THIS ONE? IT'S JUST BLACK.
IT COULD BE A PICTURE OF DARKNESS...
I THINK STARING AT PICTURES LIKE THIS IS MAKING ME FEEL FUNNY TOO...
ARE YOU HUNGRY OR SOME-THING?
I'M ALWAYS HUNGRY.

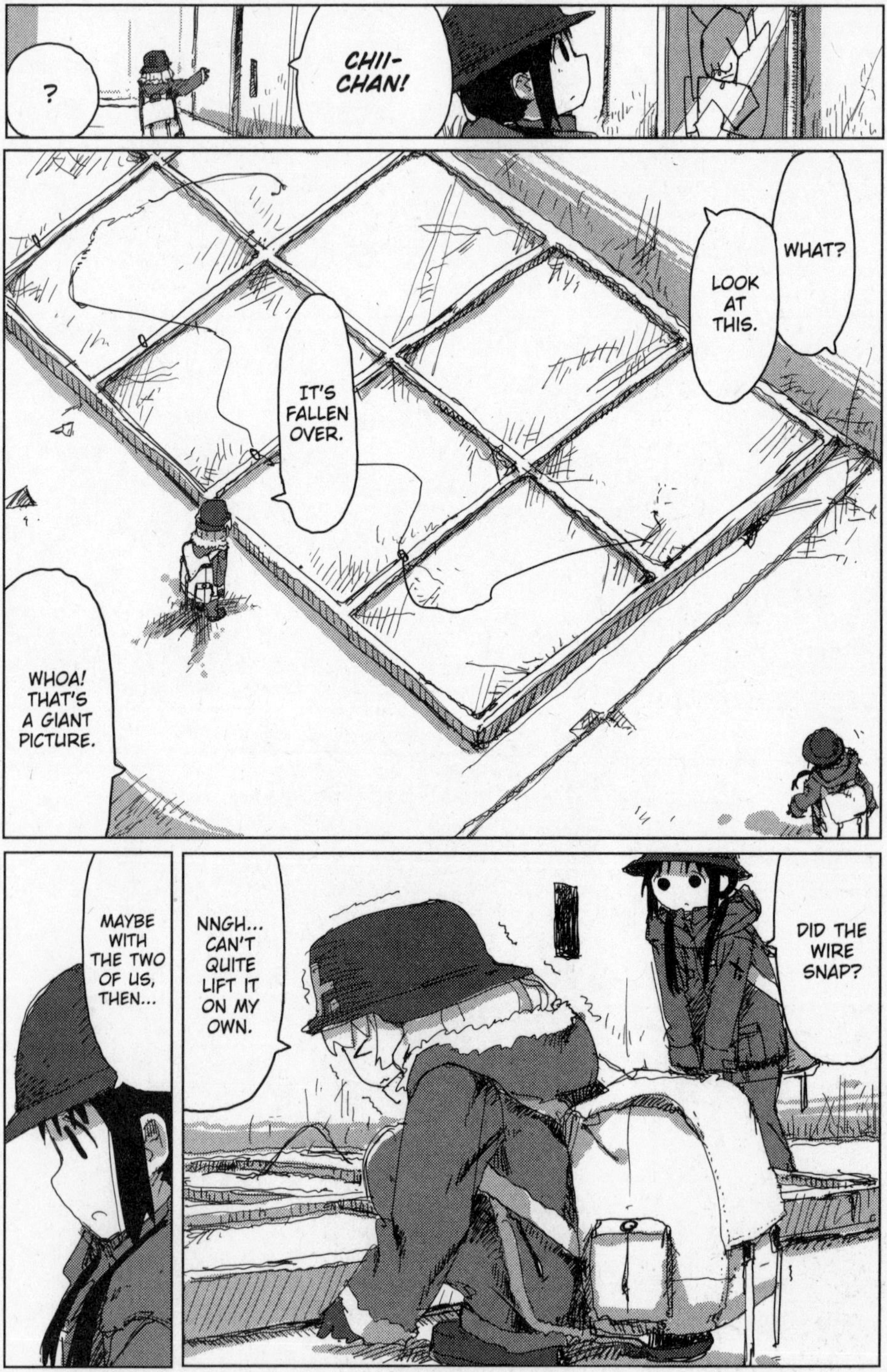
CHII-CHAN!
?
WHAT?
LOOK AT THIS.
IT'S FALLEN OVER.
WHOA! THAT'S A GIANT PICTURE.
DID THE WIRE SNAP?
NNGH... CAN'T QUITE LIFT IT ON MY OWN.
MAYBE WITH THE TWO OF US, THEN...

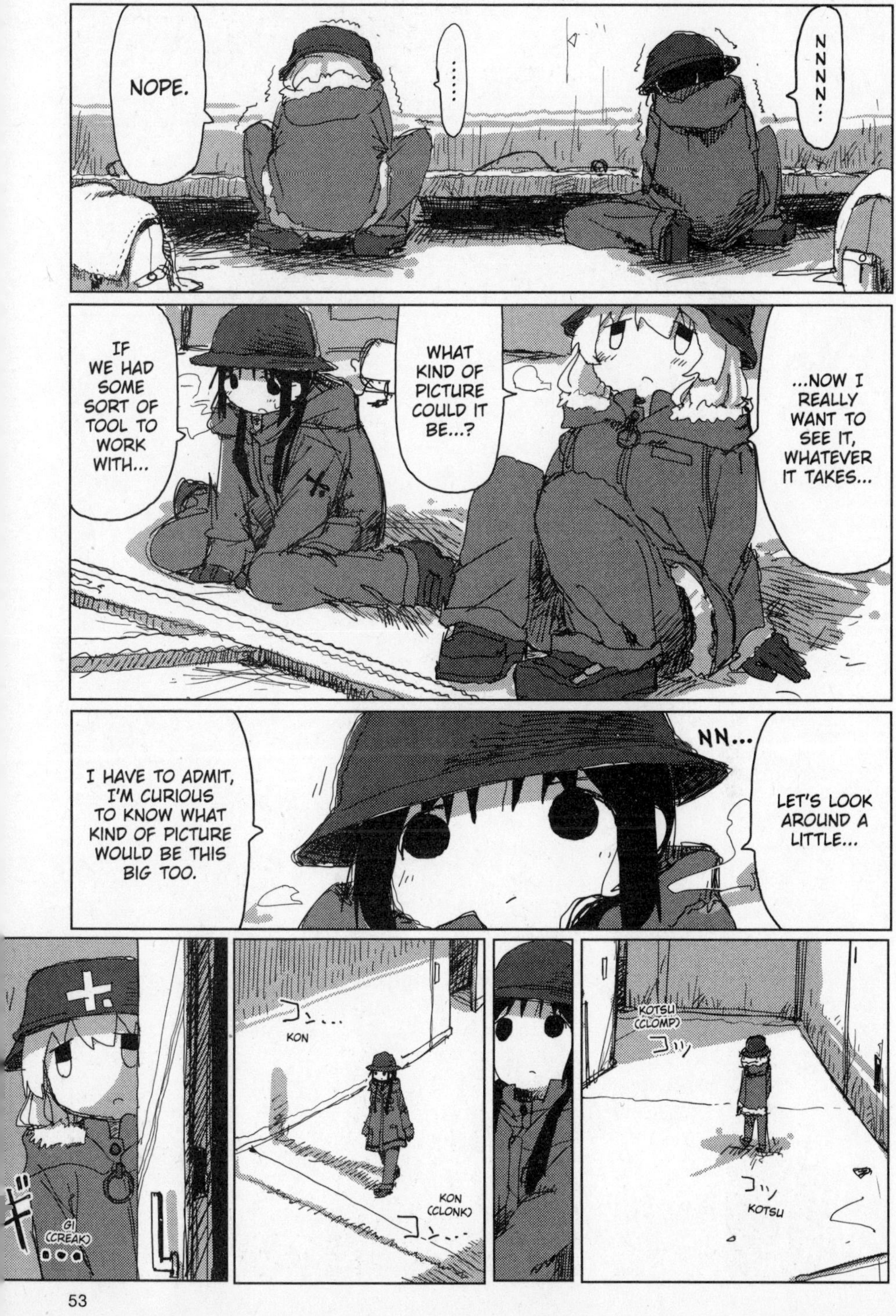
NNNN...
......
NOPE.
...NOW I REALLY WANT TO SEE IT, WHATEVER IT TAKES...
WHAT KIND OF PICTURE COULD IT BE...?
IF WE HAD SOME SORT OF TOOL TO WORK WITH...
NN...
LET'S LOOK AROUND A LITTLE...
I HAVE TO ADMIT, I'M CURIOUS TO KNOW WHAT KIND OF PICTURE WOULD BE THIS BIG TOO.
KOTSU (CLOMP)
KOTSU
KON
KON (CLONK)
GI (CREAK)

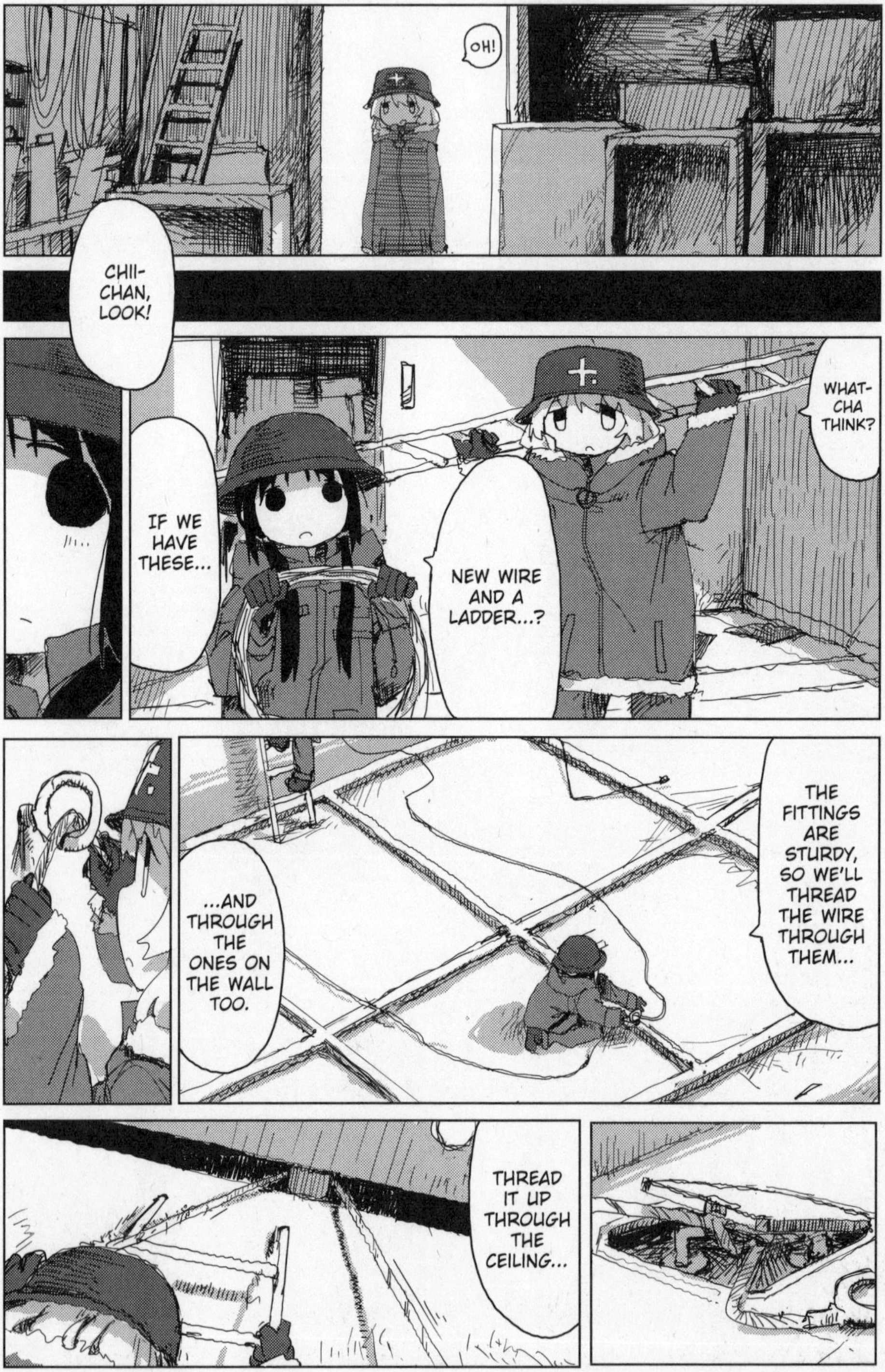
OH!
CHII-CHAN, LOOK!
WHAT-CHA THINK?
NEW WIRE AND A LADDER...?
IF WE HAVE THESE...
THE FITTINGS ARE STURDY, SO WE'LL THREAD THE WIRE THROUGH THEM...
...AND THROUGH THE ONES ON THE WALL TOO.
THREAD IT UP THROUGH THE CEILING...

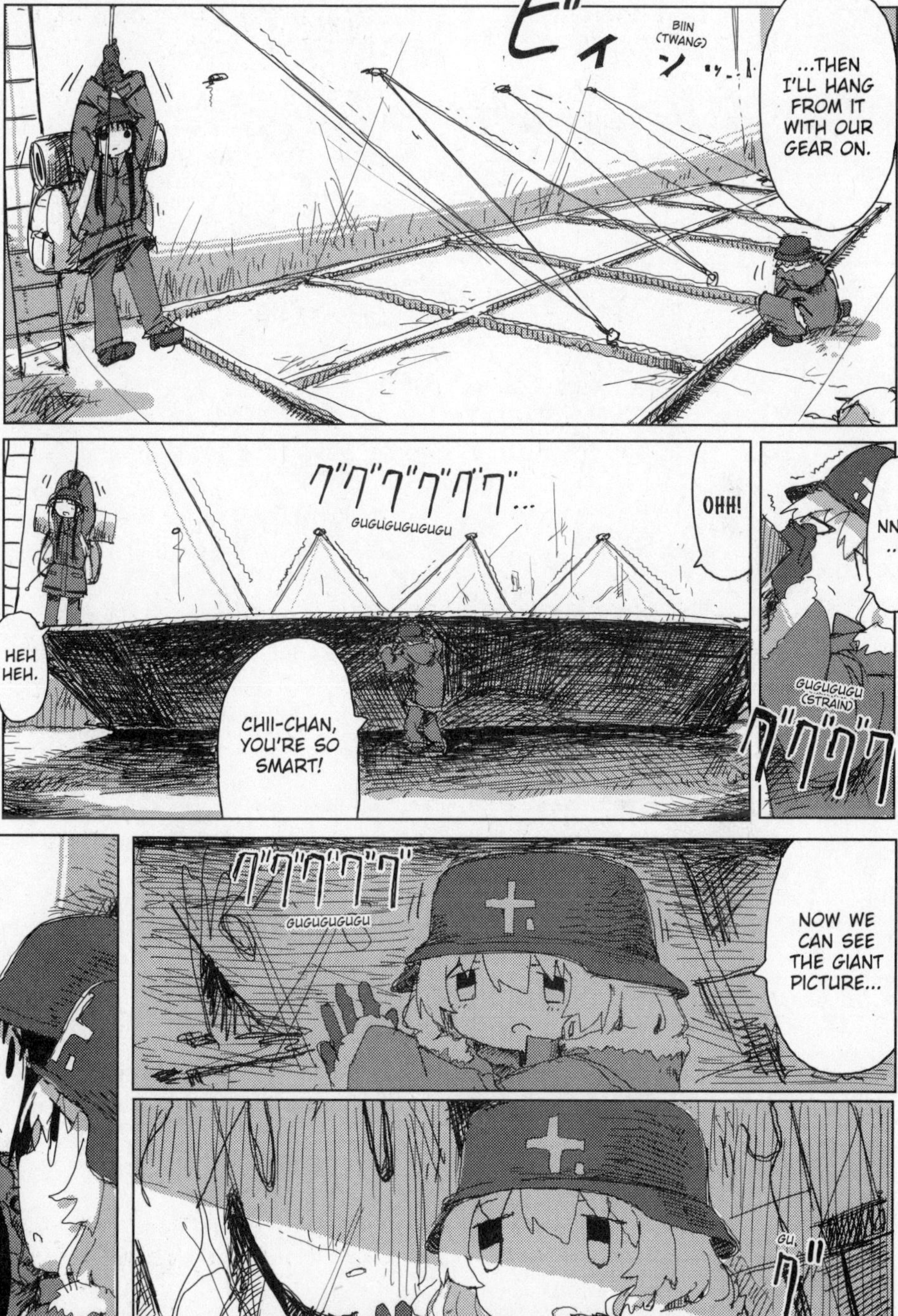

ビィン
BIIN (TWANG)
...THEN I'LL HANG FROM IT WITH OUR GEAR ON.
NNH ...
GUGUGUGU (STRAIN)
OHH!
GUGUGUGUGUGU
HEH HEH.
CHII-CHAN, YOU'RE SO SMART!
NOW WE CAN SEE THE GIANT PICTURE...
GUGUGUGUGU
GU

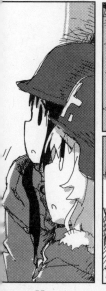

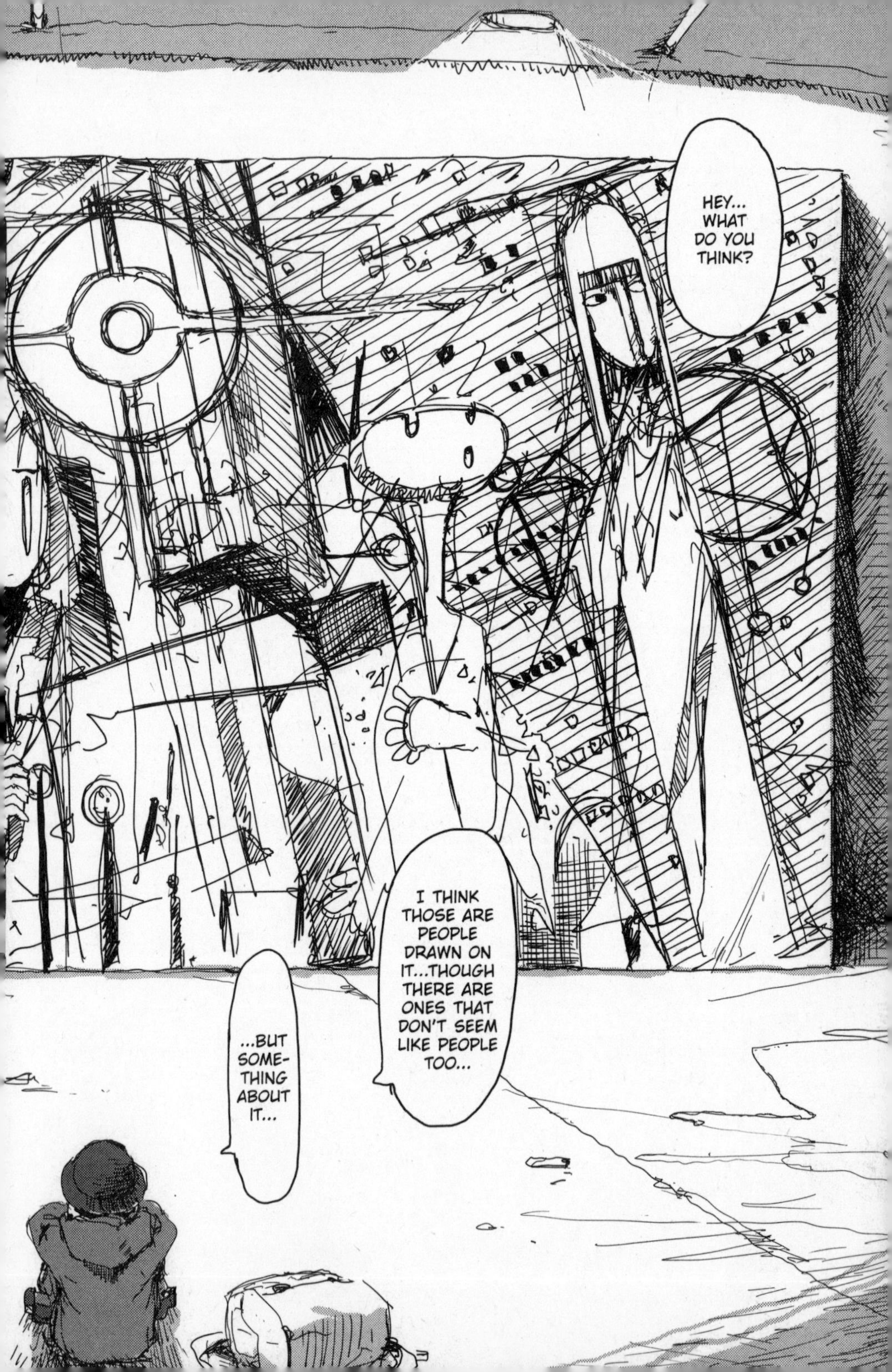
HEY... WHAT DO YOU THINK?
I THINK THOSE ARE PEOPLE DRAWN ON IT...THOUGH THERE ARE ONES THAT DON'T SEEM LIKE PEOPLE TOO...
...BUT SOMETHING ABOUT IT...

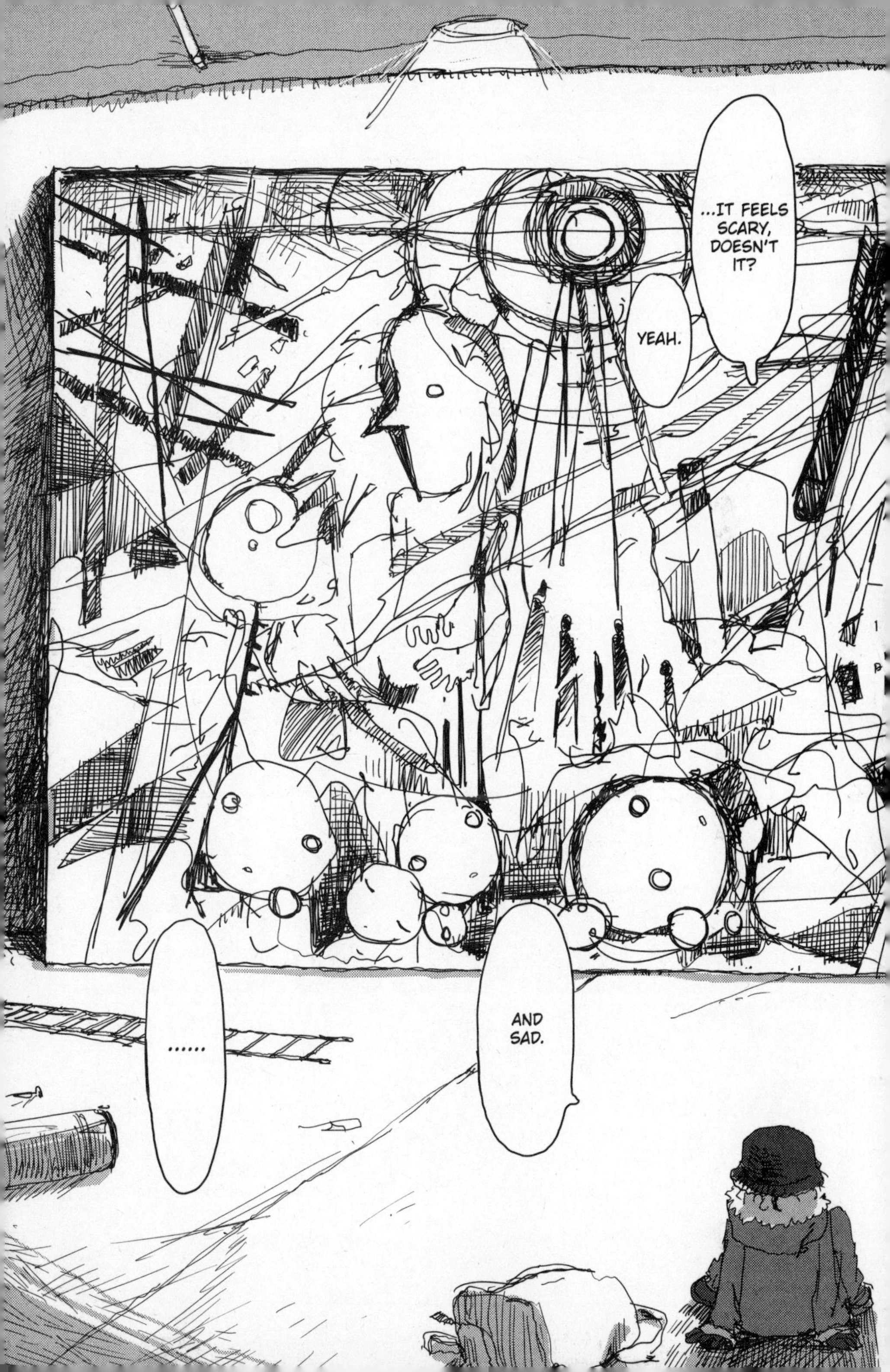
...IT FEELS SCARY, DOESN'T IT?
YEAH.
AND SAD.
......

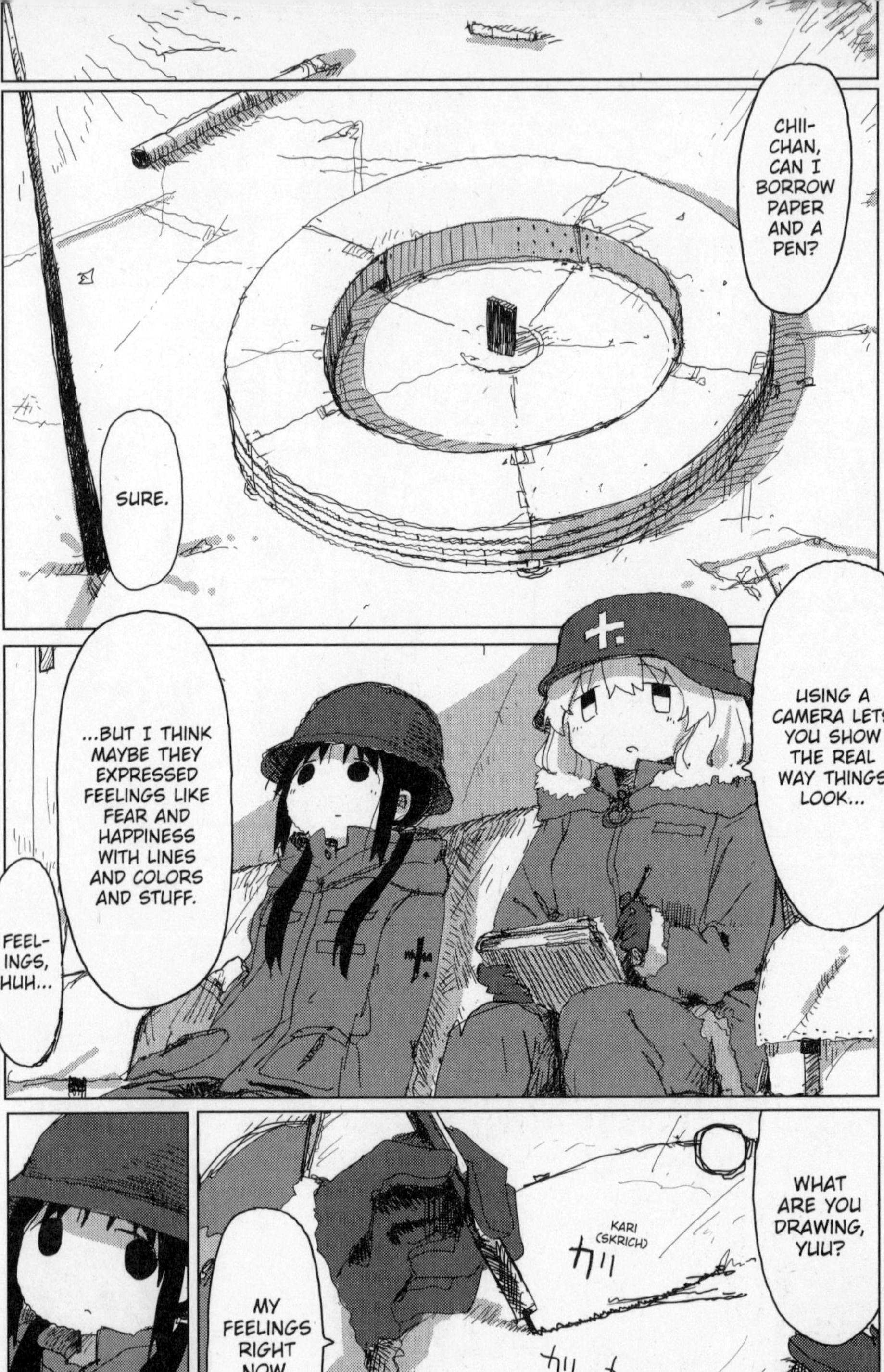
CHII-CHAN, CAN I BORROW PAPER AND A PEN?
SURE.
USING A CAMERA LETS YOU SHOW THE REAL WAY THINGS LOOK...
...BUT I THINK MAYBE THEY EXPRESSED FEELINGS LIKE FEAR AND HAPPINESS WITH LINES AND COLORS AND STUFF.
FEEL-INGS, HUH...
WHAT ARE YOU DRAWING, YUU?
カリ
KARI (SKRICH)
MY FEELINGS RIGHT NOW.
カリ
KARI
カリ
KARI

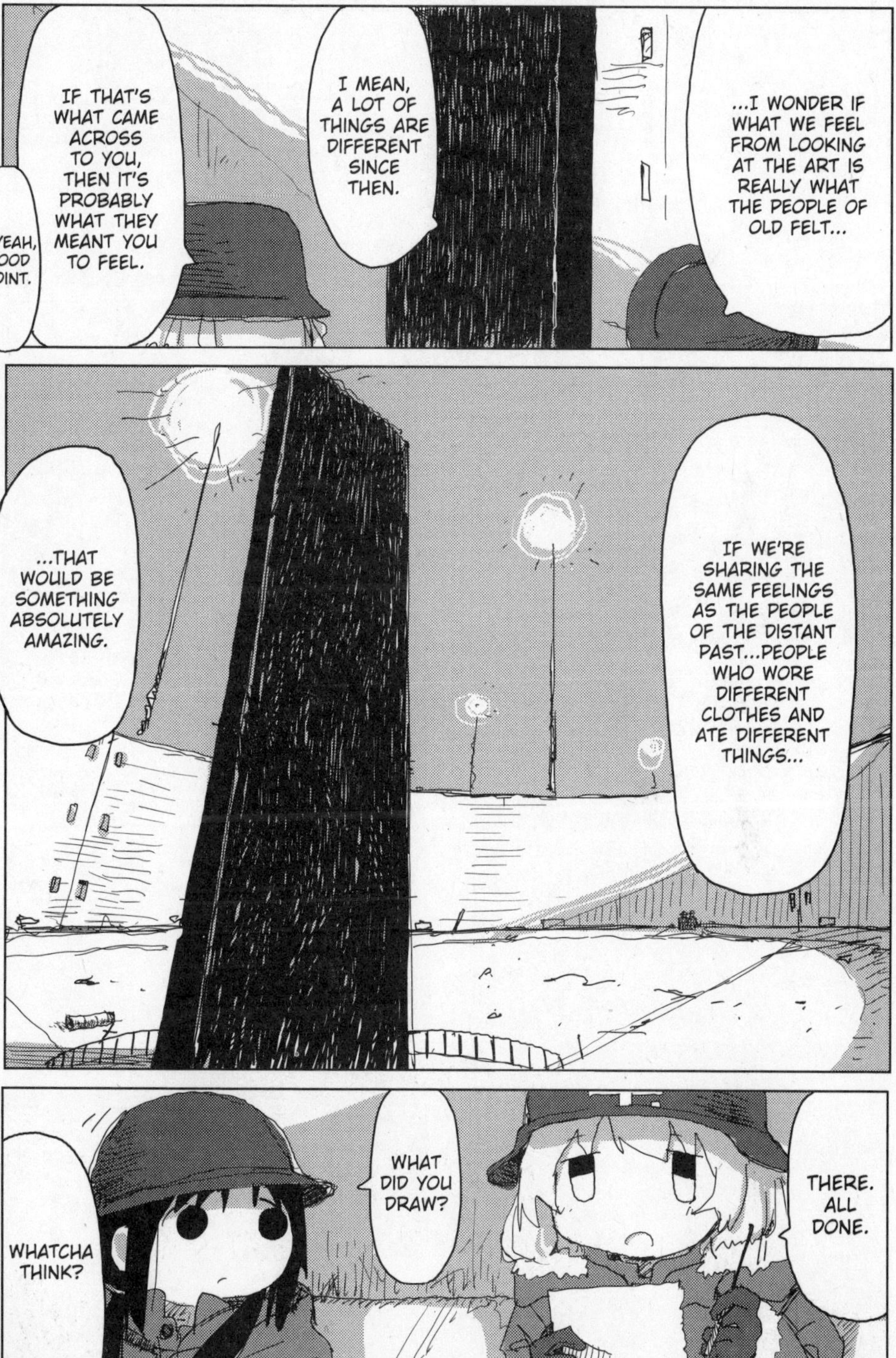
...I WONDER IF WHAT WE FEEL FROM LOOKING AT THE ART IS REALLY WHAT THE PEOPLE OF OLD FELT...
I MEAN, A LOT OF THINGS ARE DIFFERENT SINCE THEN.
IF THAT'S WHAT CAME ACROSS TO YOU, THEN IT'S PROBABLY WHAT THEY MEANT YOU TO FEEL.
...YEAH, GOOD POINT.
IF WE'RE SHARING THE SAME FEELINGS AS THE PEOPLE OF THE DISTANT PAST...PEOPLE WHO WORE DIFFERENT CLOTHES AND ATE DIFFERENT THINGS...
...THAT WOULD BE SOMETHING ABSOLUTELY AMAZING.
THERE. ALL DONE.
WHAT DID YOU DRAW?
WHATCHA THINK?

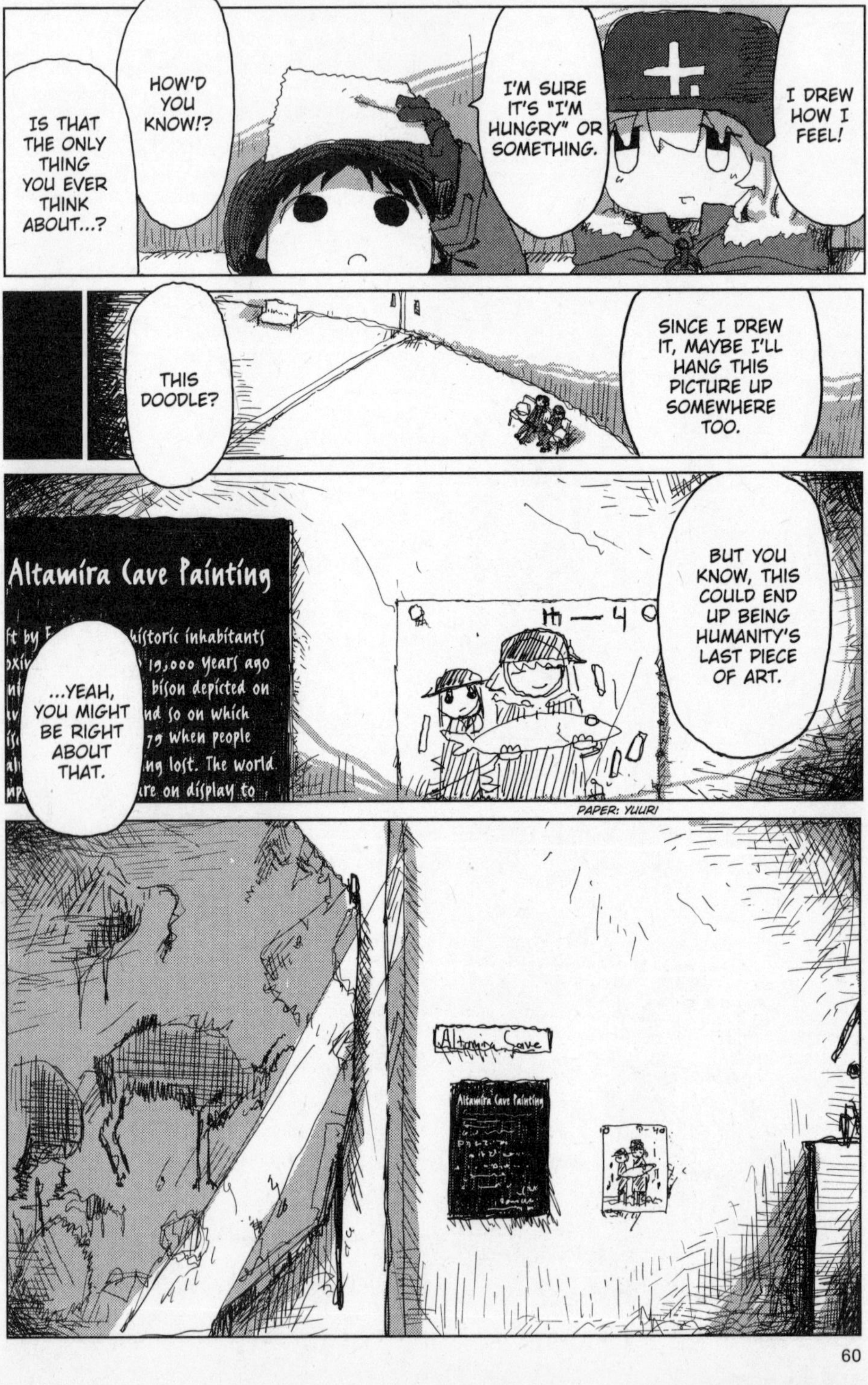
I DREW HOW I FEEL!
I'M SURE IT'S "I'M HUNGRY" OR SOMETHING.
HOW'D YOU KNOW!?
IS THAT THE ONLY THING YOU EVER THINK ABOUT...?
SINCE I DREW IT, MAYBE I'LL HANG THIS PICTURE UP SOMEWHERE TOO.
THIS DOODLE?
BUT YOU KNOW, THIS COULD END UP BEING HUMANITY'S LAST PIECE OF ART.
Altamira Cave Painting
...YEAH, YOU MIGHT BE RIGHT ABOUT THAT.
PAPER: YUURI
Altamira Cave
Altamira Cave Painting

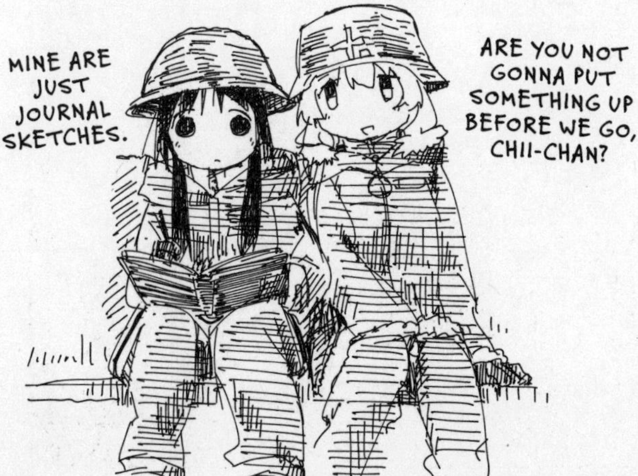
ARE YOU NOT GONNA PUT SOMETHING UP BEFORE WE GO, CHII-CHAN?
MINE ARE JUST JOURNAL SKETCHES.

GIRLS' LAST TOUR

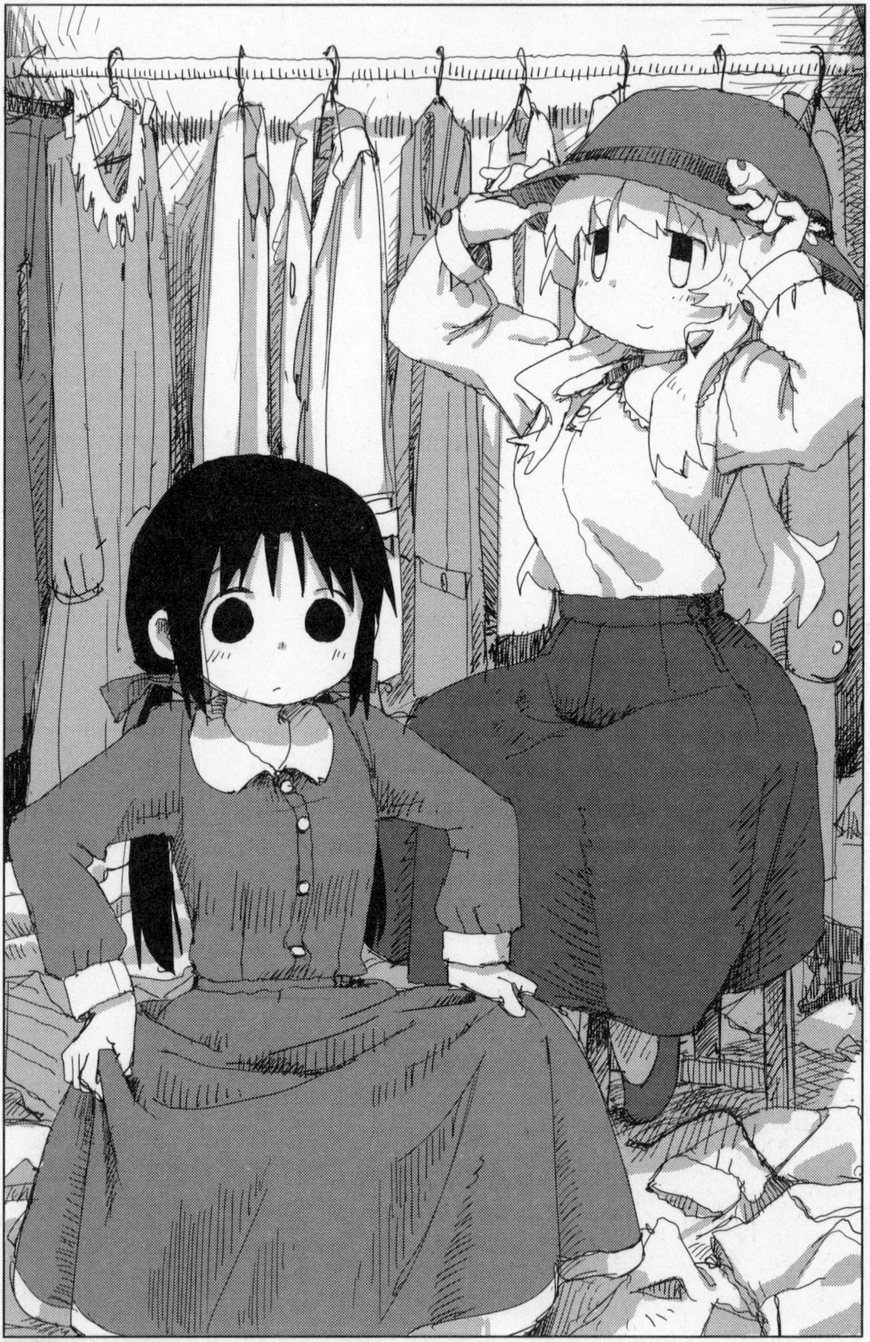

36 CLOTHING

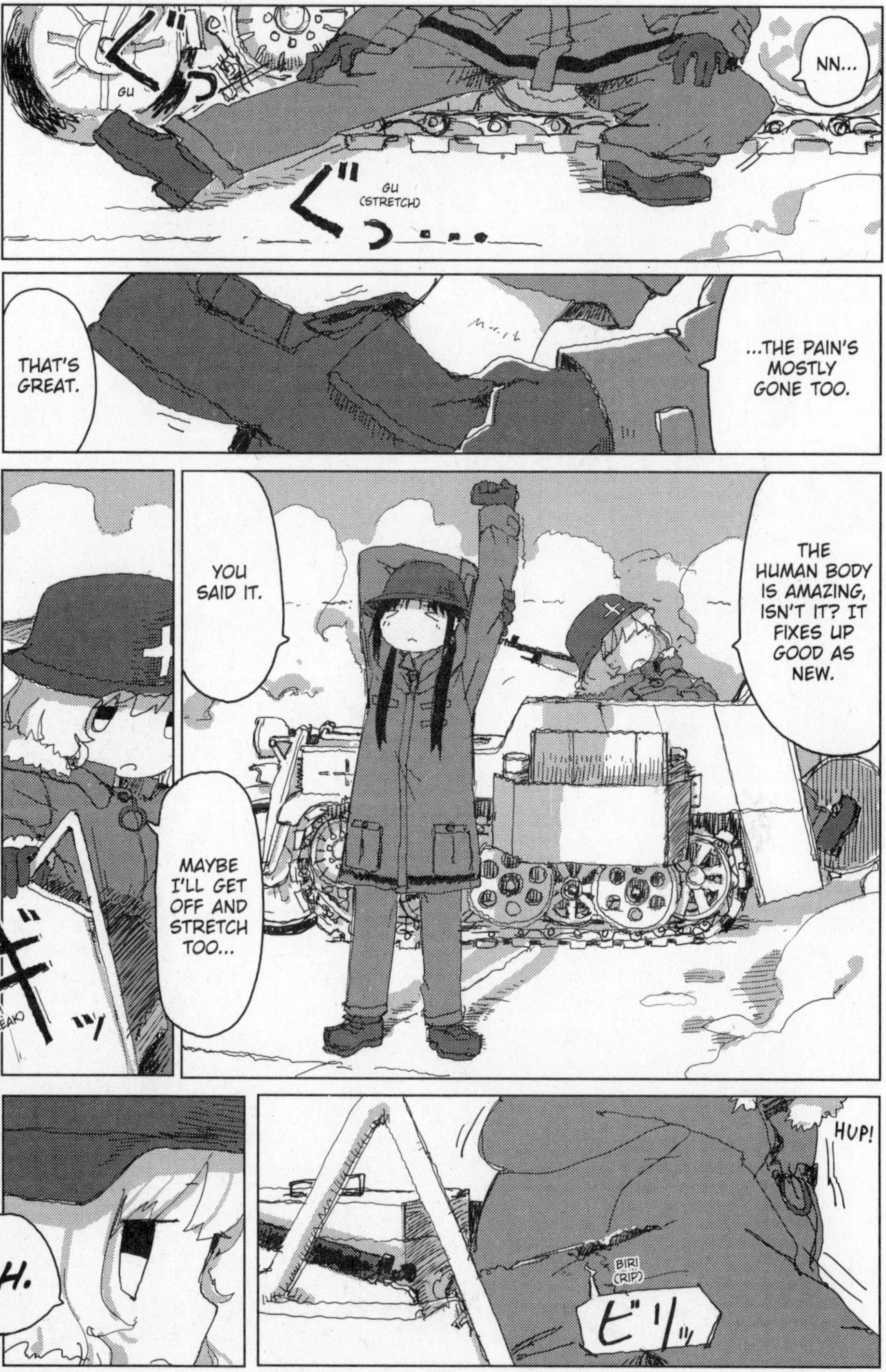
NN...
ぐっ
GU
ぐっ...
GU (STRETCH)
...THE PAIN'S MOSTLY GONE TOO.
THAT'S GREAT.
THE HUMAN BODY IS AMAZING, ISN'T IT? IT FIXES UP GOOD AS NEW.
YOU SAID IT.
MAYBE I'LL GET OFF AND STRETCH TOO...
ギッ
GI (CREAK)
HUP!
ビリッ
BIRI (RIP)
AH.

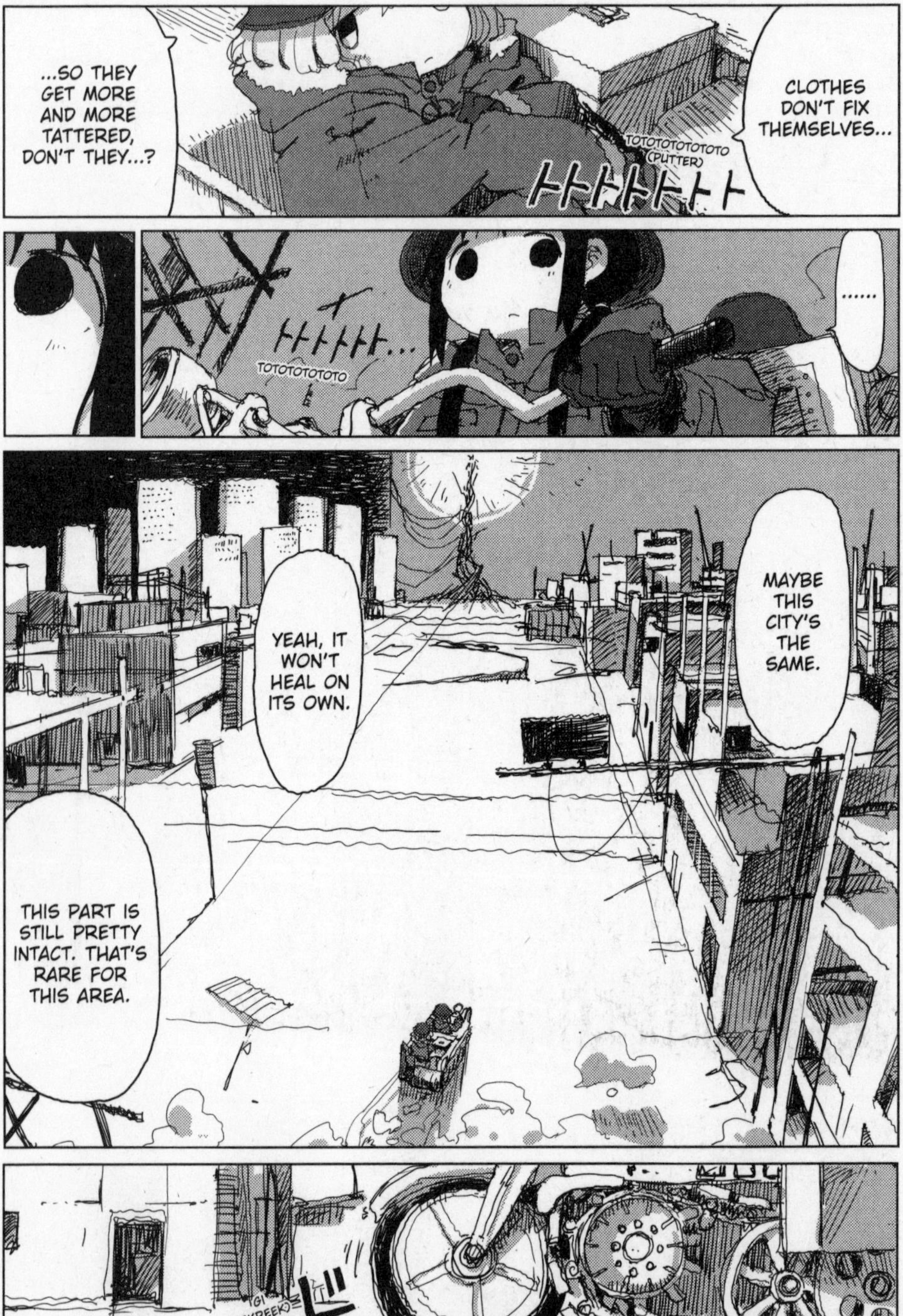
CLOTHES DON'T FIX THEMSELVES...
TOTOTOTOTOTOTO (PUTTER)
...SO THEY GET MORE AND MORE TATTERED, DON'T THEY...?
......
TOTOTOTOTOTO
MAYBE THIS CITY'S THE SAME.
YEAH, IT WON'T HEAL ON ITS OWN.
THIS PART IS STILL PRETTY INTACT. THAT'S RARE FOR THIS AREA.
GI (SKREEK)

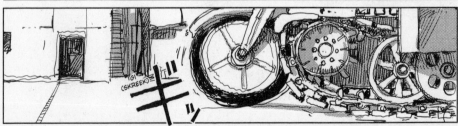

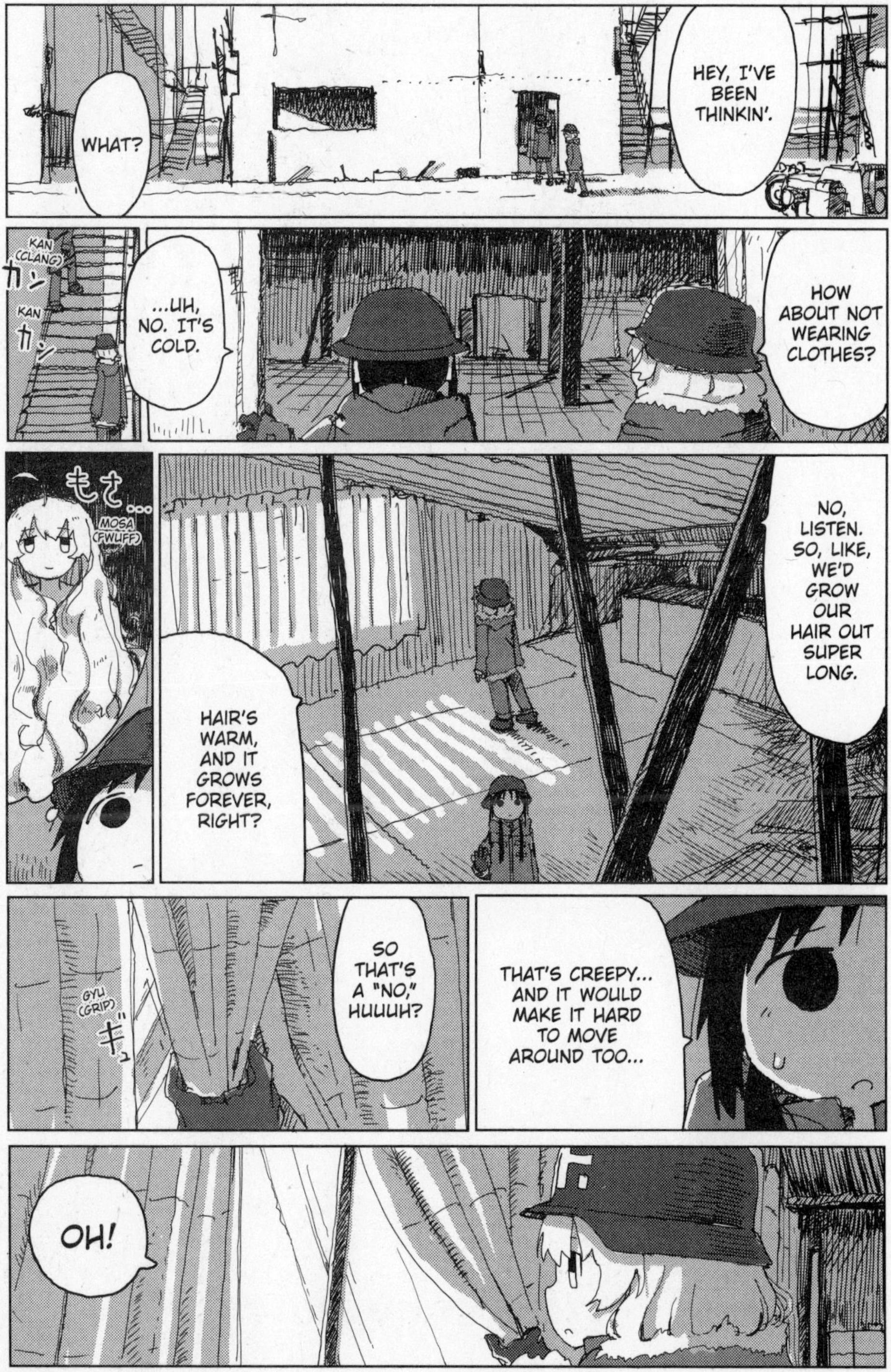
HEY, I'VE BEEN THINKIN'.
WHAT?
HOW ABOUT NOT WEARING CLOTHES?
...UH, NO. IT'S COLD.
KAN (CLANG)
カン
KAN
カン
NO, LISTEN. SO, LIKE, WE'D GROW OUR HAIR OUT SUPER LONG.
HAIR'S WARM, AND IT GROWS FOREVER, RIGHT?
もさ...
MOSA (FWUFF)
THAT'S CREEPY... AND IT WOULD MAKE IT HARD TO MOVE AROUND TOO...
SO THAT'S A "NO," HUUUH?
GYU (GRIP)
ギュ
OH!

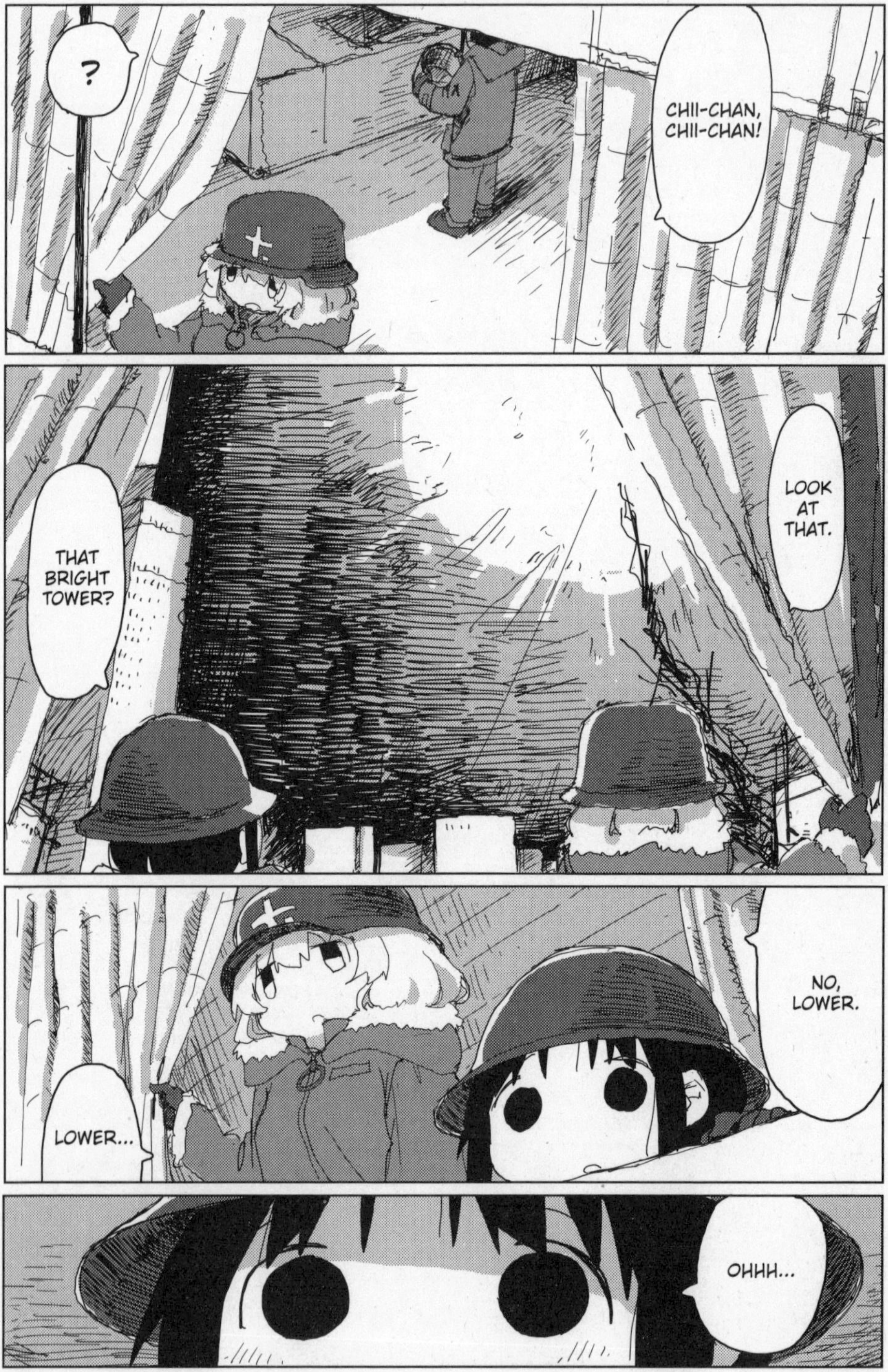
CHII-CHAN, CHII-CHAN!
?
LOOK AT THAT.
THAT BRIGHT TOWER?
NO, LOWER.
LOWER...
OHHH...

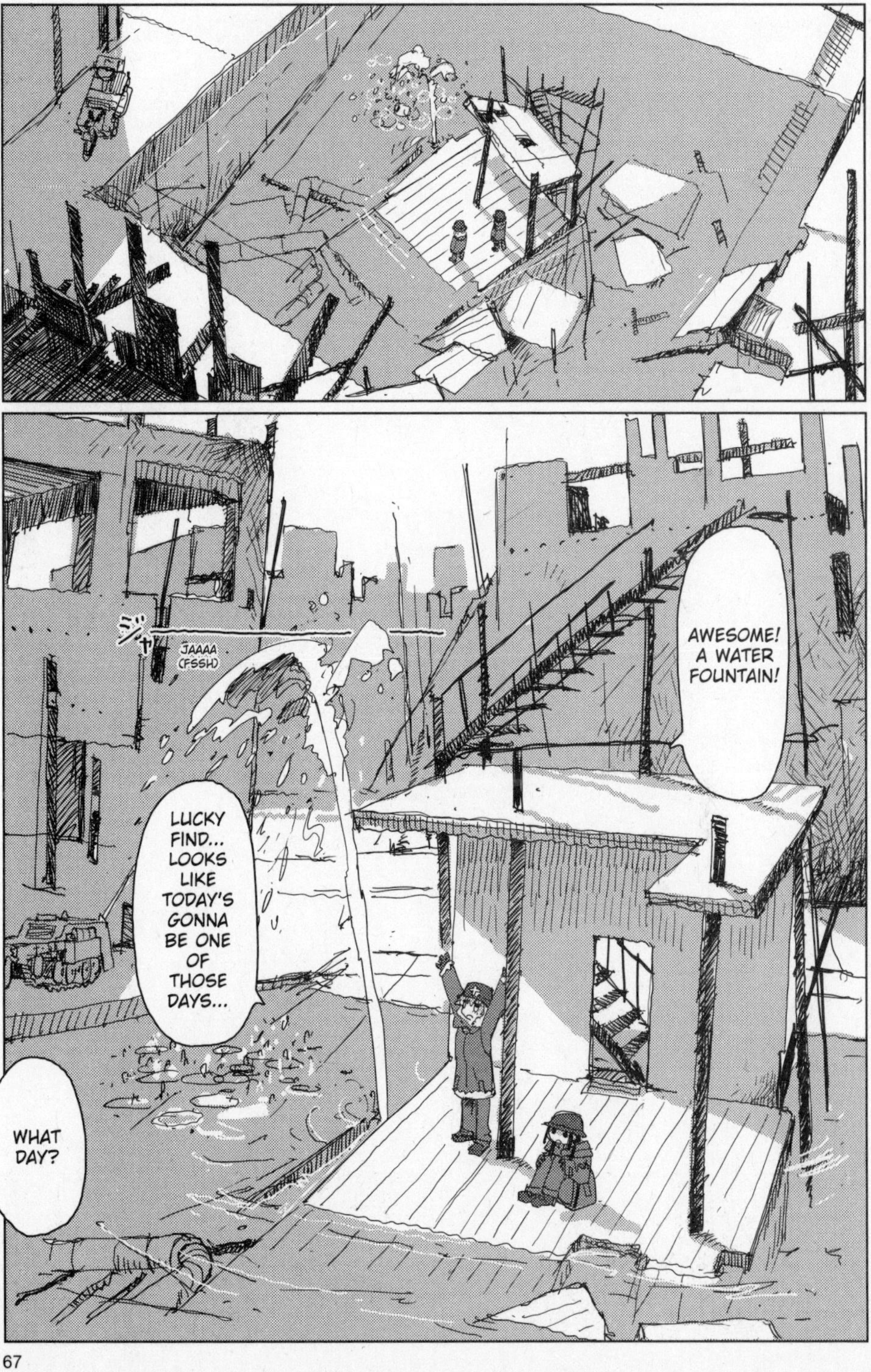
AWESOME! A WATER FOUNTAIN!
ジャ
JAAAA (FSSH)
LUCKY FIND... LOOKS LIKE TODAY'S GONNA BE ONE OF THOSE DAYS...
WHAT DAY?

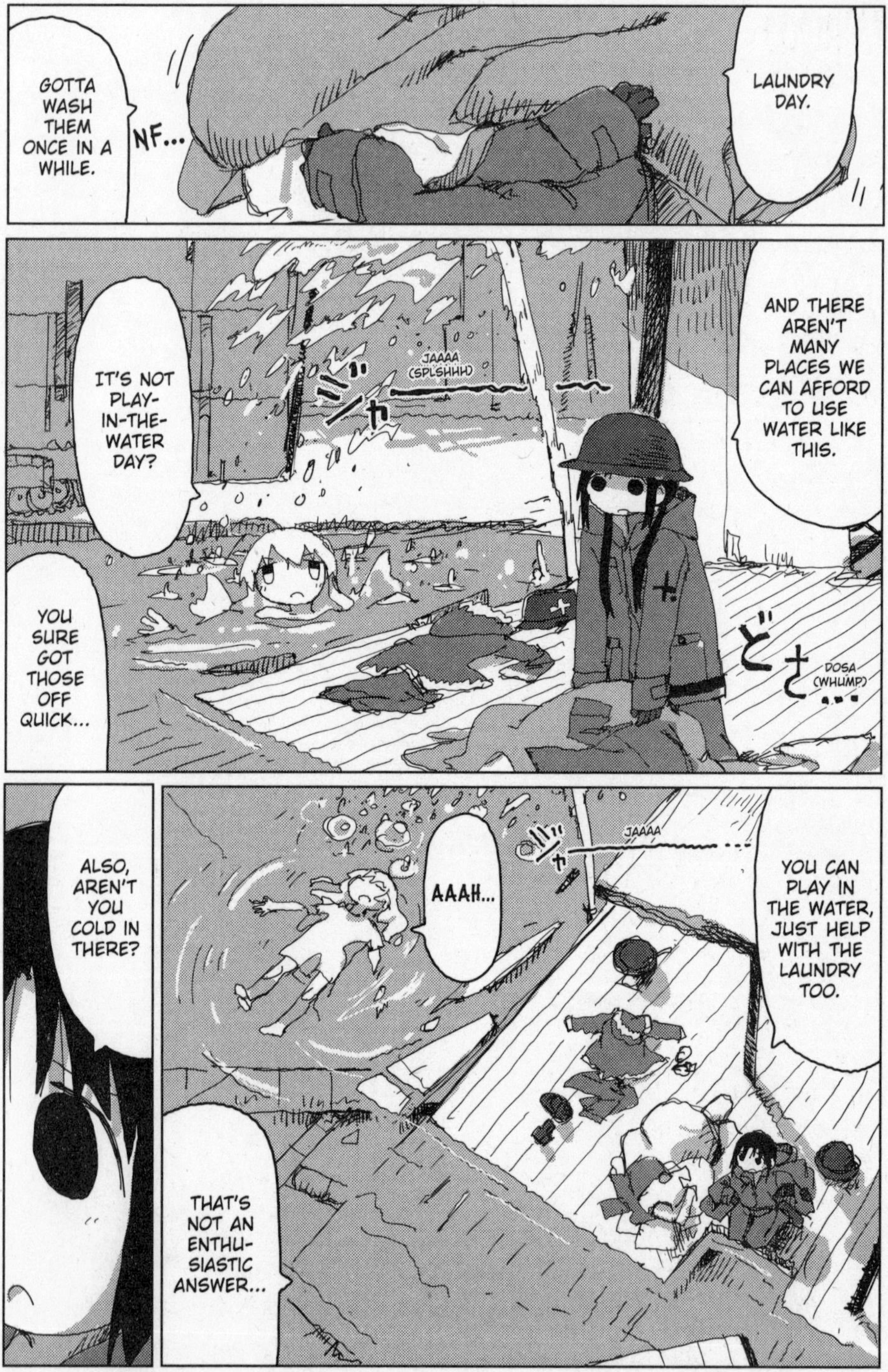
LAUNDRY DAY.
NF...
GOTTA WASH THEM ONCE IN A WHILE.
AND THERE AREN'T MANY PLACES WE CAN AFFORD TO USE WATER LIKE THIS.
IT'S NOT PLAY-IN-THE-WATER DAY?
JAAAA (SPLSHHH)
DOSA (WHUMP)
YOU SURE GOT THOSE OFF QUICK...
YOU CAN PLAY IN THE WATER, JUST HELP WITH THE LAUNDRY TOO.
JAAAA
AAAH...
THAT'S NOT AN ENTHUSIASTIC ANSWER...
ALSO, AREN'T YOU COLD IN THERE?

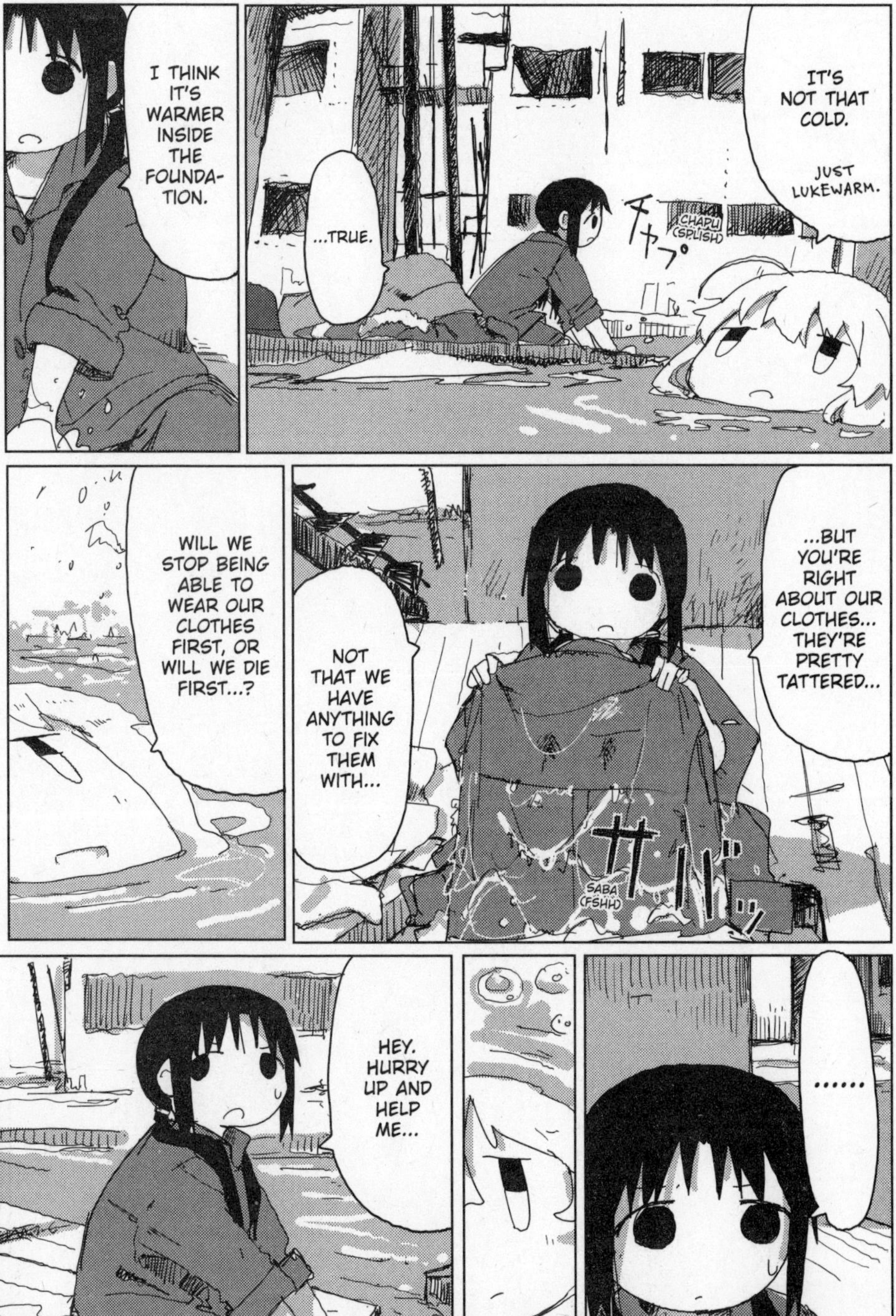
IT'S NOT THAT COLD.
JUST LUKEWARM.
チャプ
CHAPU (SPLISH)
...TRUE.
I THINK IT'S WARMER INSIDE THE FOUNDA-TION.
...BUT YOU'RE RIGHT ABOUT OUR CLOTHES... THEY'RE PRETTY TATTERED...
ザバッ
SABA (FSHH)
NOT THAT WE HAVE ANYTHING TO FIX THEM WITH...
WILL WE STOP BEING ABLE TO WEAR OUR CLOTHES FIRST, OR WILL WE DIE FIRST...?
......
HEY. HURRY UP AND HELP ME...

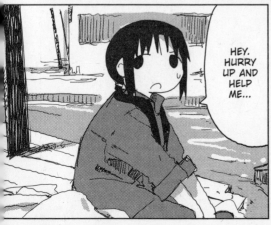

ビャァァァ
BYAAAA
(SQUIIIIIRT)

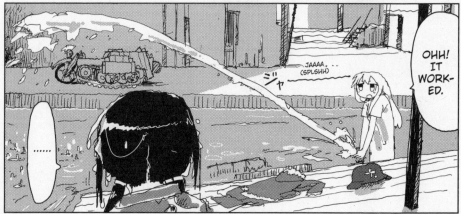

JAAAA...
(SPLSHH)

OHH! IT WORKED.

......

OW!

GO
(KONK)

BYABYABYA
ビャビャビャ

COVER THE WATER JET LIKE THIS AND IT SQUIRTS, SEE?

HEY!

COME INTO THE WATER, CHII-CHAN!

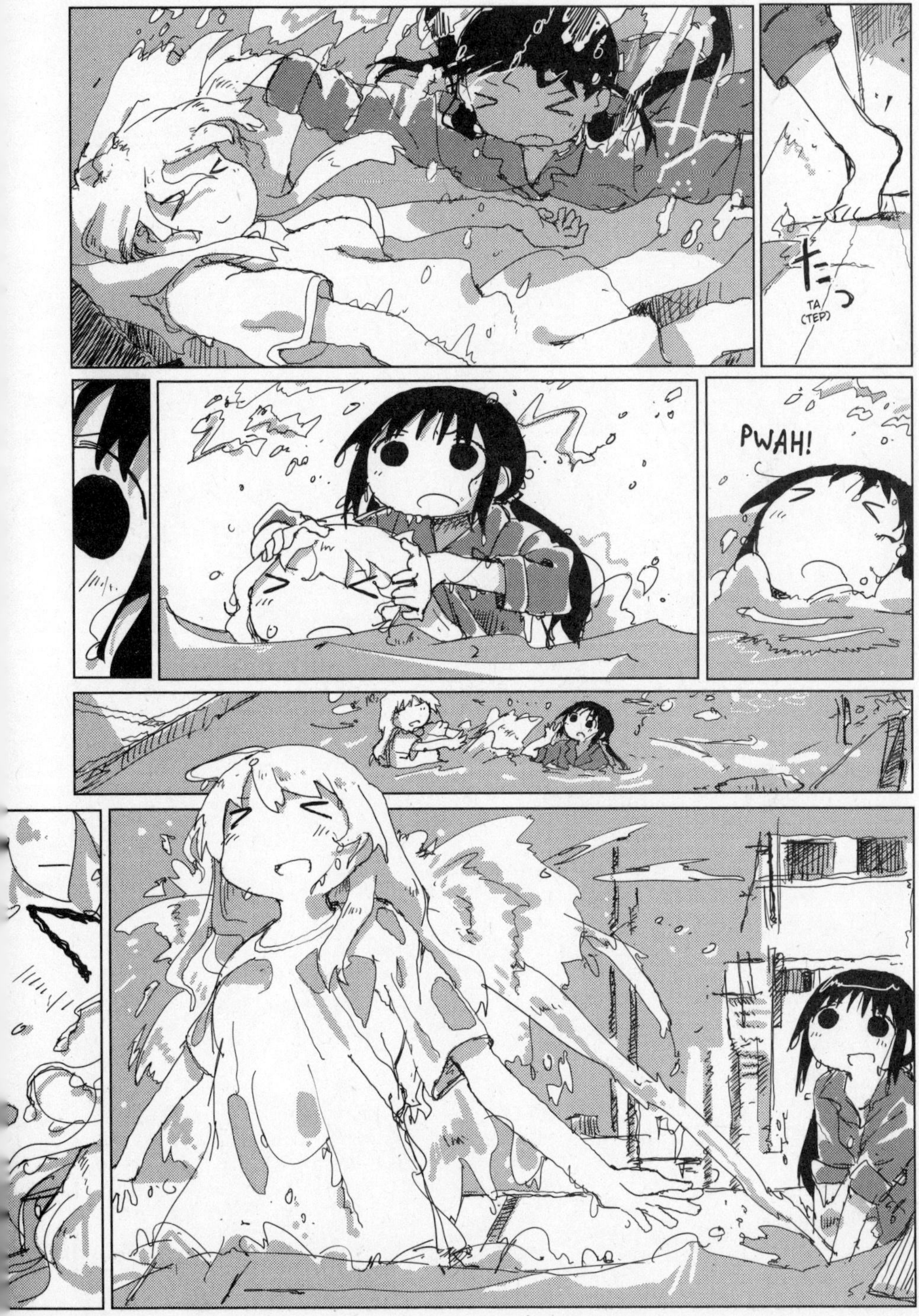
たっ
TA
(TEP)
PWAH!

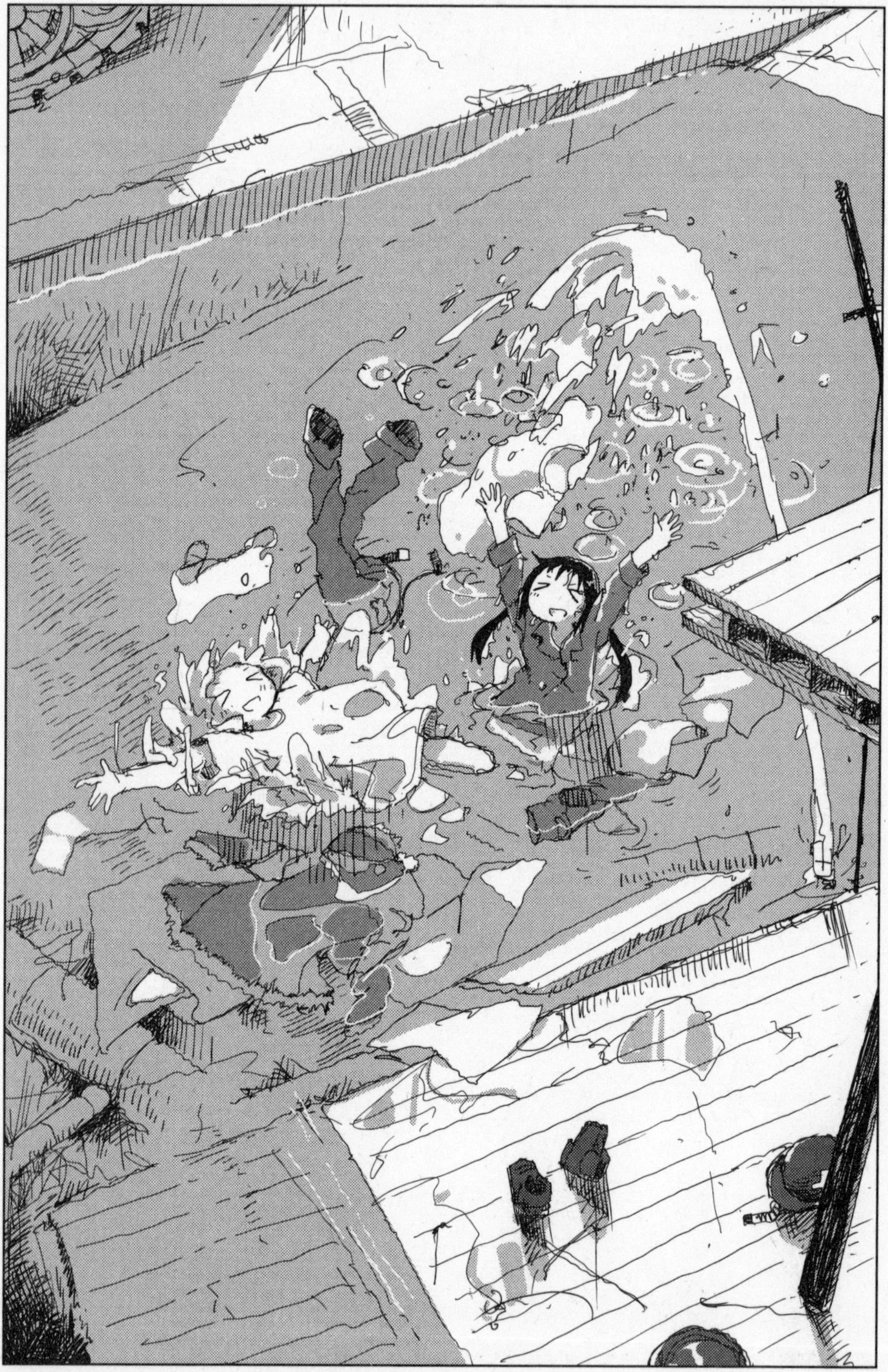

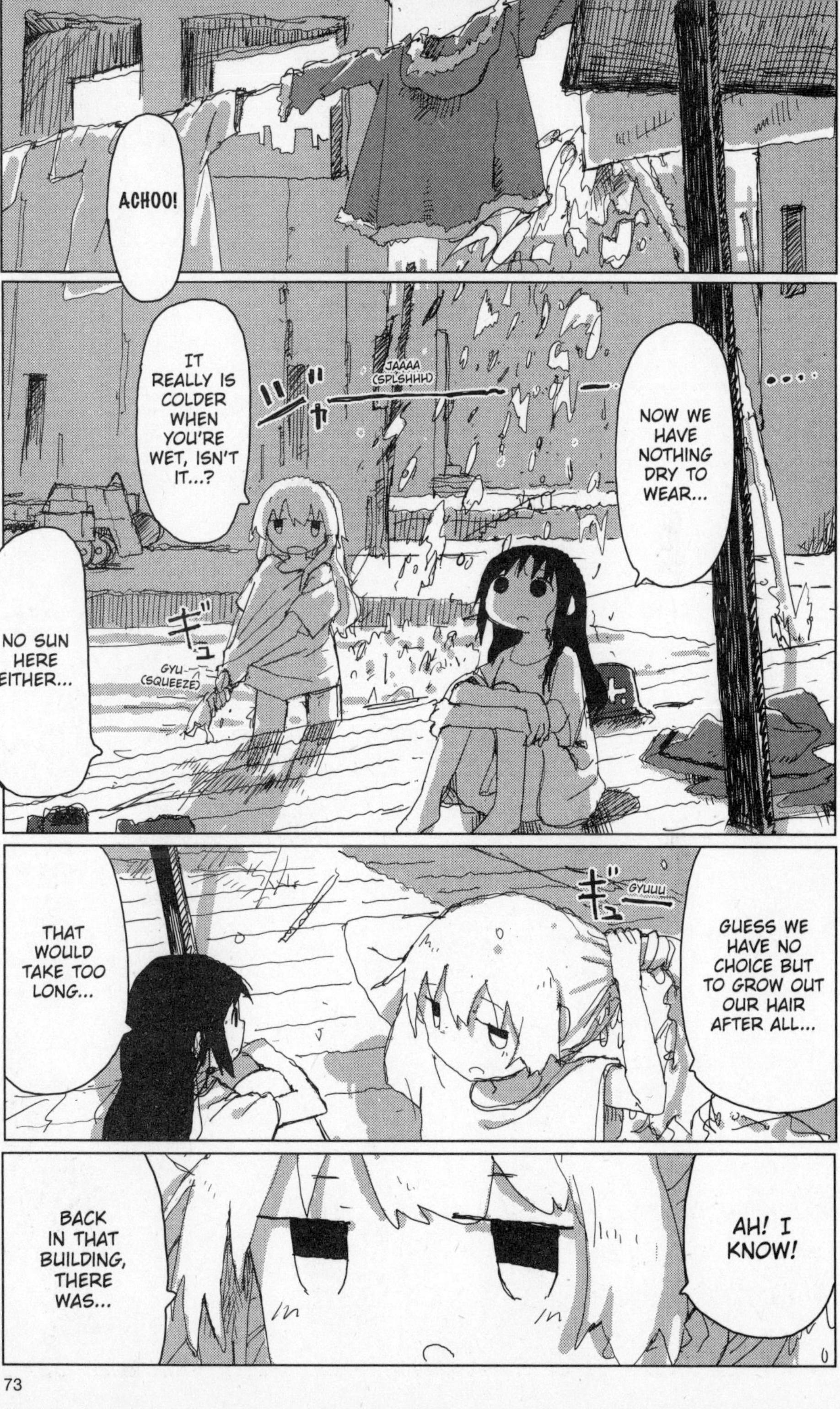
ACHOO!
NOW WE HAVE NOTHING DRY TO WEAR...
...
ジャー
JAAAA (SPLSHHH)
IT REALLY IS COLDER WHEN YOU'RE WET, ISN'T IT...?
ギュ
GYU (SQUEEZE)
NO SUN HERE EITHER...
GUESS WE HAVE NO CHOICE BUT TO GROW OUT OUR HAIR AFTER ALL...
ギュー
GYUUU
THAT WOULD TAKE TOO LONG...
AH! I KNOW!
BACK IN THAT BUILDING, THERE WAS...

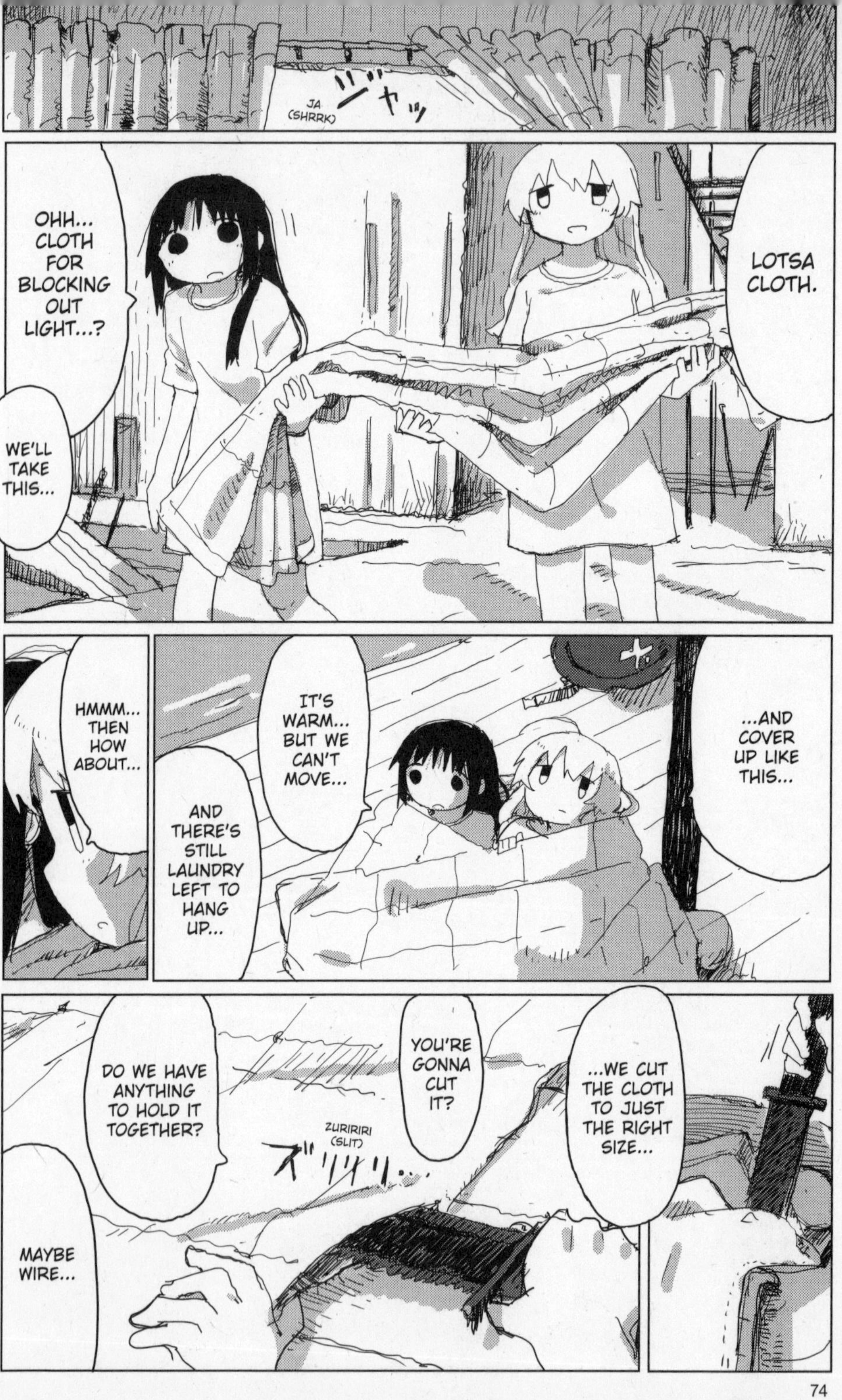
ジャッ
JA (SHRRK)
LOTSA CLOTH.
OHH... CLOTH FOR BLOCKING OUT LIGHT...?
WE'LL TAKE THIS...
...AND COVER UP LIKE THIS...
IT'S WARM... BUT WE CAN'T MOVE...
AND THERE'S STILL LAUNDRY LEFT TO HANG UP...
HMMM... THEN HOW ABOUT...
...WE CUT THE CLOTH TO JUST THE RIGHT SIZE...
YOU'RE GONNA CUT IT?
ZURIRIRI (SLIT)
ズリリリ...
DO WE HAVE ANYTHING TO HOLD IT TOGETHER?
MAYBE WIRE...

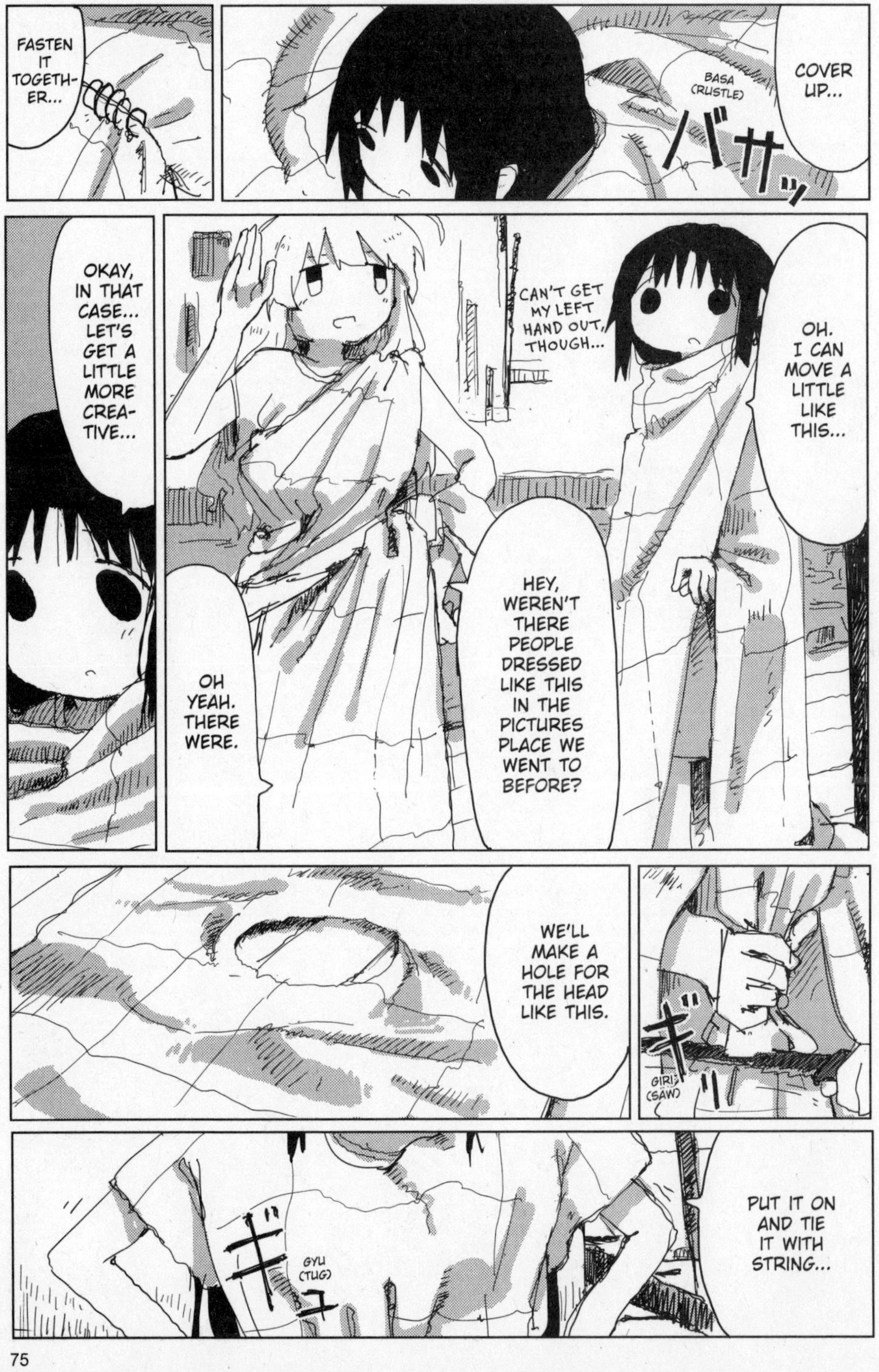
COVER UP...
BASA (RUSTLE)
バサッ
FASTEN IT TOGETHER...
OH. I CAN MOVE A LITTLE LIKE THIS...
CAN'T GET MY LEFT HAND OUT, THOUGH...
HEY, WEREN'T THERE PEOPLE DRESSED LIKE THIS IN THE PICTURES PLACE WE WENT TO BEFORE?
OH YEAH. THERE WERE.
OKAY, IN THAT CASE... LET'S GET A LITTLE MORE CREATIVE...
ギリ
GIRI (SAW)
WE'LL MAKE A HOLE FOR THE HEAD LIKE THIS.
PUT IT ON AND TIE IT WITH STRING...
GYU (TUG)
ギュ

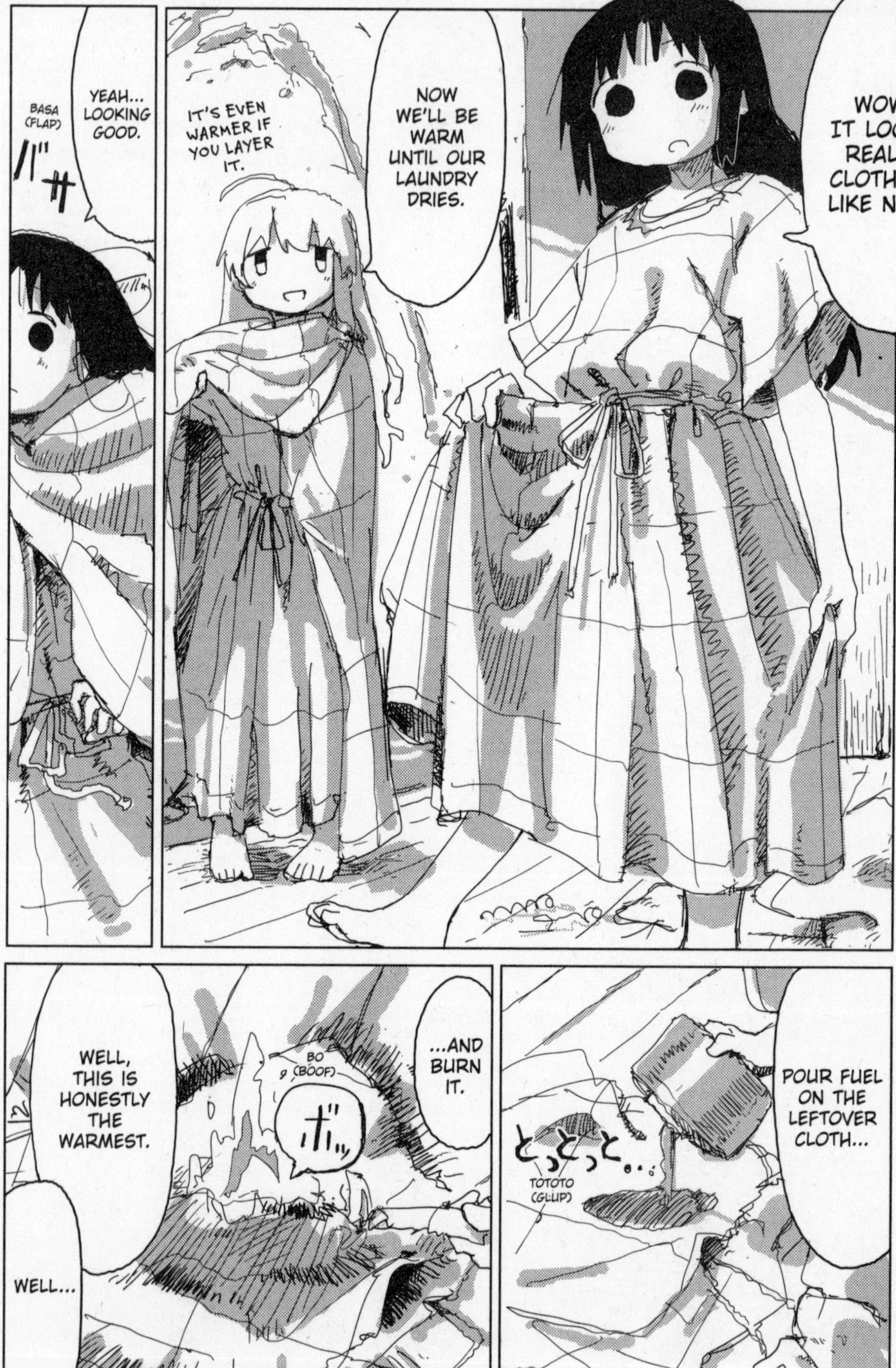
WOW. IT LOOKS REALLY CLOTHES-LIKE NOW.
NOW WE'LL BE WARM UNTIL OUR LAUNDRY DRIES.
IT'S EVEN WARMER IF YOU LAYER IT.
YEAH... LOOKING GOOD.
バサ
BASA (FLAP)
POUR FUEL ON THE LEFTOVER CLOTH...
とっとっと。。。
TOTOTO (GLUP)
...AND BURN IT.
ボッ
BO (BOOF)
WELL, THIS IS HONESTLY THE WARMEST.
WELL...

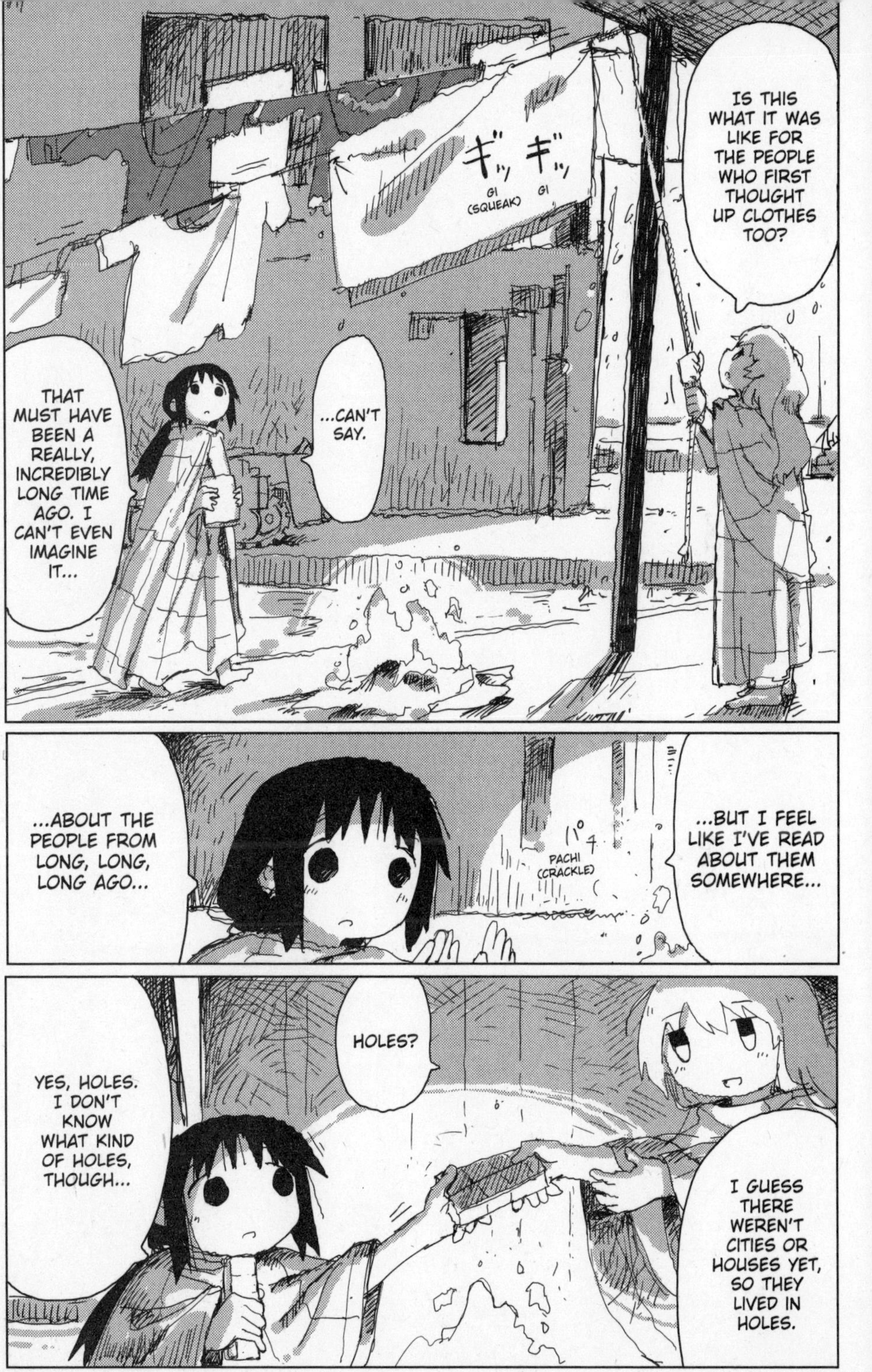

IS THIS WHAT IT WAS LIKE FOR THE PEOPLE WHO FIRST THOUGHT UP CLOTHES TOO?
ギッ ギッ
GI GI (SQUEAK)
...CAN'T SAY.
THAT MUST HAVE BEEN A REALLY, INCREDIBLY LONG TIME AGO. I CAN'T EVEN IMAGINE IT...
...BUT I FEEL LIKE I'VE READ ABOUT THEM SOMEWHERE...
パチ
PACHI (CRACKLE)
...ABOUT THE PEOPLE FROM LONG, LONG, LONG AGO...
I GUESS THERE WEREN'T CITIES OR HOUSES YET, SO THEY LIVED IN HOLES.
HOLES?
YES, HOLES. I DON'T KNOW WHAT KIND OF HOLES, THOUGH...

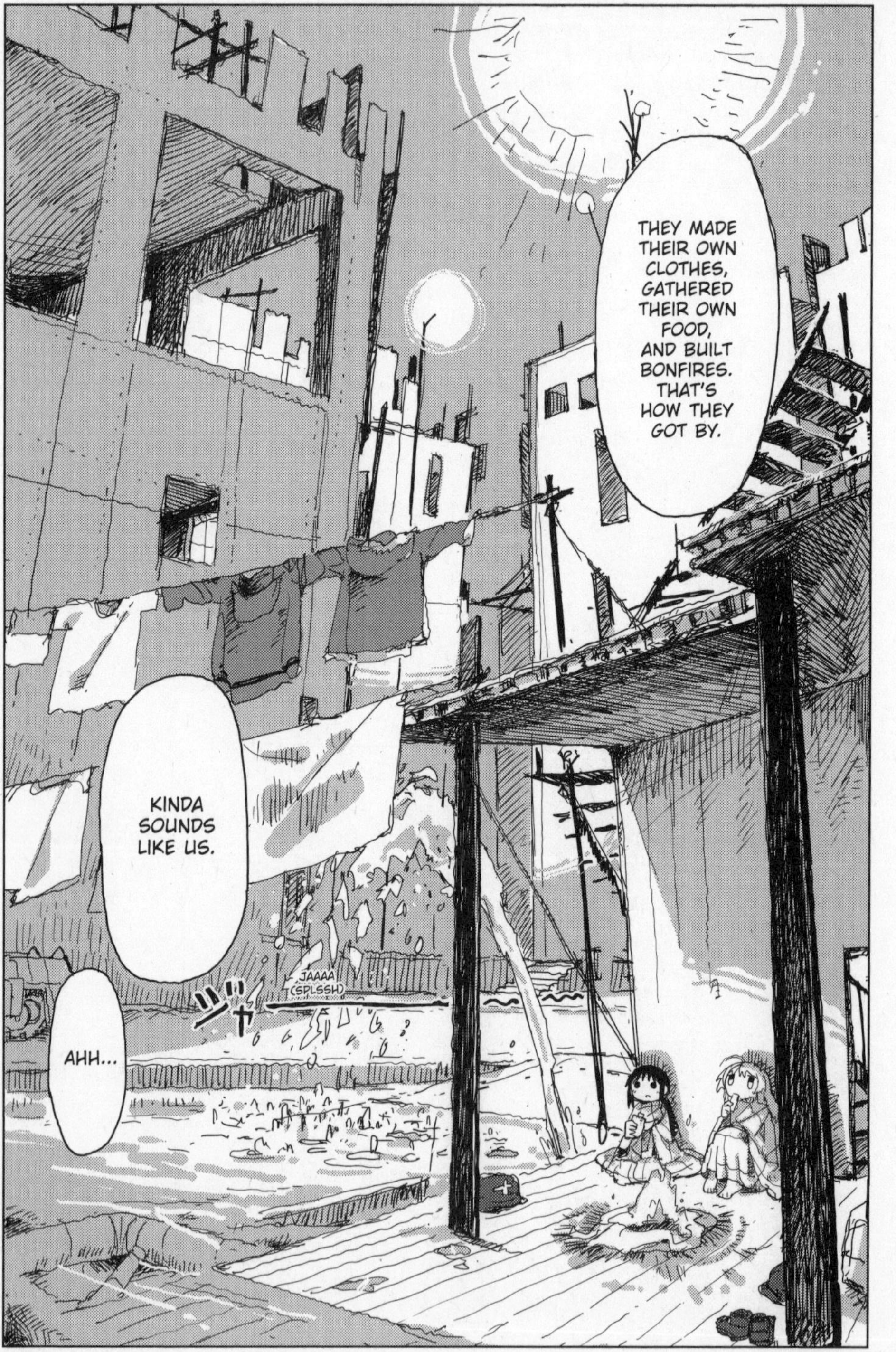
THEY MADE THEIR OWN CLOTHES, GATHERED THEIR OWN FOOD, AND BUILT BONFIRES. THAT'S HOW THEY GOT BY.
KINDA SOUNDS LIKE US.
ジャ
JAAAA (SPLSSH)
AHH...

FASTEN A GEAR TO THE CLOTH...
...AND WITH THAT, WE HAVE A BUTTON.
DO YOU NEED THAT?
I MEAN, NOT REALLY, BUT...

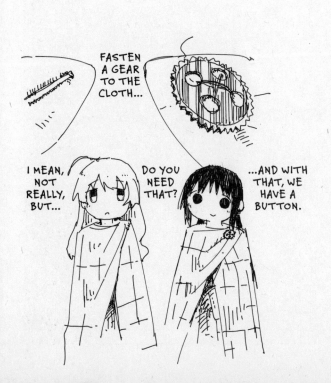

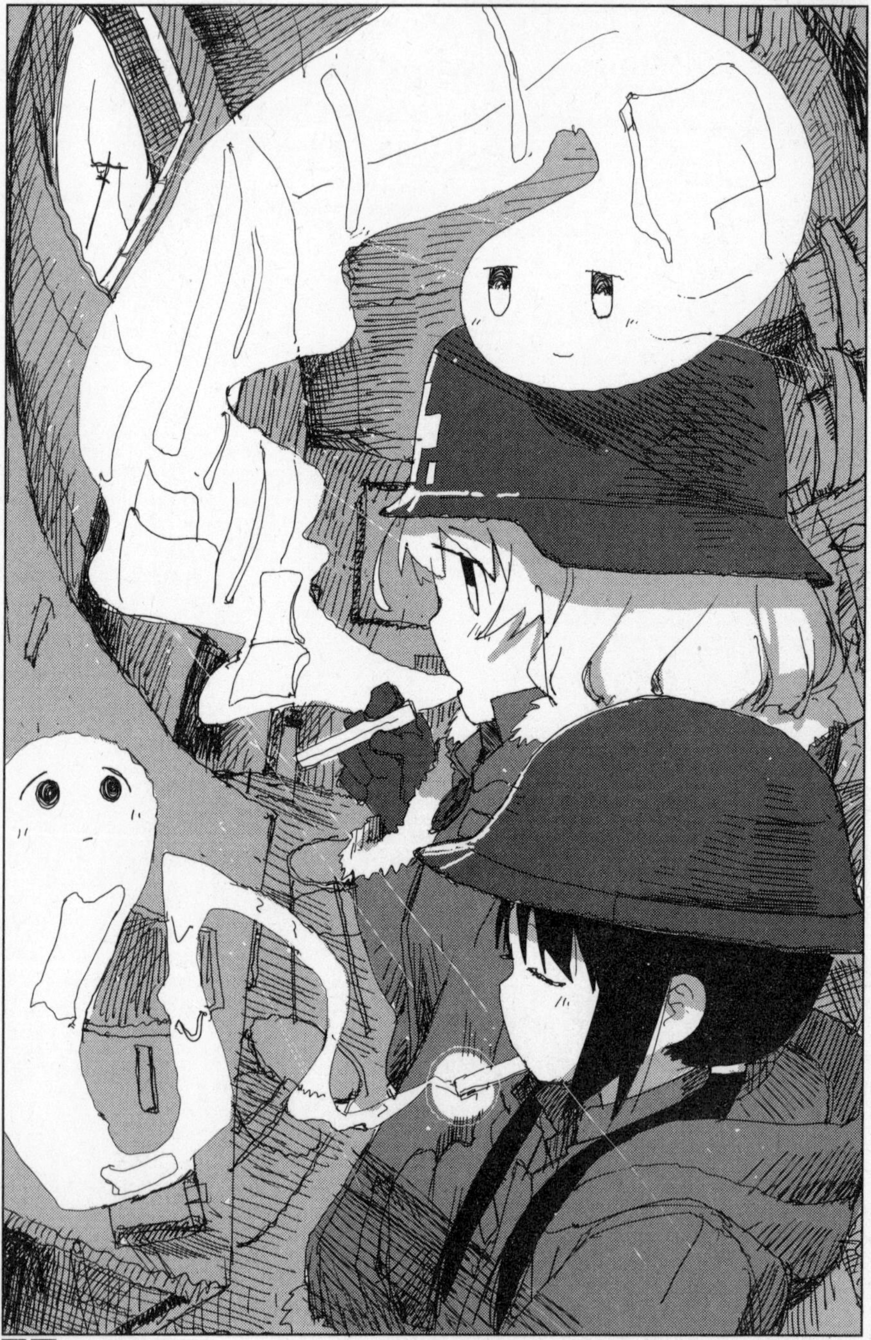

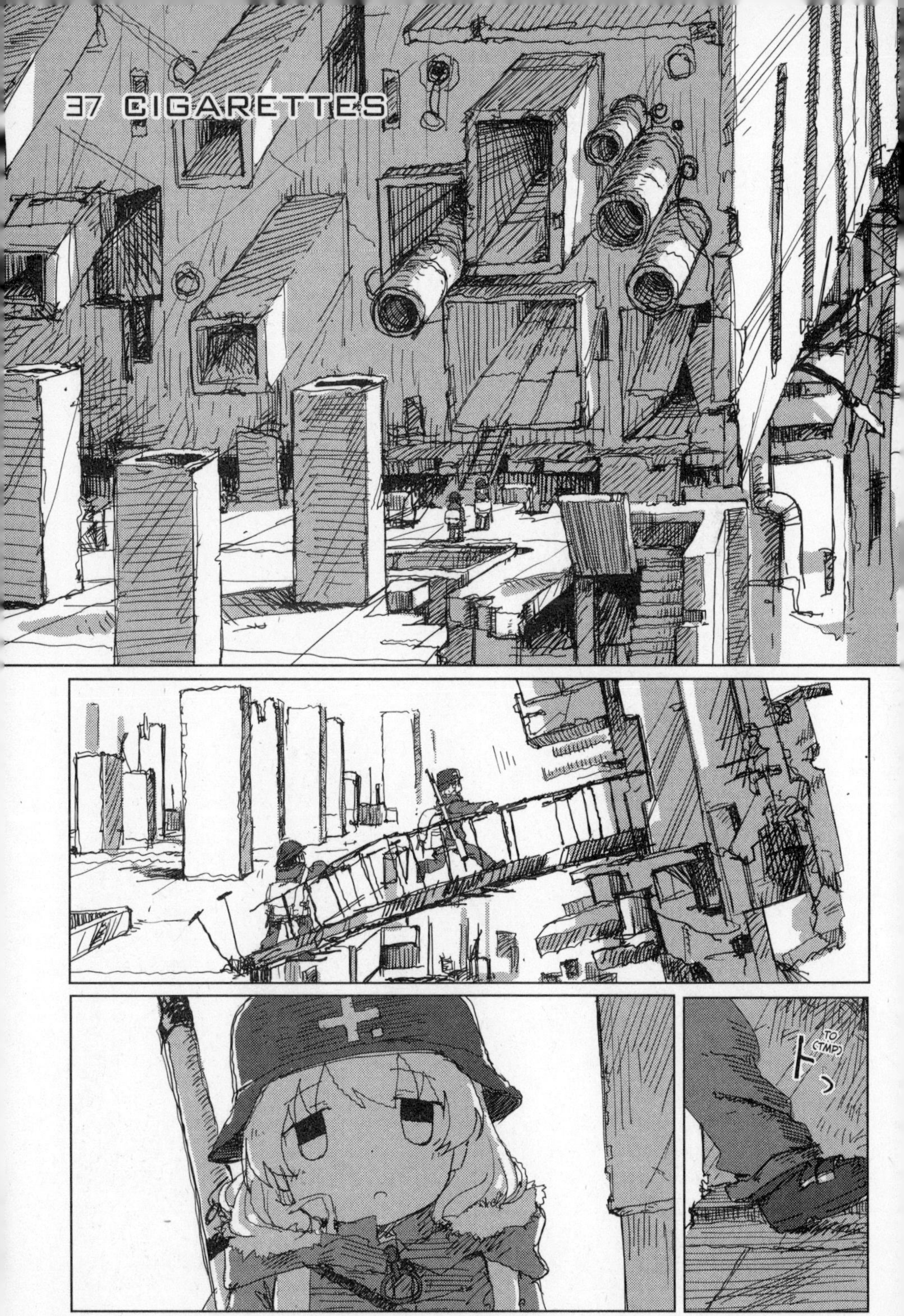
37 CIGARETTES
ト TO (TMP)
っ

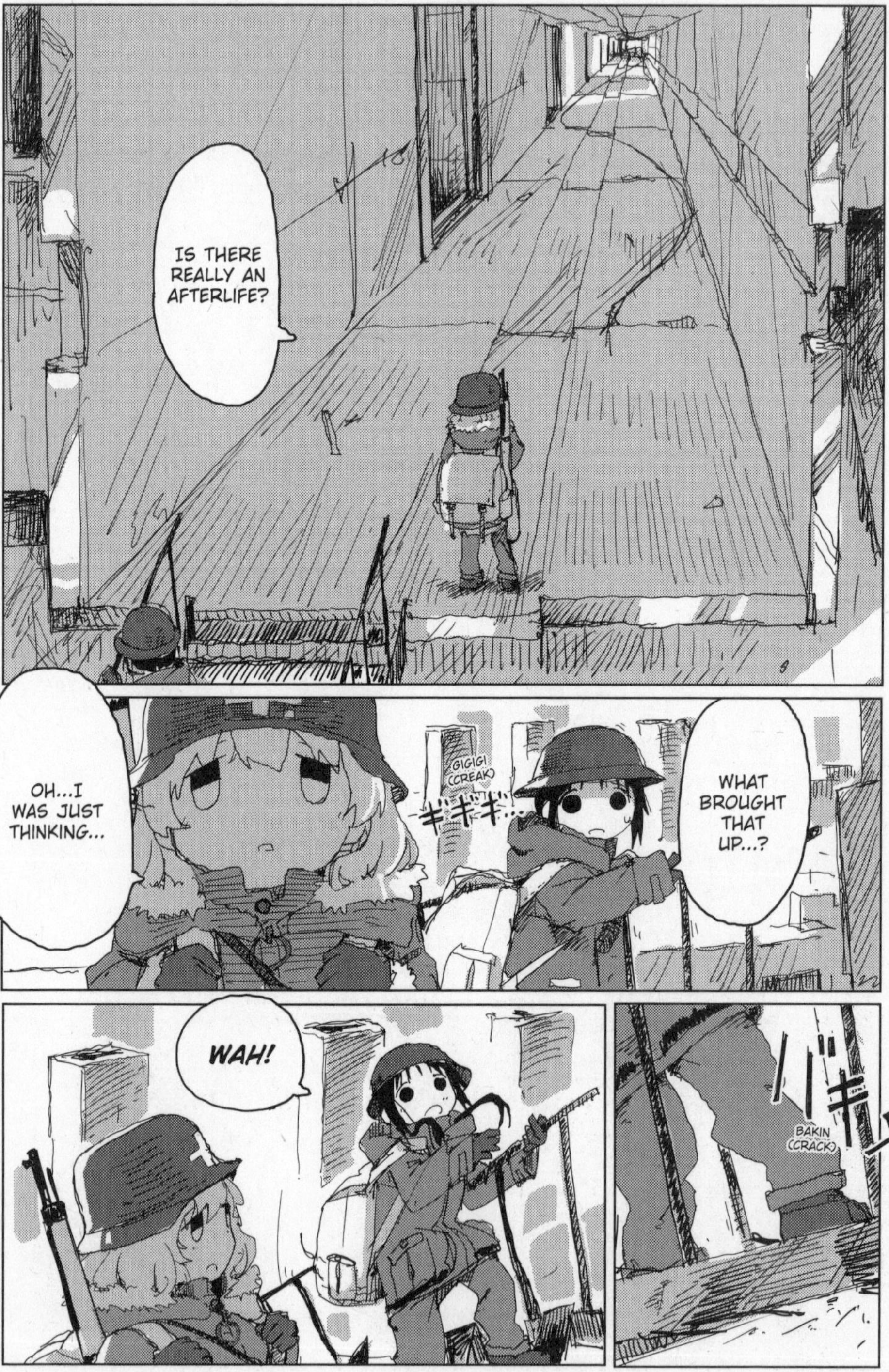
IS THERE REALLY AN AFTERLIFE?
WHAT BROUGHT THAT UP...?
GIGIGI (CREAK)
ギギギ...
OH...I WAS JUST THINKING...
BAKIN (CRACK)
バギィッ
WAH!

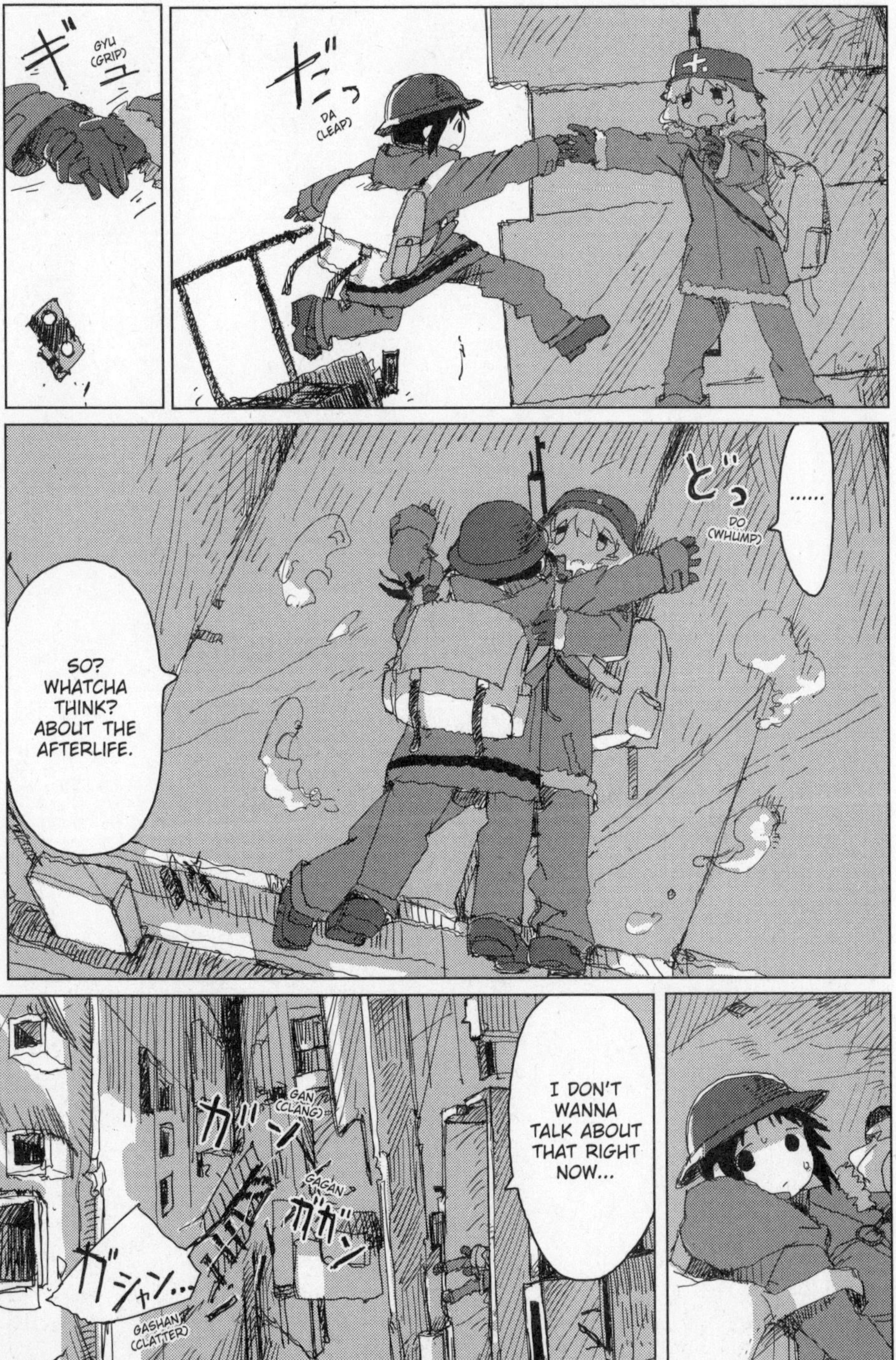
ダッ
DA (LEAP)
ギュ
GYU (GRIP)
......
どっ
DO (WHUMP)
SO? WHATCHA THINK? ABOUT THE AFTERLIFE.
I DON'T WANNA TALK ABOUT THAT RIGHT NOW...
ガーン
GAN (CLANG)
ガガン
GAGAN
ガシャン...
GASHAN (CLATTER)

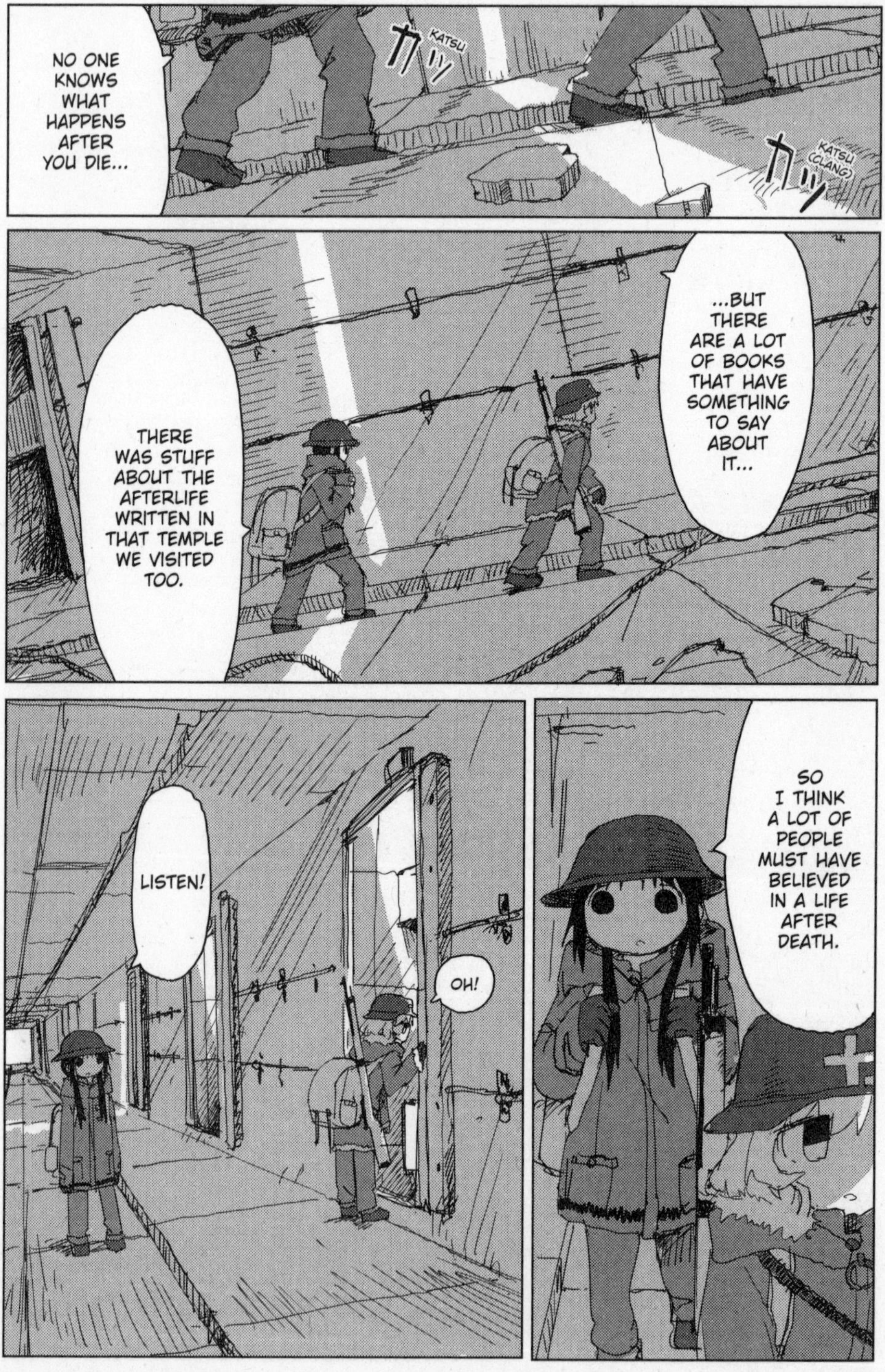
KATSU
KATSU (CLANG)
NO ONE KNOWS WHAT HAPPENS AFTER YOU DIE...
...BUT THERE ARE A LOT OF BOOKS THAT HAVE SOMETHING TO SAY ABOUT IT...
THERE WAS STUFF ABOUT THE AFTERLIFE WRITTEN IN THAT TEMPLE WE VISITED TOO.
SO I THINK A LOT OF PEOPLE MUST HAVE BELIEVED IN A LIFE AFTER DEATH.
LISTEN!
OH!

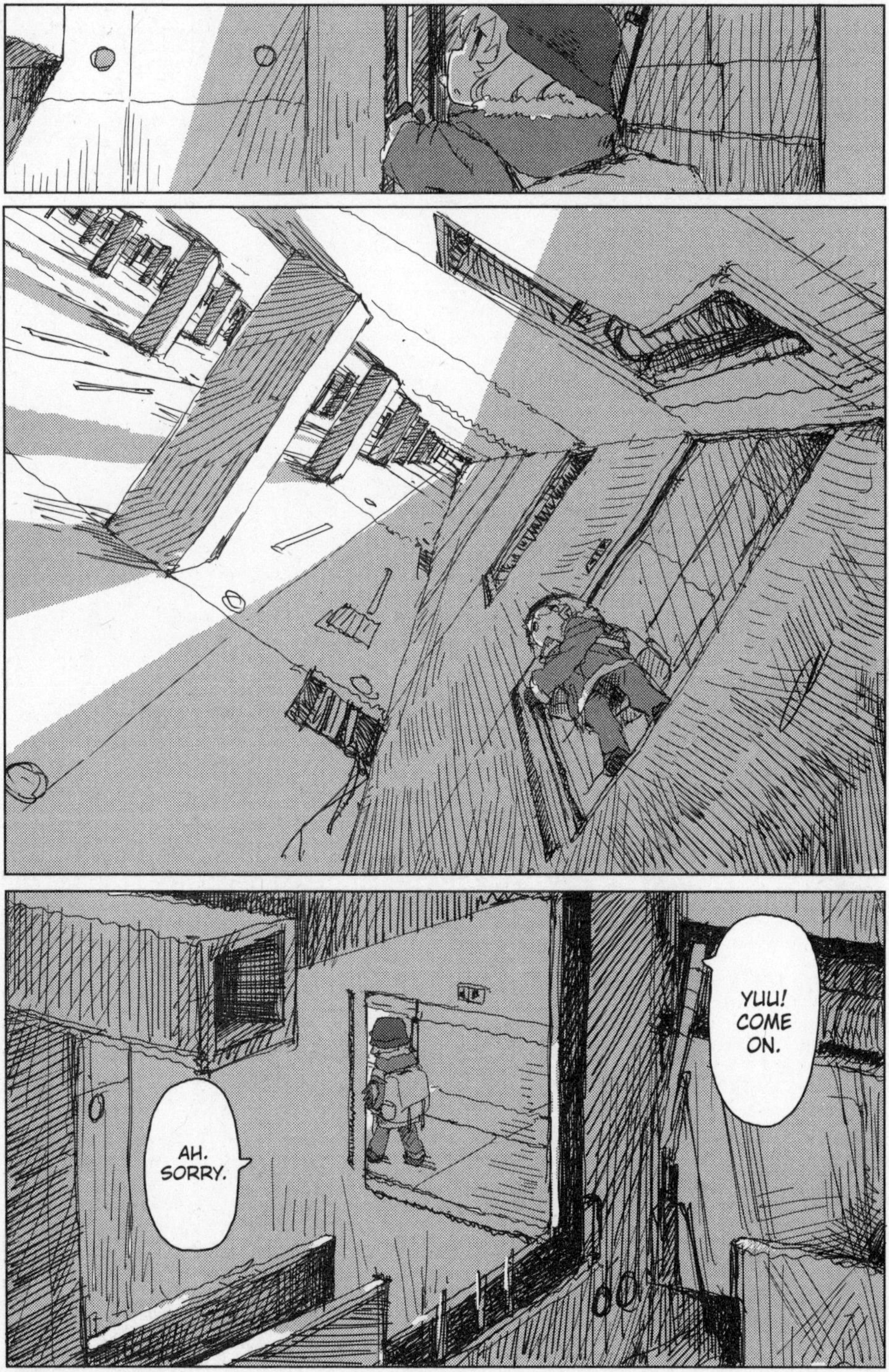
YUU! COME ON.
AH. SORRY.

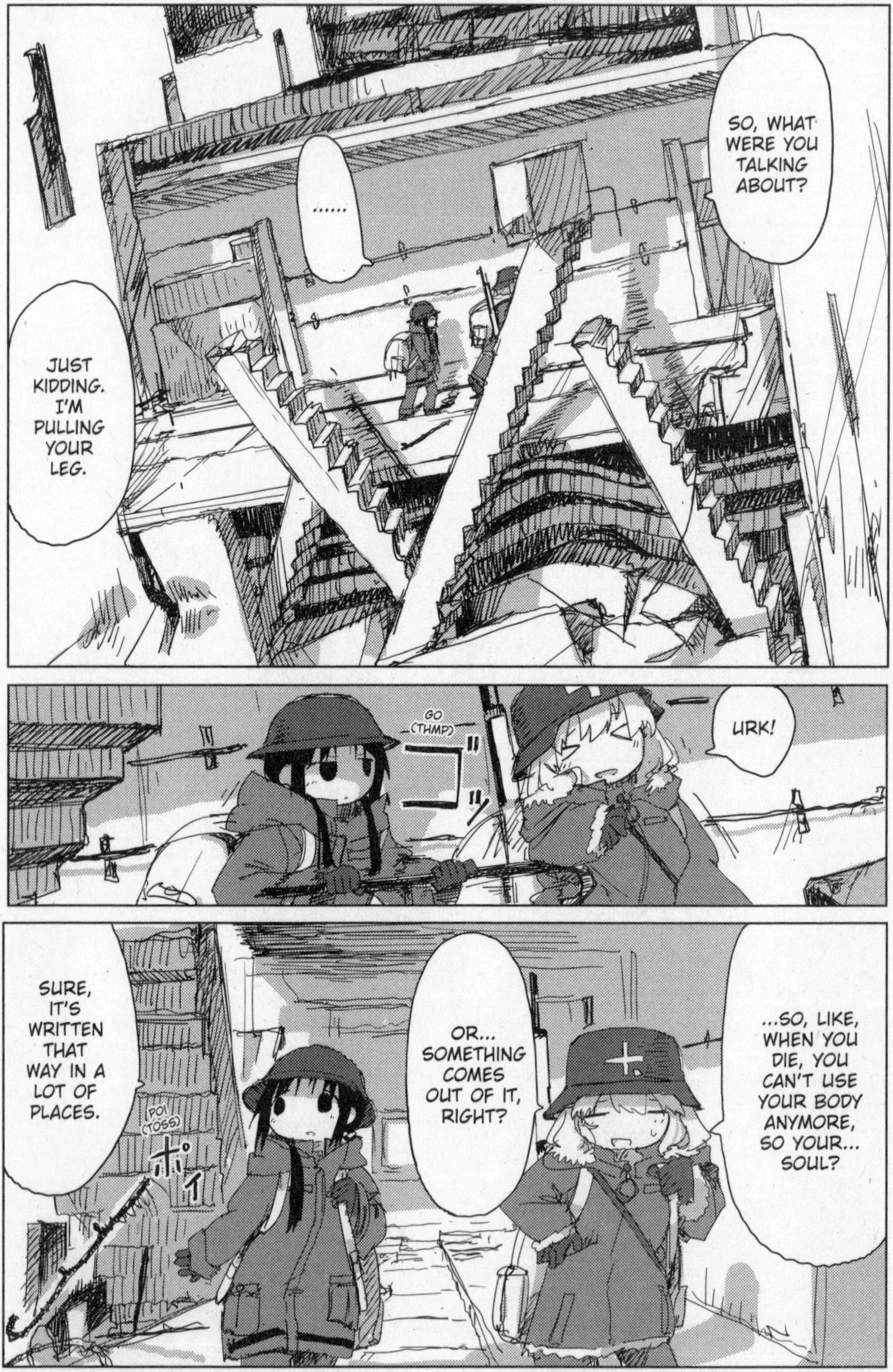

SO, WHAT WERE YOU TALKING ABOUT?
......
JUST KIDDING. I'M PULLING YOUR LEG.
URK!
GO (THMP)
...SO, LIKE, WHEN YOU DIE, YOU CAN'T USE YOUR BODY ANYMORE, SO YOUR... SOUL?
OR... SOMETHING COMES OUT OF IT, RIGHT?
SURE, IT'S WRITTEN THAT WAY IN A LOT OF PLACES.
POI (TOSS)

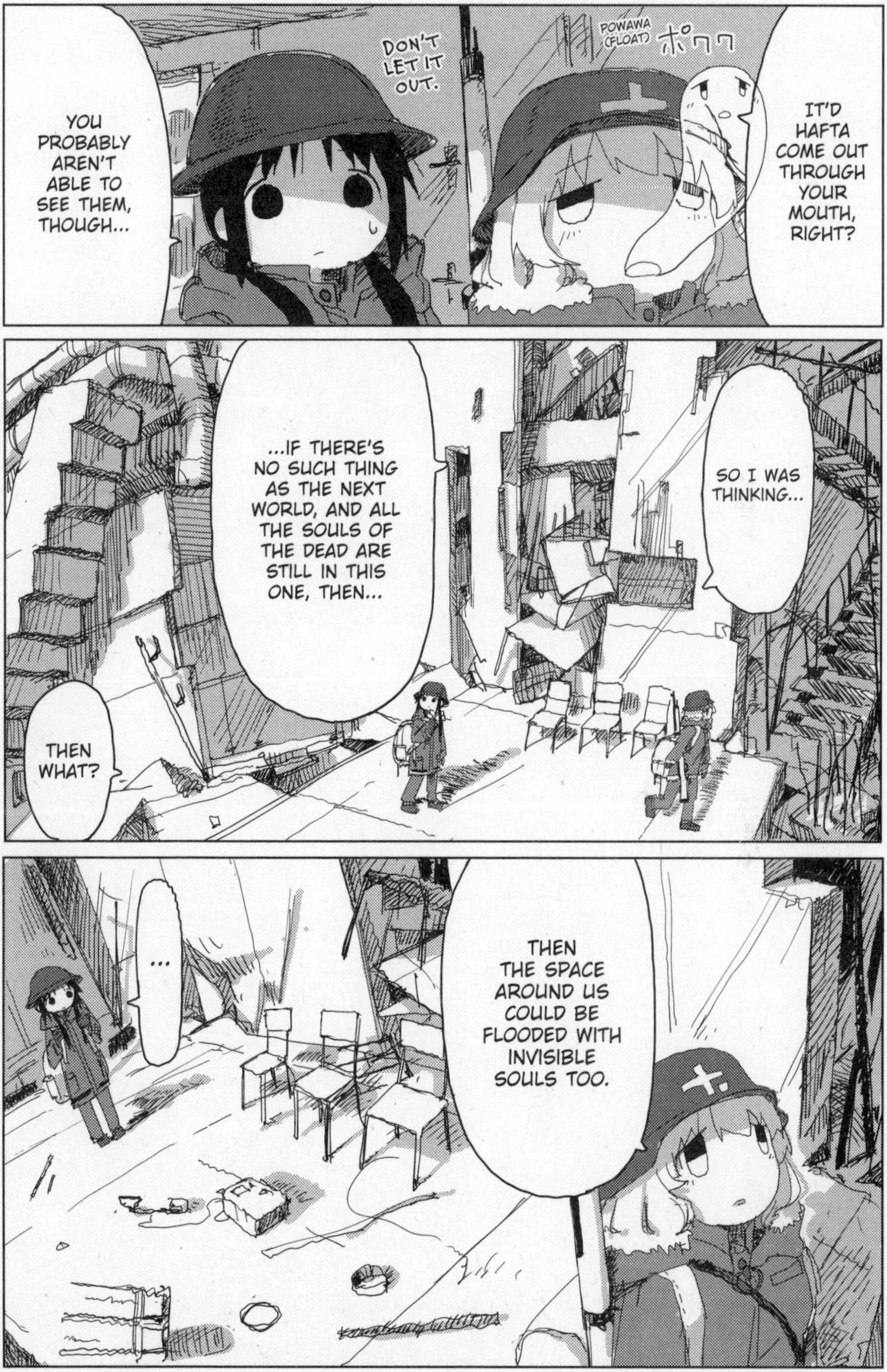
IT'D HAFTA COME OUT THROUGH YOUR MOUTH, RIGHT?
POWAWA (FLOAT) ポワワ
DON'T LET IT OUT.
YOU PROBABLY AREN'T ABLE TO SEE THEM, THOUGH...
SO I WAS THINKING...
...IF THERE'S NO SUCH THING AS THE NEXT WORLD, AND ALL THE SOULS OF THE DEAD ARE STILL IN THIS ONE, THEN...
THEN WHAT?
THEN THE SPACE AROUND US COULD BE FLOODED WITH INVISIBLE SOULS TOO.
...

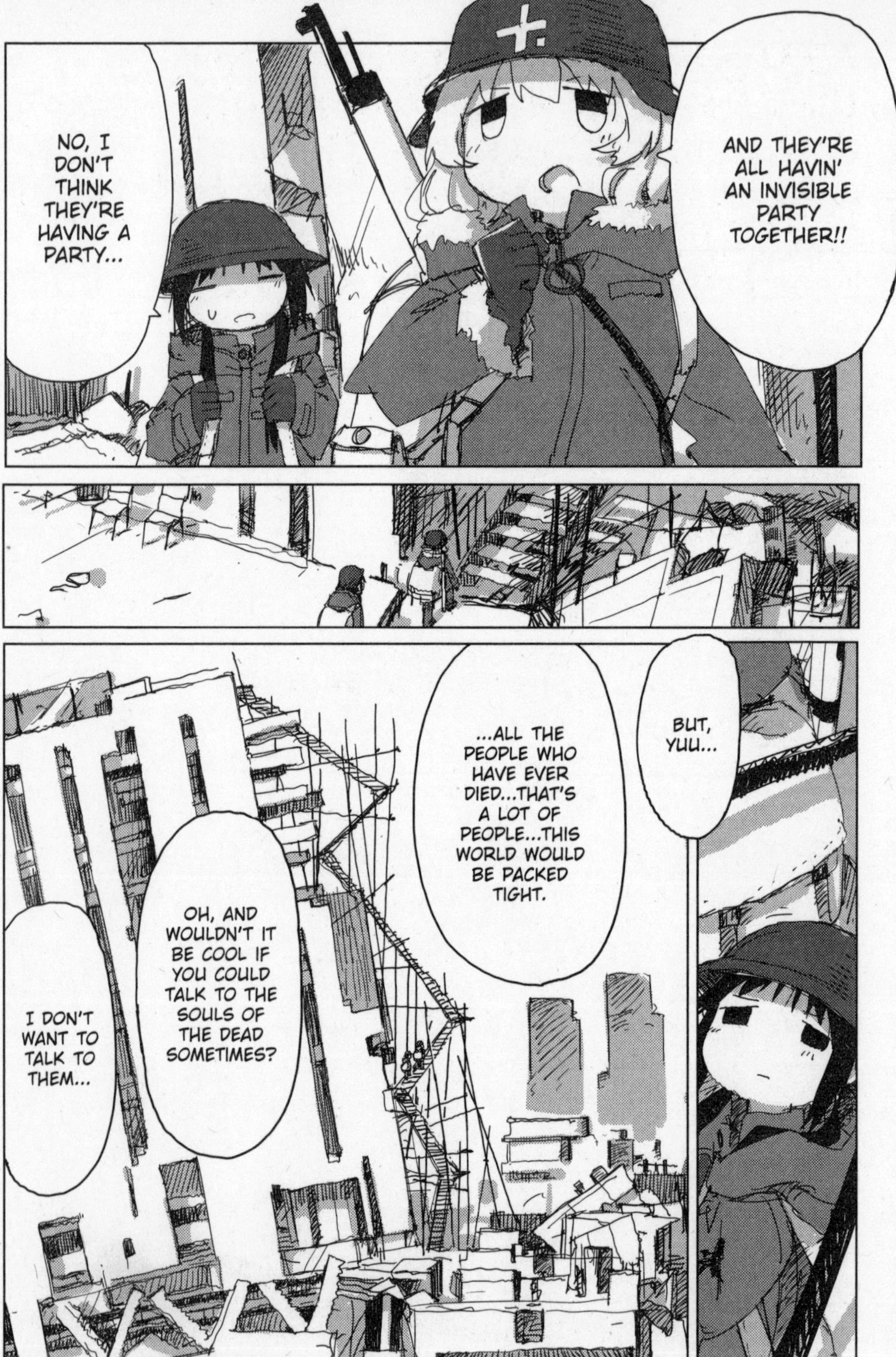
AND THEY'RE ALL HAVIN' AN INVISIBLE PARTY TOGETHER!!
NO, I DON'T THINK THEY'RE HAVING A PARTY...
BUT, YUU...
...ALL THE PEOPLE WHO HAVE EVER DIED...THAT'S A LOT OF PEOPLE...THIS WORLD WOULD BE PACKED TIGHT.
OH, AND WOULDN'T IT BE COOL IF YOU COULD TALK TO THE SOULS OF THE DEAD SOMETIMES?
I DON'T WANT TO TALK TO THEM...

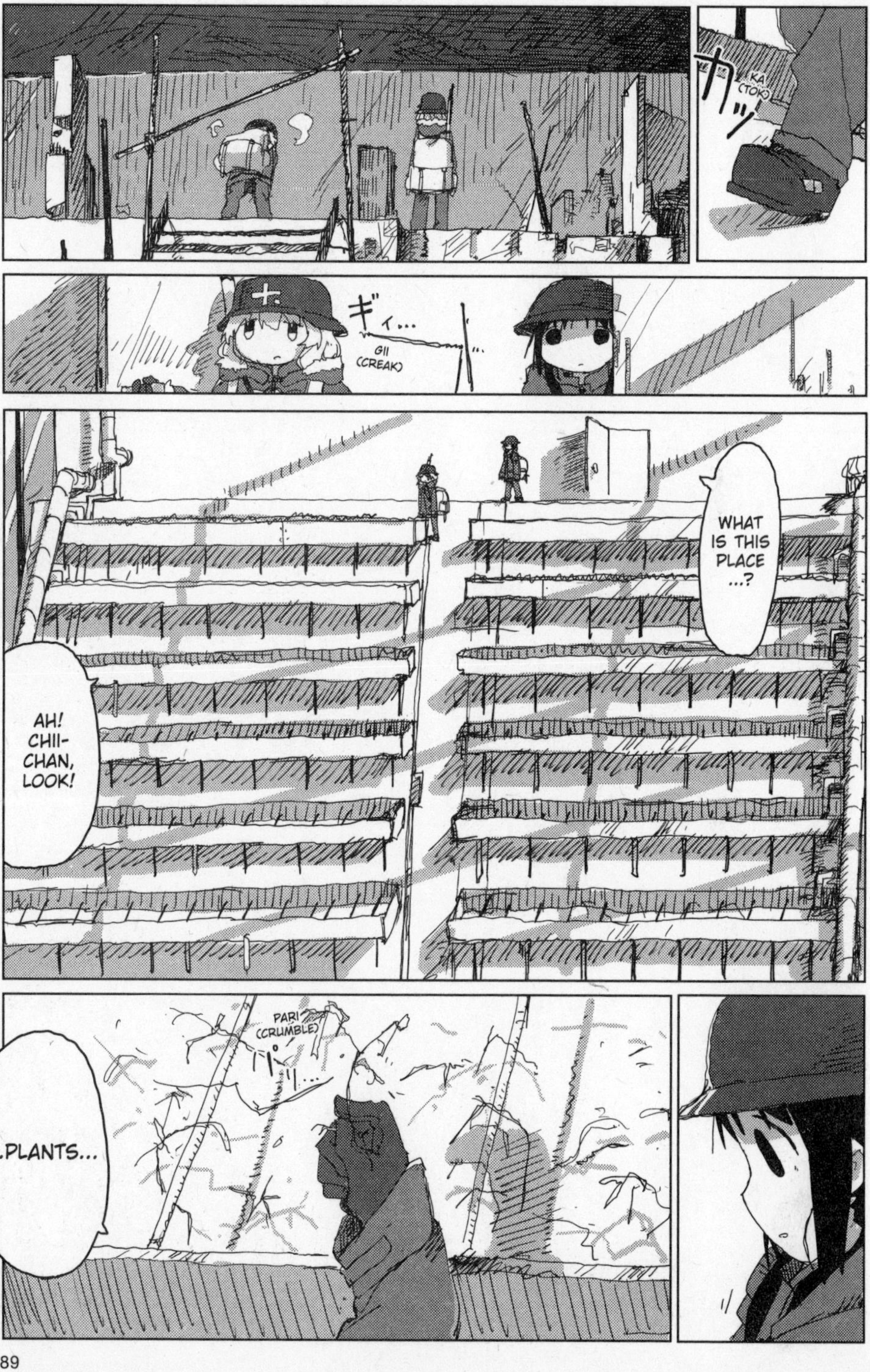
カッ
KA (TOK)
ギィ…
GII (CREAK)
…
WHAT IS THIS PLACE ...?
AH! CHII-CHAN, LOOK!
PARI (CRUMBLE)
パリ…
...PLANTS...

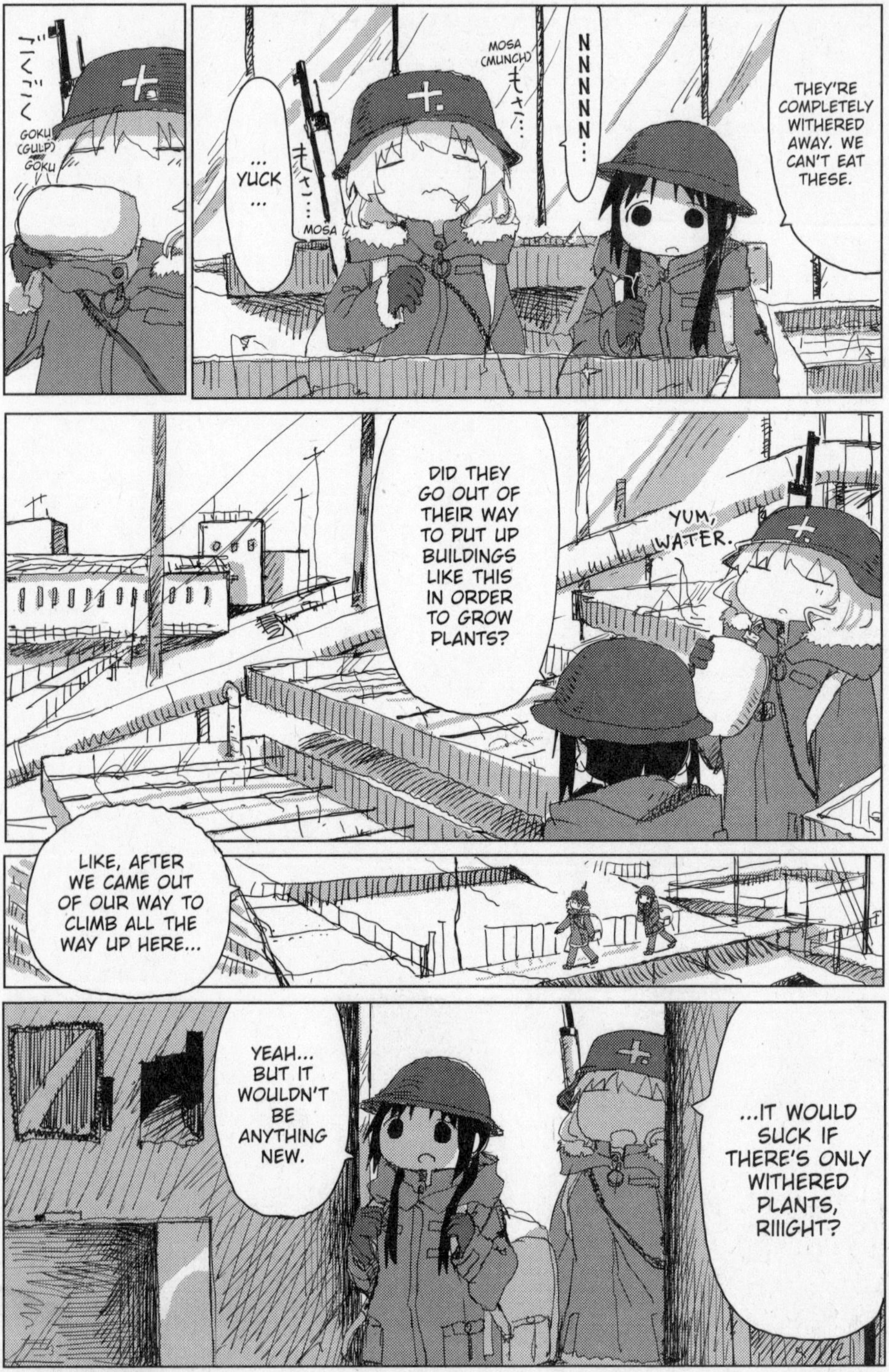
THEY'RE COMPLETELY WITHERED AWAY. WE CAN'T EAT THESE.
NNNNN...
MOSA (MUNCH) もさ…
... YUCK ...
もさ… MOSA
ごくごく
GOKU (GULP) GOKU
YUM, WATER.
DID THEY GO OUT OF THEIR WAY TO PUT UP BUILDINGS LIKE THIS IN ORDER TO GROW PLANTS?
LIKE, AFTER WE CAME OUT OF OUR WAY TO CLIMB ALL THE WAY UP HERE...
...IT WOULD SUCK IF THERE'S ONLY WITHERED PLANTS, RIIIGHT?
YEAH... BUT IT WOULDN'T BE ANYTHING NEW.

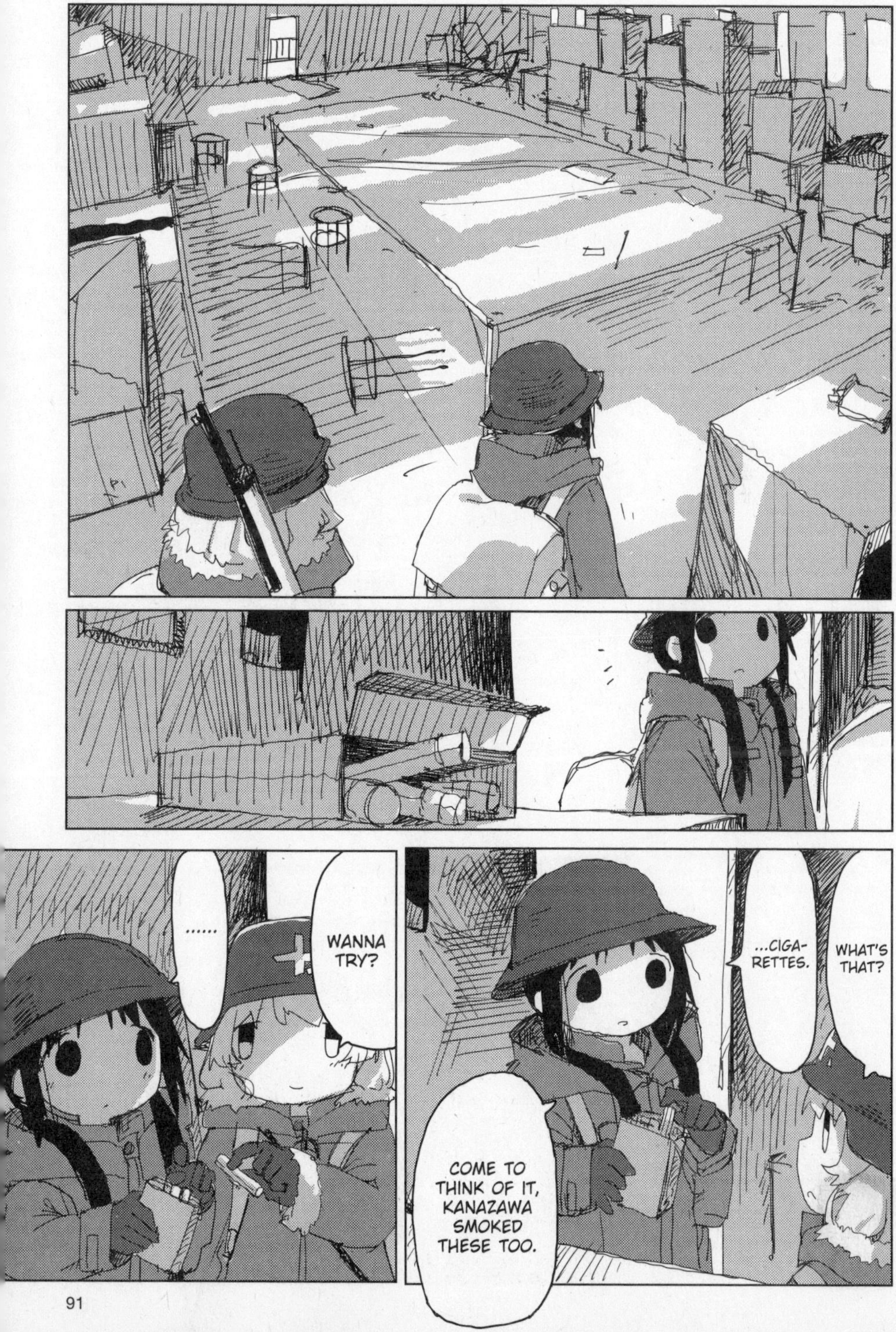
WHAT'S THAT?
...CIGA-
RETTES.
COME TO THINK OF IT, KANAZAWA SMOKED THESE TOO.
WANNA TRY?
......

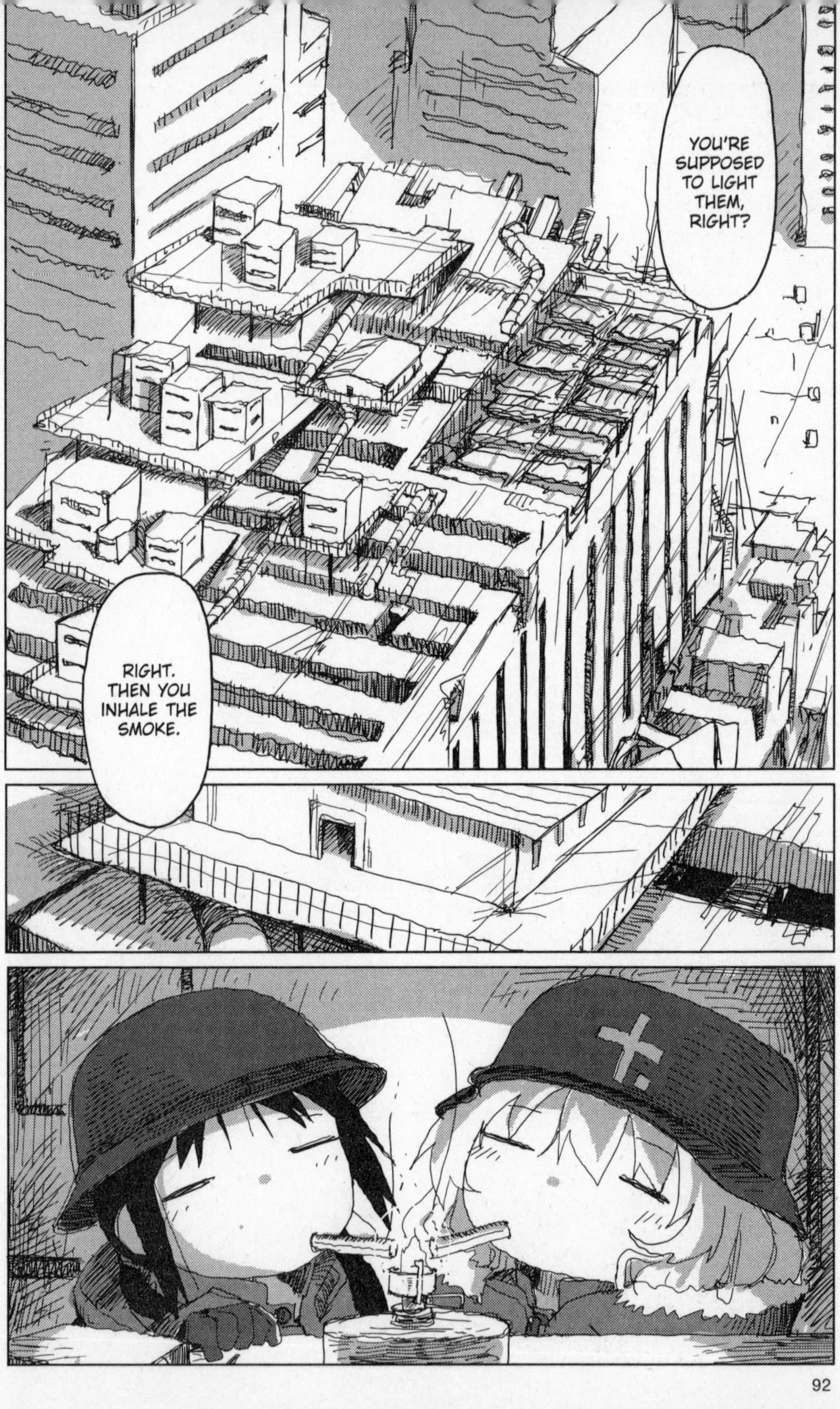
YOU'RE SUPPOSED TO LIGHT THEM, RIGHT?
RIGHT. THEN YOU INHALE THE SMOKE.

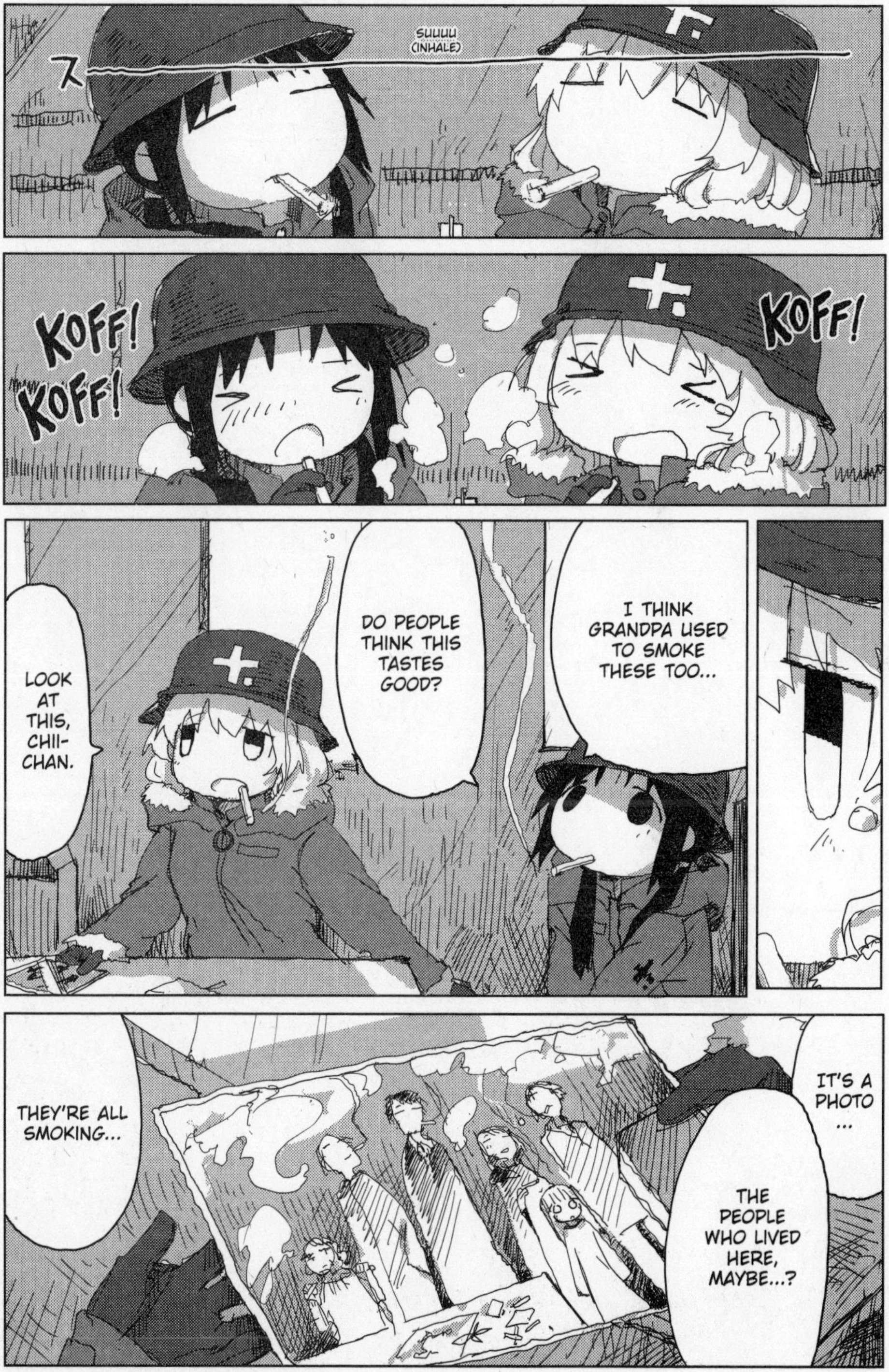
SUUUU (INHALE)
ス
KOFF!
KOFF! KOFF!
I THINK GRANDPA USED TO SMOKE THESE TOO...
DO PEOPLE THINK THIS TASTES GOOD?
LOOK AT THIS, CHII-CHAN.
IT'S A PHOTO...
THE PEOPLE WHO LIVED HERE, MAYBE...?
THEY'RE ALL SMOKING...

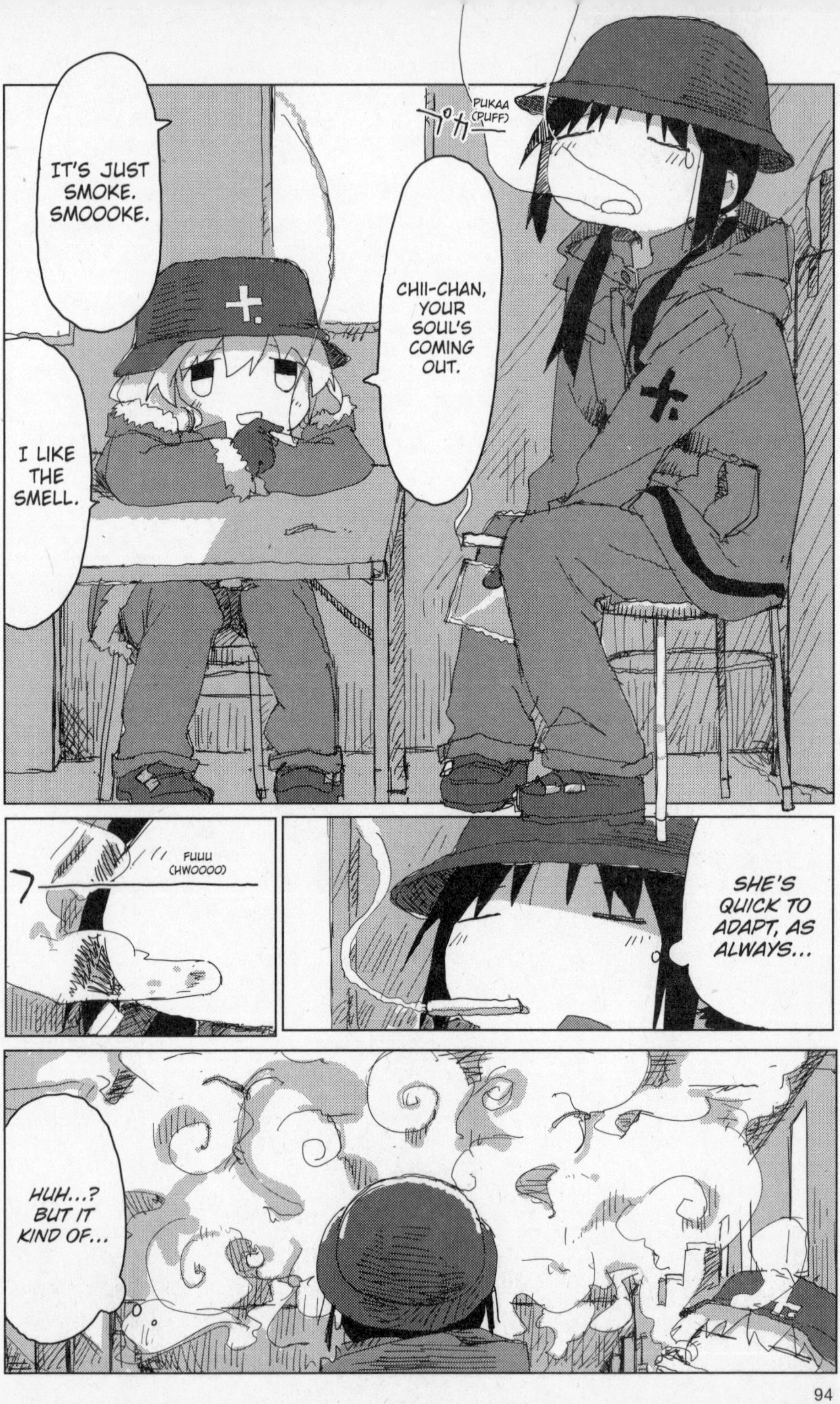
PUKAA (PUFF)
CHII-CHAN, YOUR SOUL'S COMING OUT.
IT'S JUST SMOKE. SMOOOKE.
I LIKE THE SMELL.
SHE'S QUICK TO ADAPT, AS ALWAYS...
FUUU (HWOOOO)
HUH...? BUT IT KIND OF...

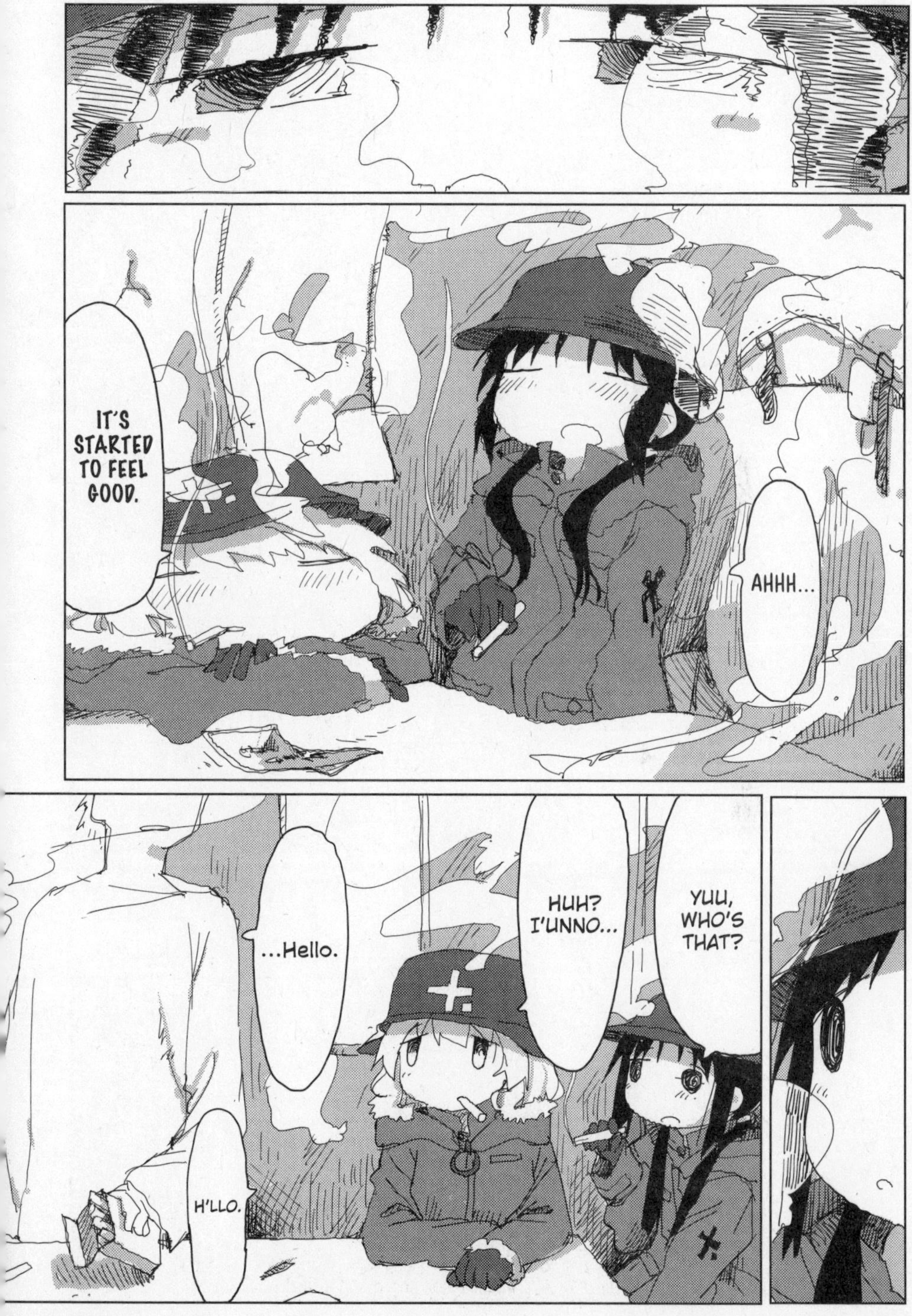
AHHH...
IT'S STARTED TO FEEL GOOD.
YUU, WHO'S THAT?
HUH? I'UNNO...
...Hello.
H'LLO.

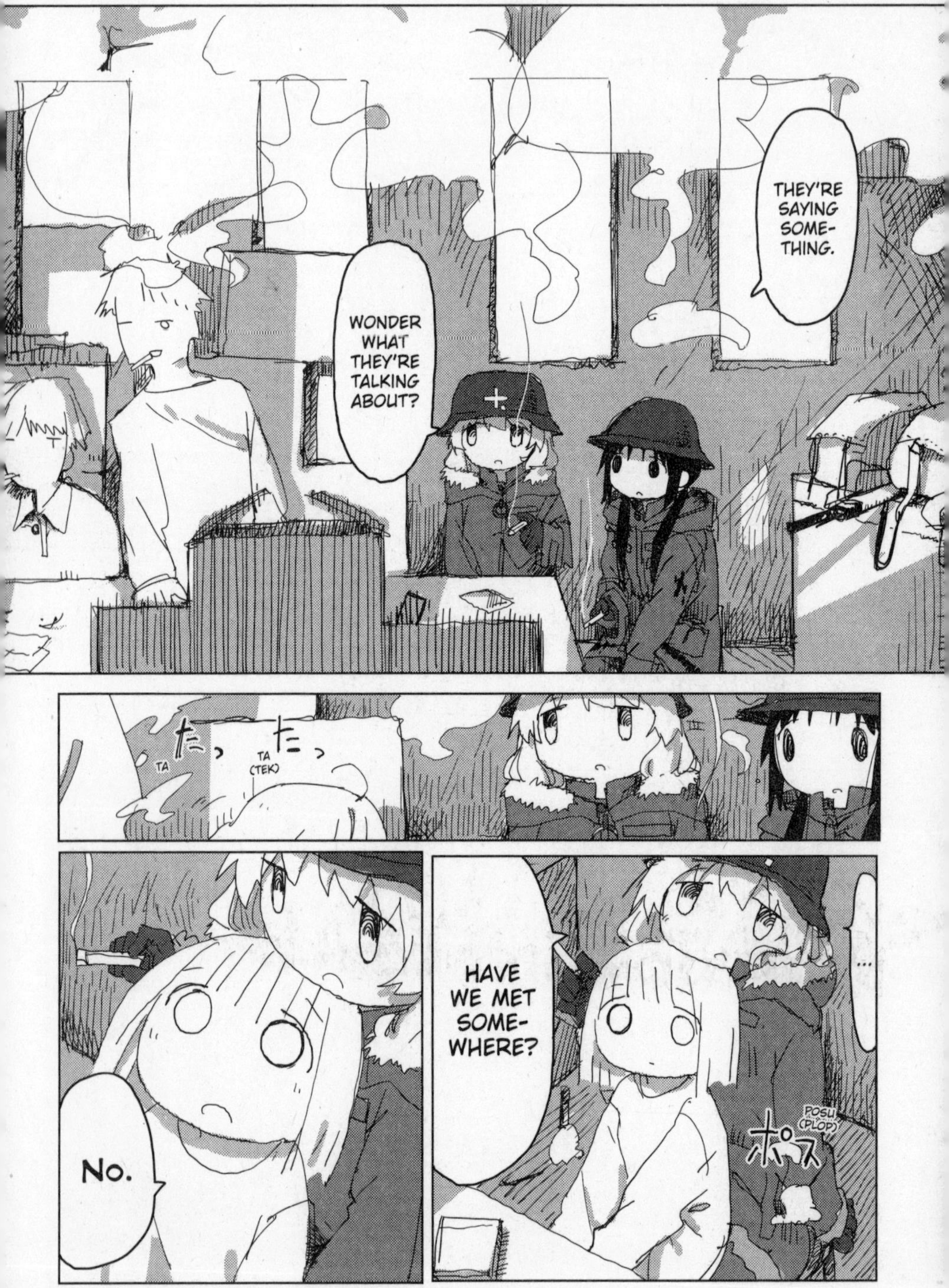
THEY'RE SAYING SOME-THING.
WONDER WHAT THEY'RE TALKING ABOUT?
たっ
TA (TEK)
たっ
TA
...
HAVE WE MET SOME-WHERE?
ポス
POSU (PLOP)
No.

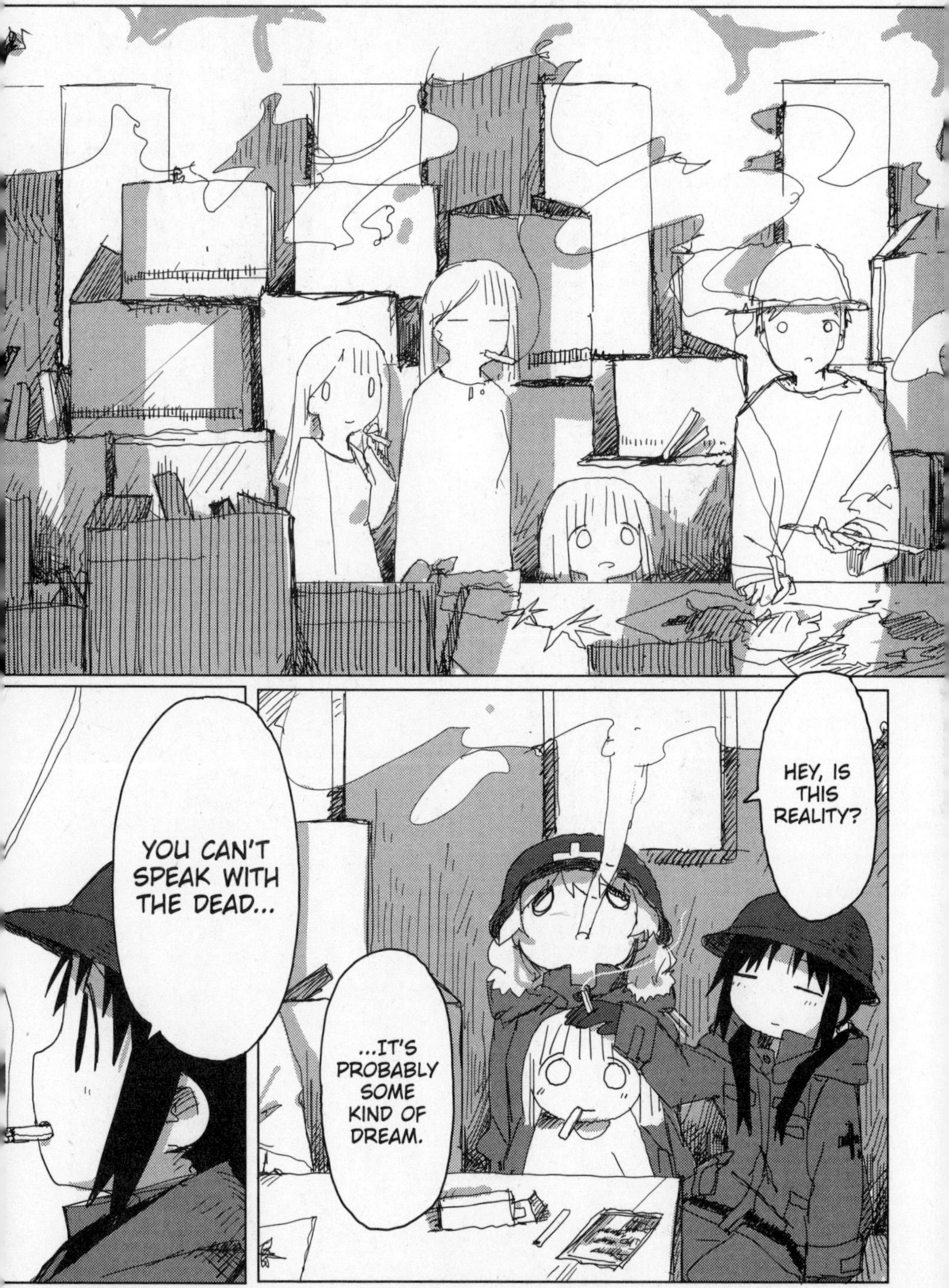
HEY, IS THIS REALITY?
...IT'S PROBABLY SOME KIND OF DREAM.
YOU CAN'T SPEAK WITH THE DEAD...

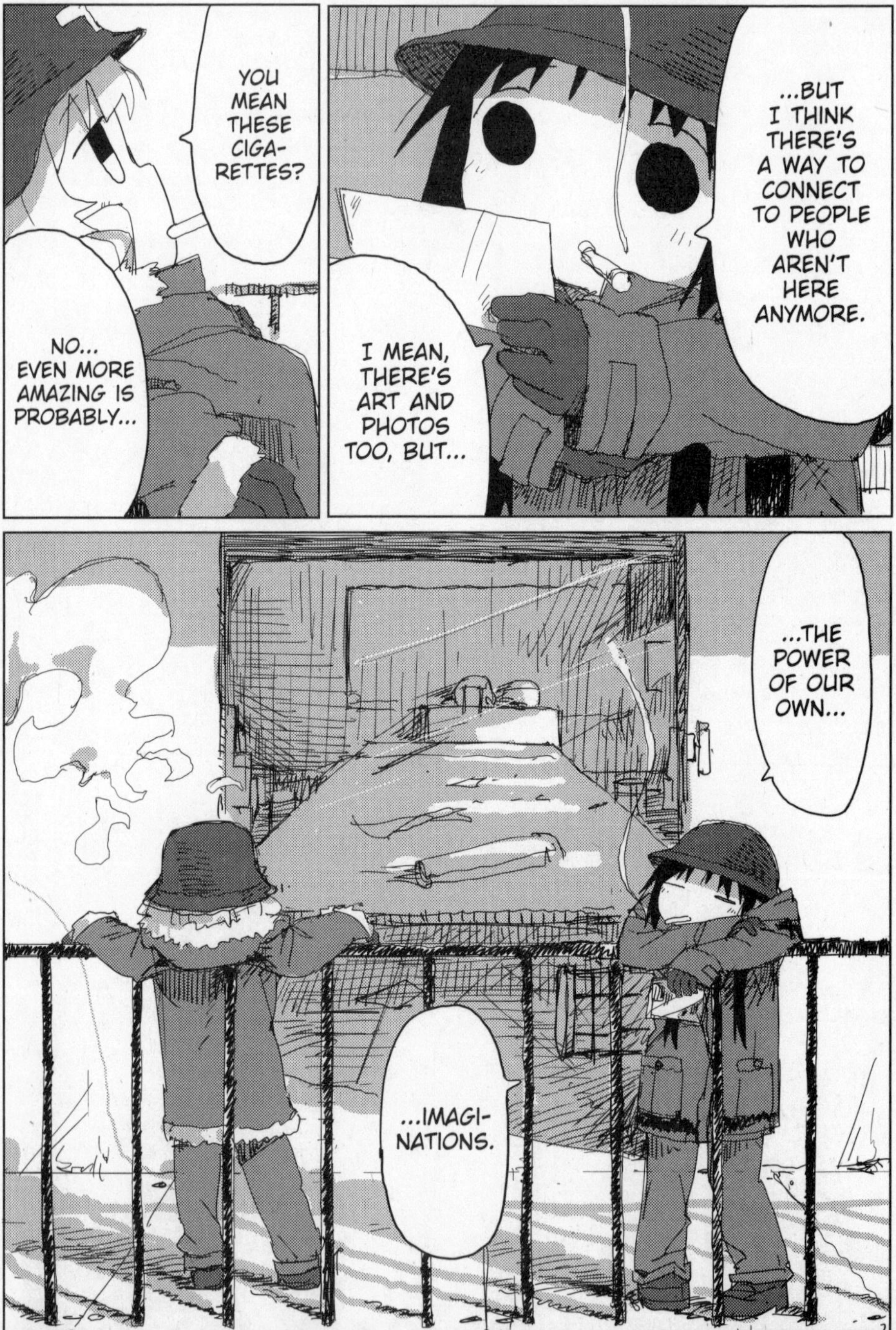
...BUT I THINK THERE'S A WAY TO CONNECT TO PEOPLE WHO AREN'T HERE ANYMORE.
I MEAN, THERE'S ART AND PHOTOS TOO, BUT...
YOU MEAN THESE CIGA-RETTES?
NO... EVEN MORE AMAZING IS PROBABLY...
...THE POWER OF OUR OWN...
...IMAGI-NATIONS.

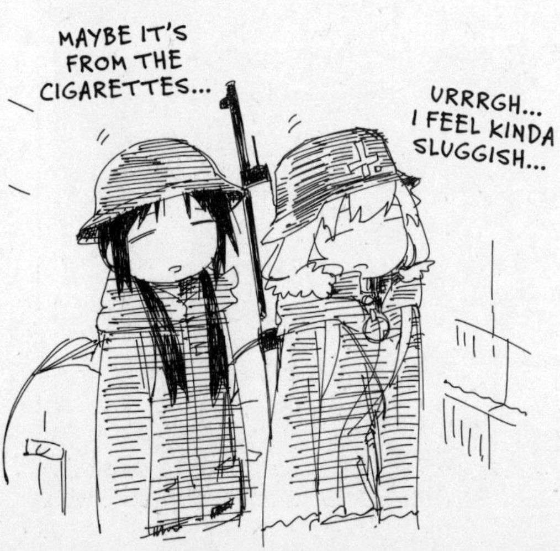
URRRGH... I FEEL KINDA SLUGGISH...
MAYBE IT'S FROM THE CIGARETTES...

GIRLS' LAST TOUR

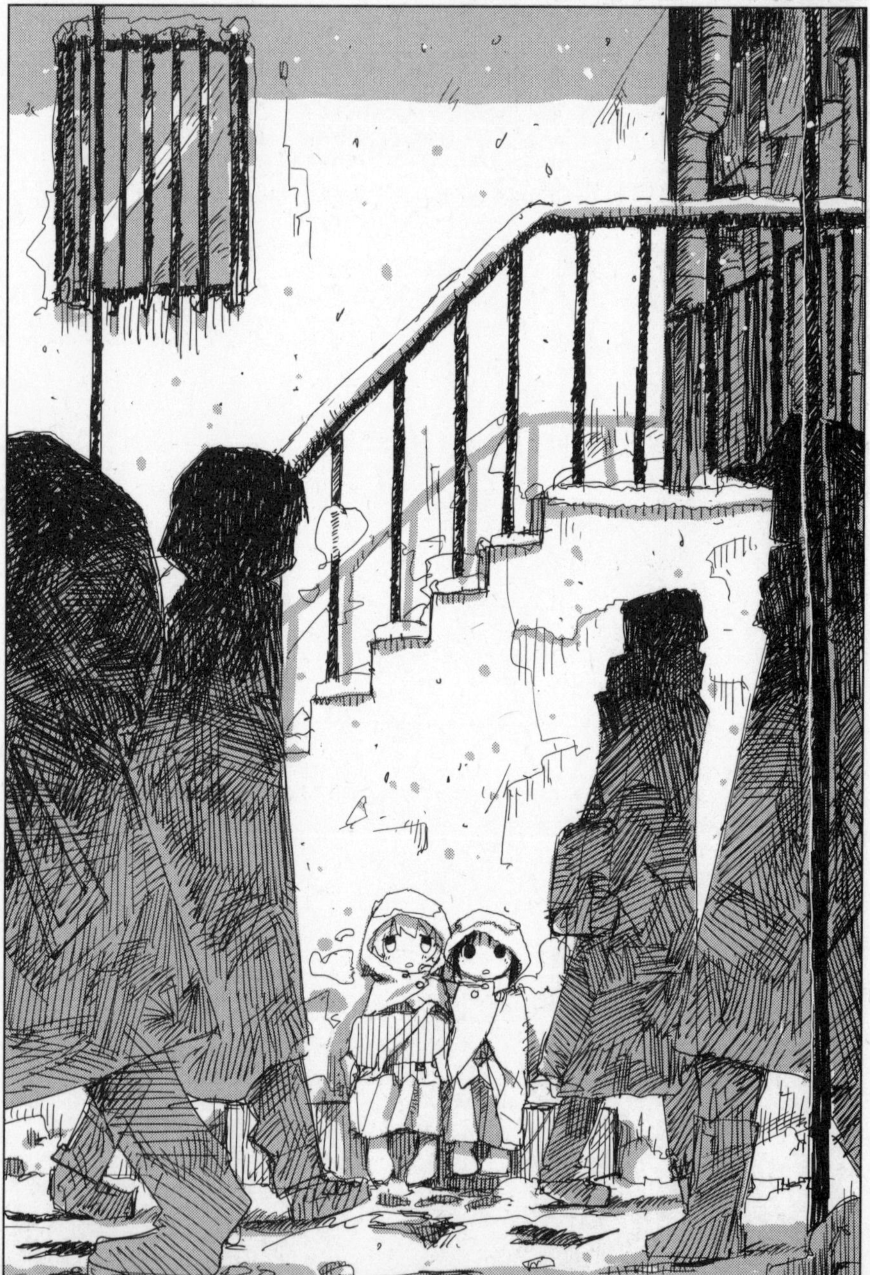

38/39/40

38 EXPLOSION

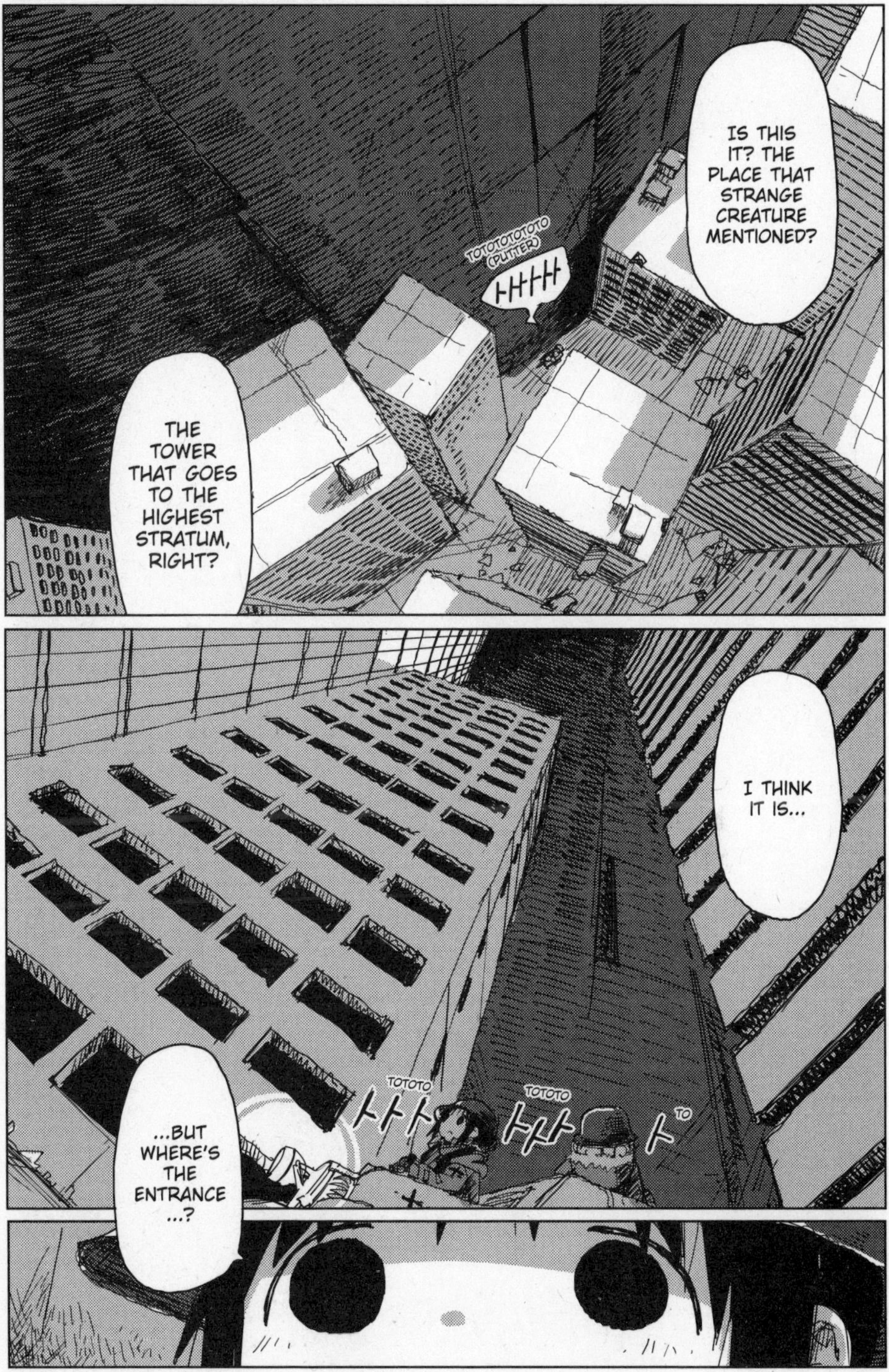
IS THIS IT? THE PLACE THAT STRANGE CREATURE MENTIONED?
TOTOTOTOTOTO (PUTTER)
THE TOWER THAT GOES TO THE HIGHEST STRATUM, RIGHT?
I THINK IT IS...
TO
TOTOTO
TOTOTO
...BUT WHERE'S THE ENTRANCE...?

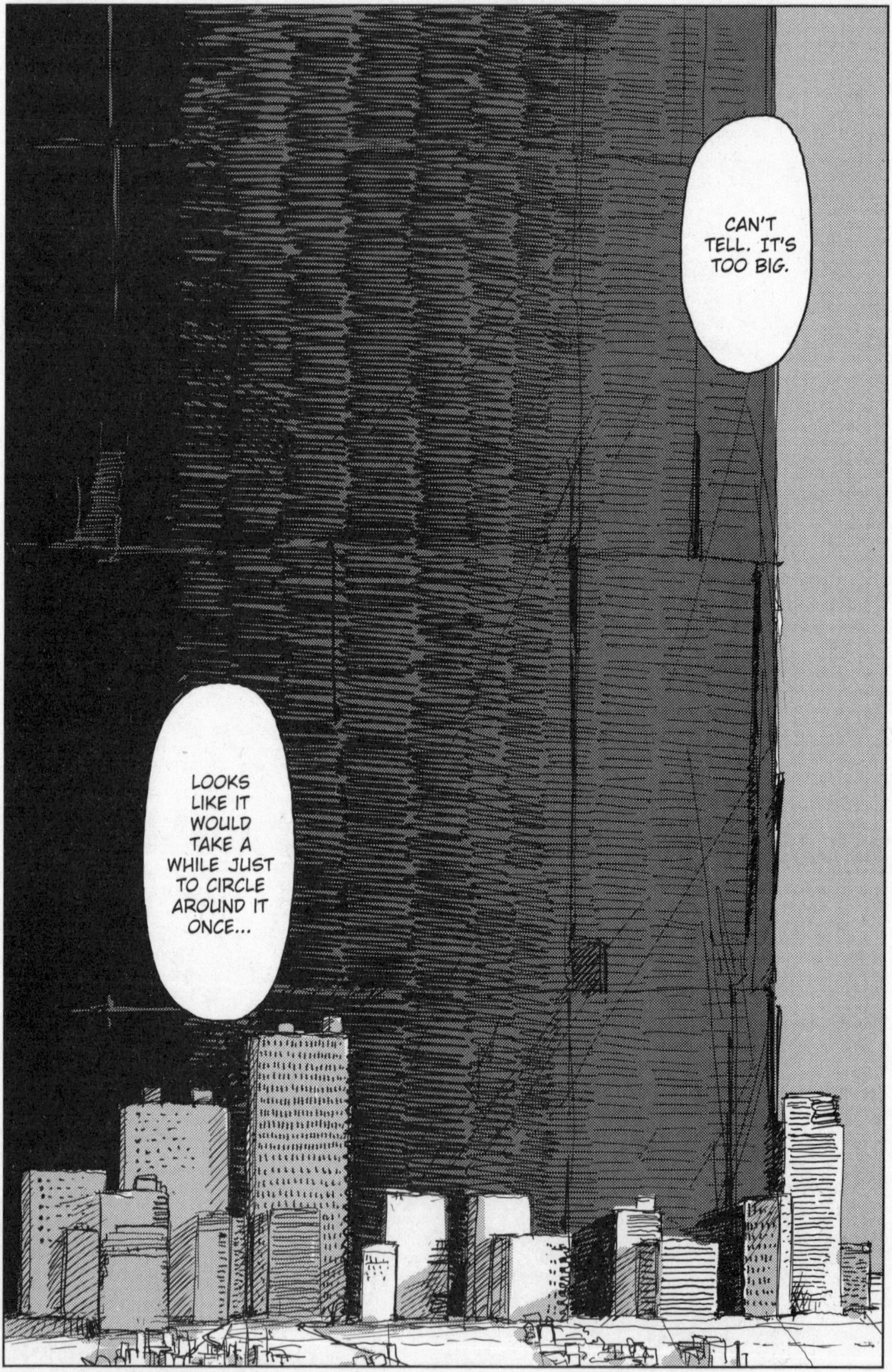
CAN'T TELL. IT'S TOO BIG.
LOOKS LIKE IT WOULD TAKE A WHILE JUST TO CIRCLE AROUND IT ONCE...

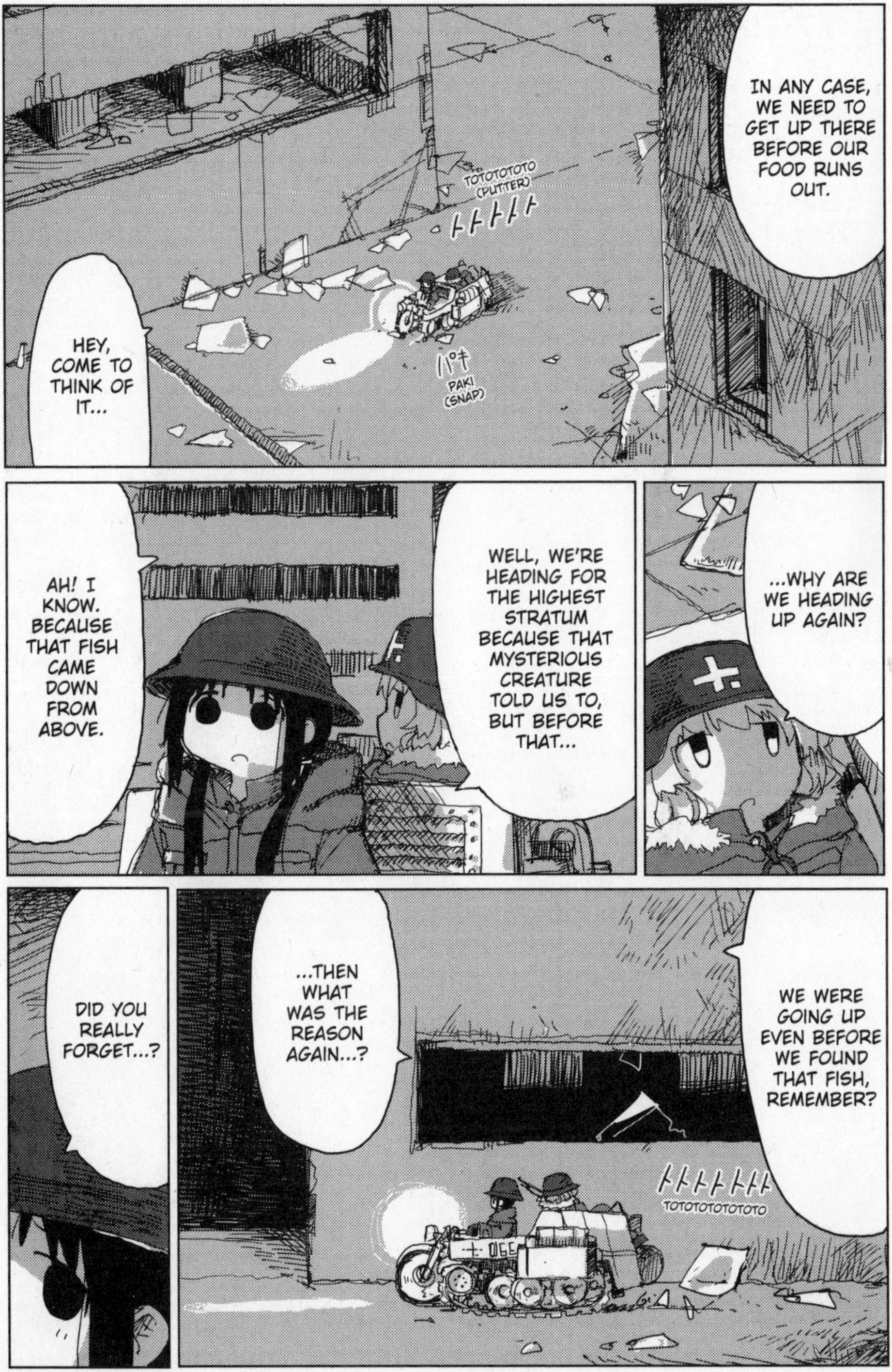

IN ANY CASE, WE NEED TO GET UP THERE BEFORE OUR FOOD RUNS OUT.
トトトトト
TOTOTOTOTO (PUTTER)
パキ
PAKI (SNAP)
HEY, COME TO THINK OF IT...
...WHY ARE WE HEADING UP AGAIN?
WELL, WE'RE HEADING FOR THE HIGHEST STRATUM BECAUSE THAT MYSTERIOUS CREATURE TOLD US TO, BUT BEFORE THAT...
AH! I KNOW. BECAUSE THAT FISH CAME DOWN FROM ABOVE.
WE WERE GOING UP EVEN BEFORE WE FOUND THAT FISH, REMEMBER?
トトトトトトト
TOTOTOTOTOTOTO
...THEN WHAT WAS THE REASON AGAIN...?
DID YOU REALLY FORGET...?

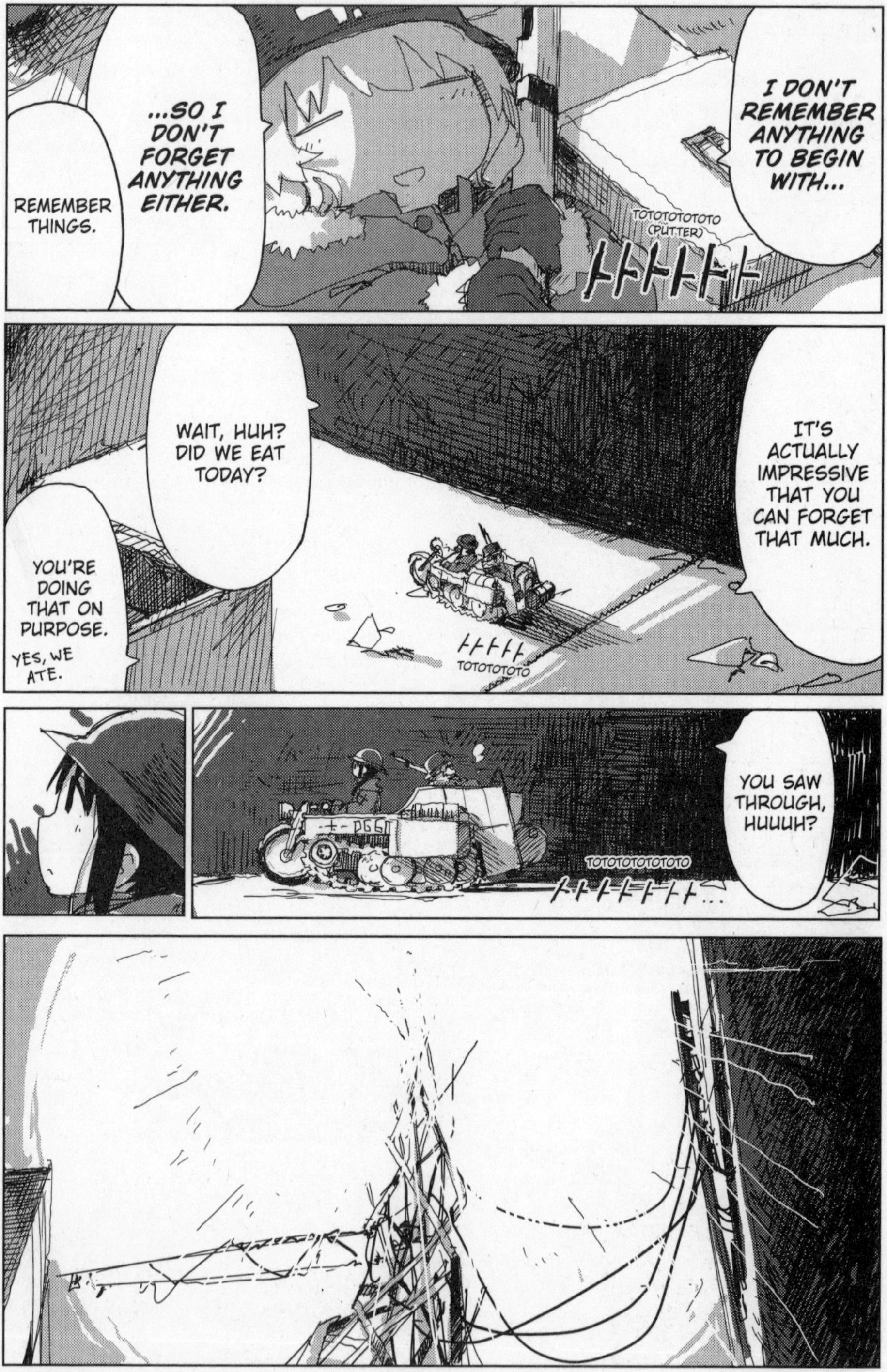
I DON'T REMEMBER ANYTHING TO BEGIN WITH...
TOTOTOTOTOTO (PUTTER)
...SO I DON'T FORGET ANYTHING EITHER.
REMEMBER THINGS.
IT'S ACTUALLY IMPRESSIVE THAT YOU CAN FORGET THAT MUCH.
WAIT, HUH? DID WE EAT TODAY?
TOTOTOTOTO
YOU'RE DOING THAT ON PURPOSE.
YES, WE ATE.
YOU SAW THROUGH, HUUUH?
TOTOTOTOTOTOTO

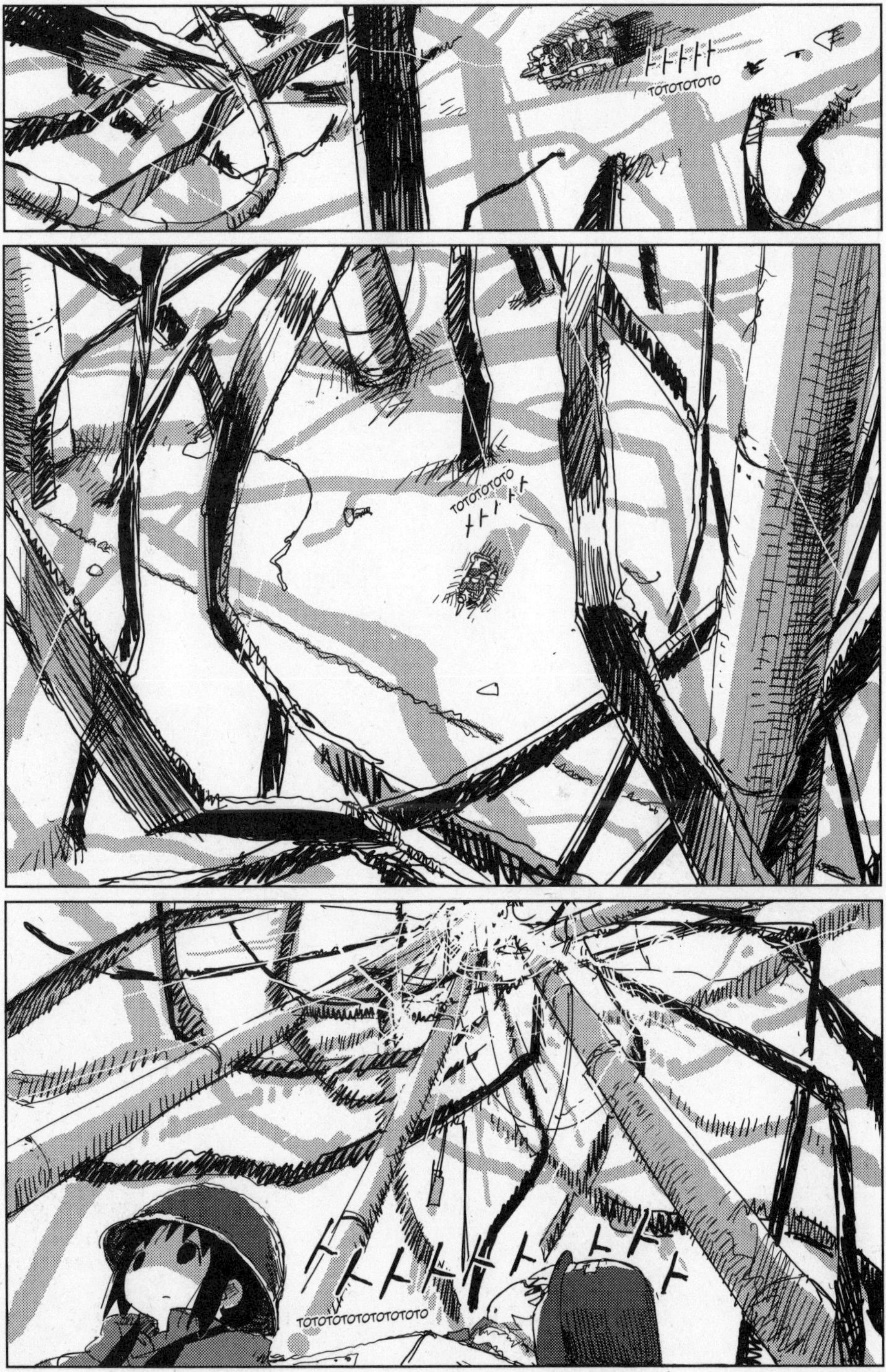
TOTOTOTOTO
TOTOTOTOTO
TOTOTOTOTOTOTOTOTO

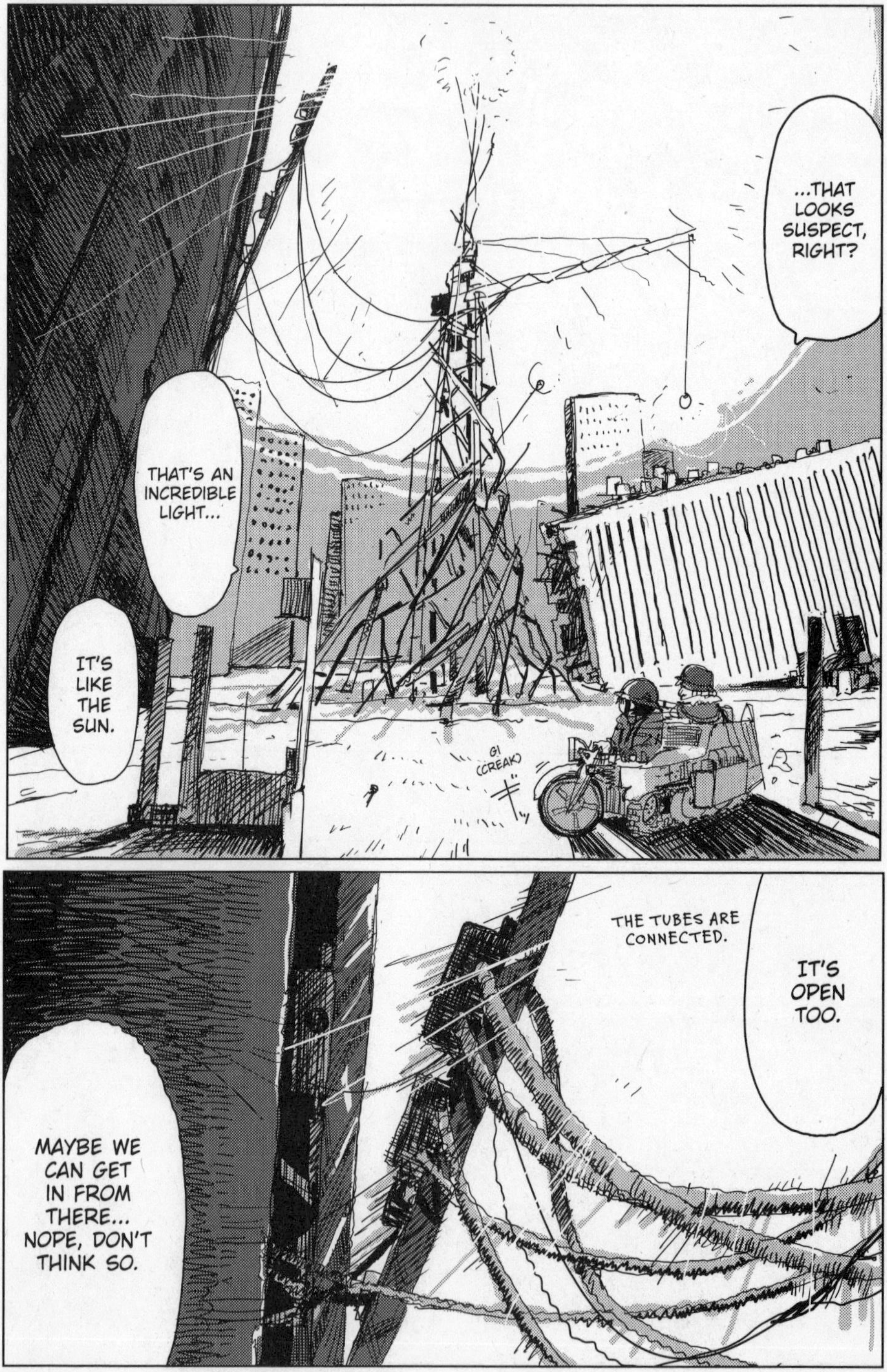
...THAT LOOKS SUSPECT, RIGHT?
THAT'S AN INCREDIBLE LIGHT...
GI (CREAK)
IT'S LIKE THE SUN.
THE TUBES ARE CONNECTED.
IT'S OPEN TOO.
MAYBE WE CAN GET IN FROM THERE... NOPE, DON'T THINK SO.

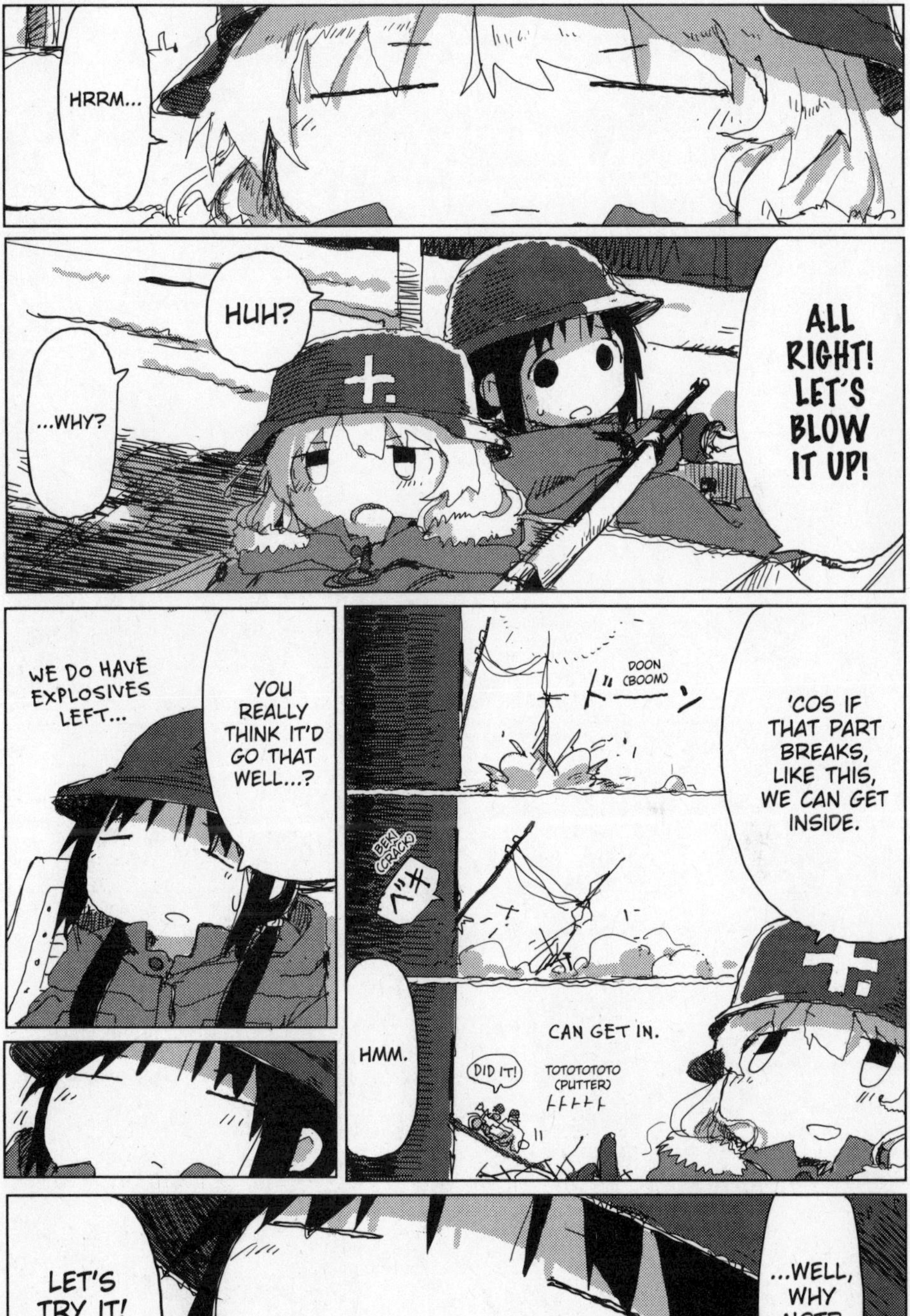
HRRM...
ALL RIGHT! LET'S BLOW IT UP!
HUH?
...WHY?
'COS IF THAT PART BREAKS, LIKE THIS, WE CAN GET INSIDE.
DOON (BOOM)
BEKI (CRACK)
CAN GET IN.
DID IT!
TOTOTOTOTO (PUTTER)
HMM.
YOU REALLY THINK IT'D GO THAT WELL...?
WE DO HAVE EXPLOSIVES LEFT...
...WELL, WHY NOT?
LET'S TRY IT!

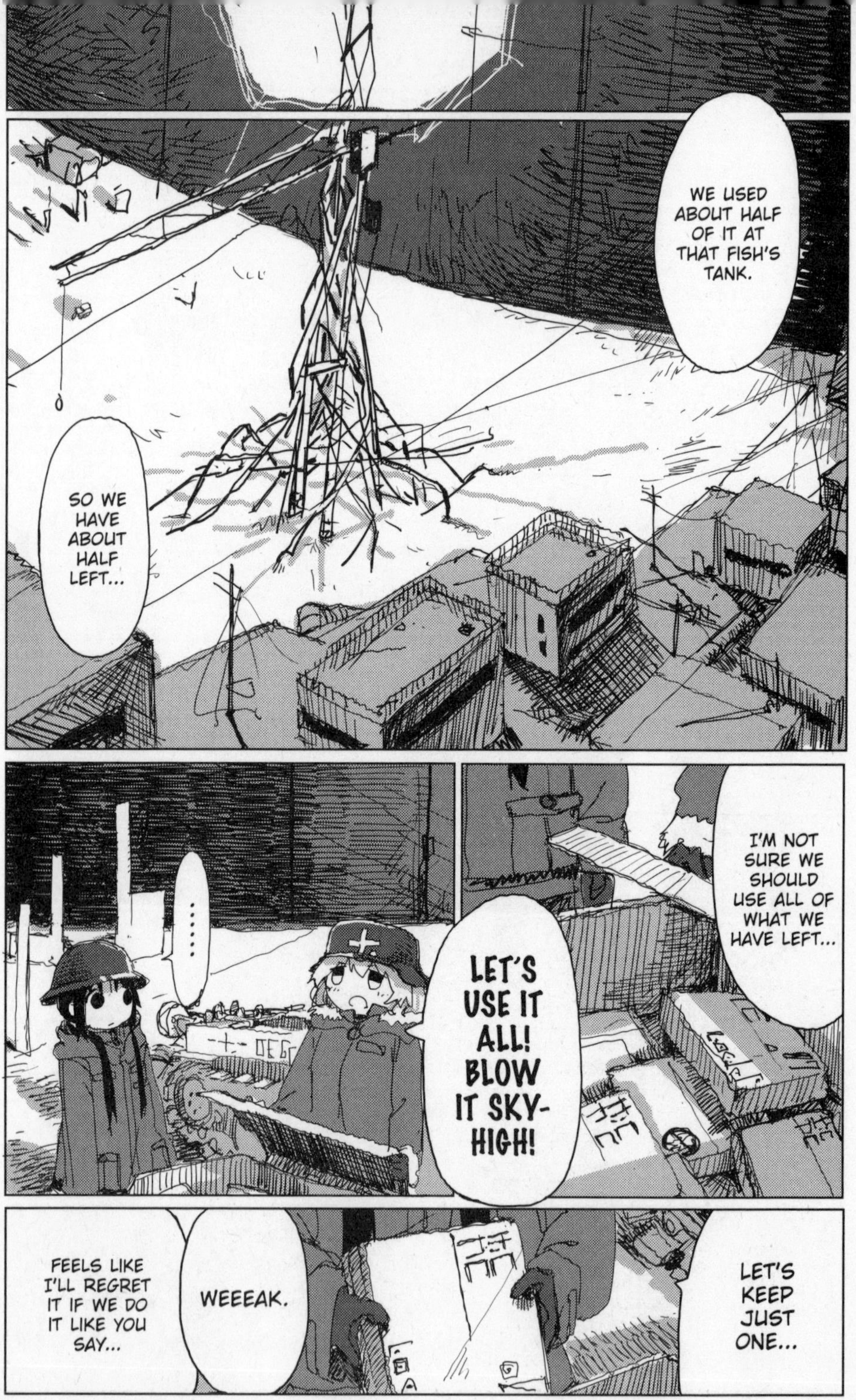
WE USED ABOUT HALF OF IT AT THAT FISH'S TANK.
SO WE HAVE ABOUT HALF LEFT...
I'M NOT SURE WE SHOULD USE ALL OF WHAT WE HAVE LEFT...
LET'S USE IT ALL! BLOW IT SKY-HIGH!
......
LET'S KEEP JUST ONE...
WEEEAK.
FEELS LIKE I'LL REGRET IT IF WE DO IT LIKE YOU SAY...

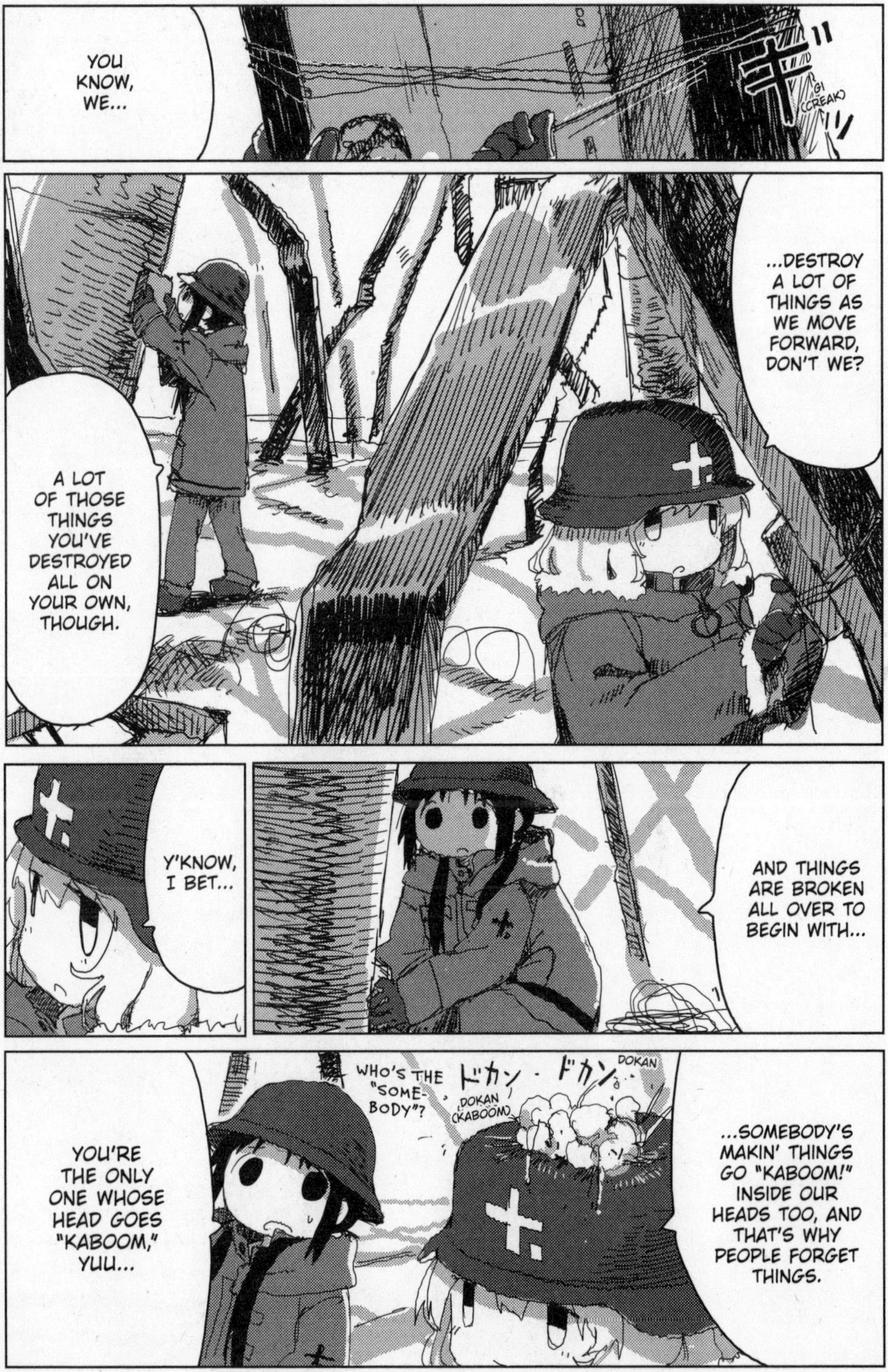
ギッ
GI (CREAK)
YOU KNOW, WE...
...DESTROY A LOT OF THINGS AS WE MOVE FORWARD, DON'T WE?
A LOT OF THOSE THINGS YOU'VE DESTROYED ALL ON YOUR OWN, THOUGH.
AND THINGS ARE BROKEN ALL OVER TO BEGIN WITH...
Y'KNOW, I BET...
...SOMEBODY'S MAKIN' THINGS GO "KABOOM!" INSIDE OUR HEADS TOO, AND THAT'S WHY PEOPLE FORGET THINGS.
ドカン
DOKAN
ドカン
DOKAN (KABOOM)
WHO'S THE "SOMEBODY"?
YOU'RE THE ONLY ONE WHOSE HEAD GOES "KABOOM," YUU...

...WE HAVE TO MOVE FORWARD, EVEN IF IT MEANS DESTROYING THINGS.

IN ANY CASE...

IT'S READY.

ALL RIGHT.

WE CAN'T USE THE TRIGGER DEVICE FROM THIS DISTANCE... SO...

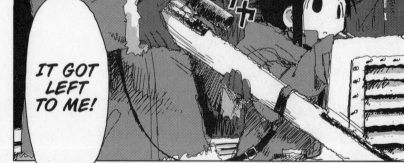

GACHA
(KCHAK)

...I LEAVE THIS TO YOU.

IT GOT LEFT TO ME!

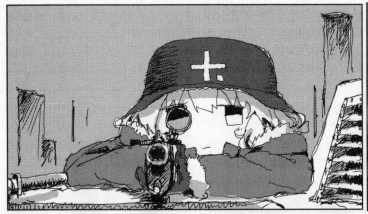

KACHA
(KCHUNK)

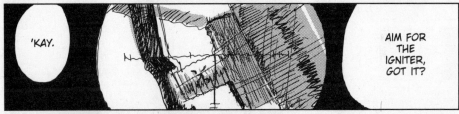

'KAY.

AIM FOR THE IGNITER, GOT IT?

PAN
(BANG)

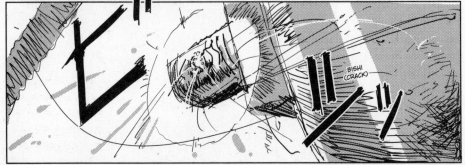

BISHI
(CRACK)

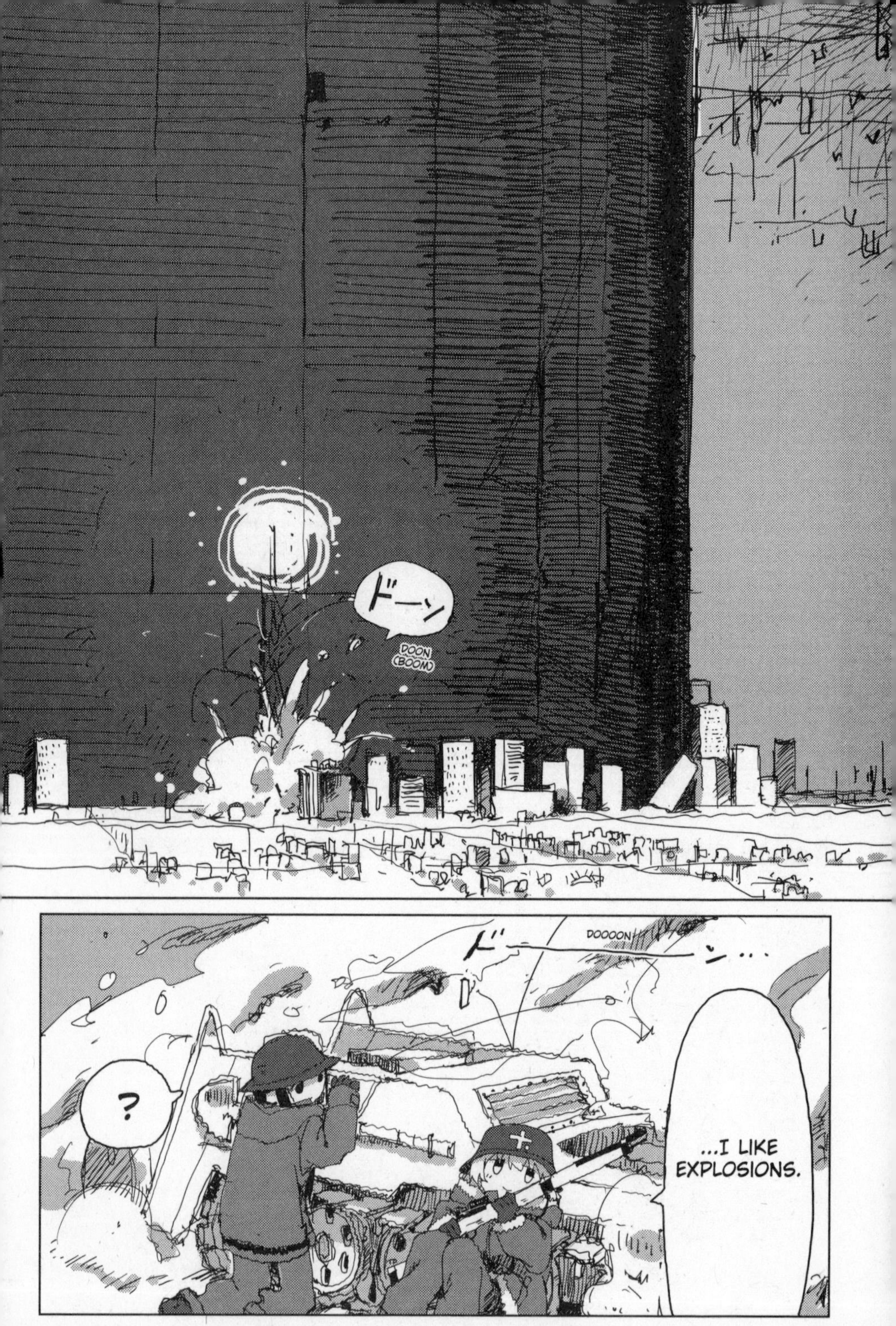
ドーン
DOON (BOOM)
ドーーン…
DOOOON
...I LIKE EXPLOSIONS.
?

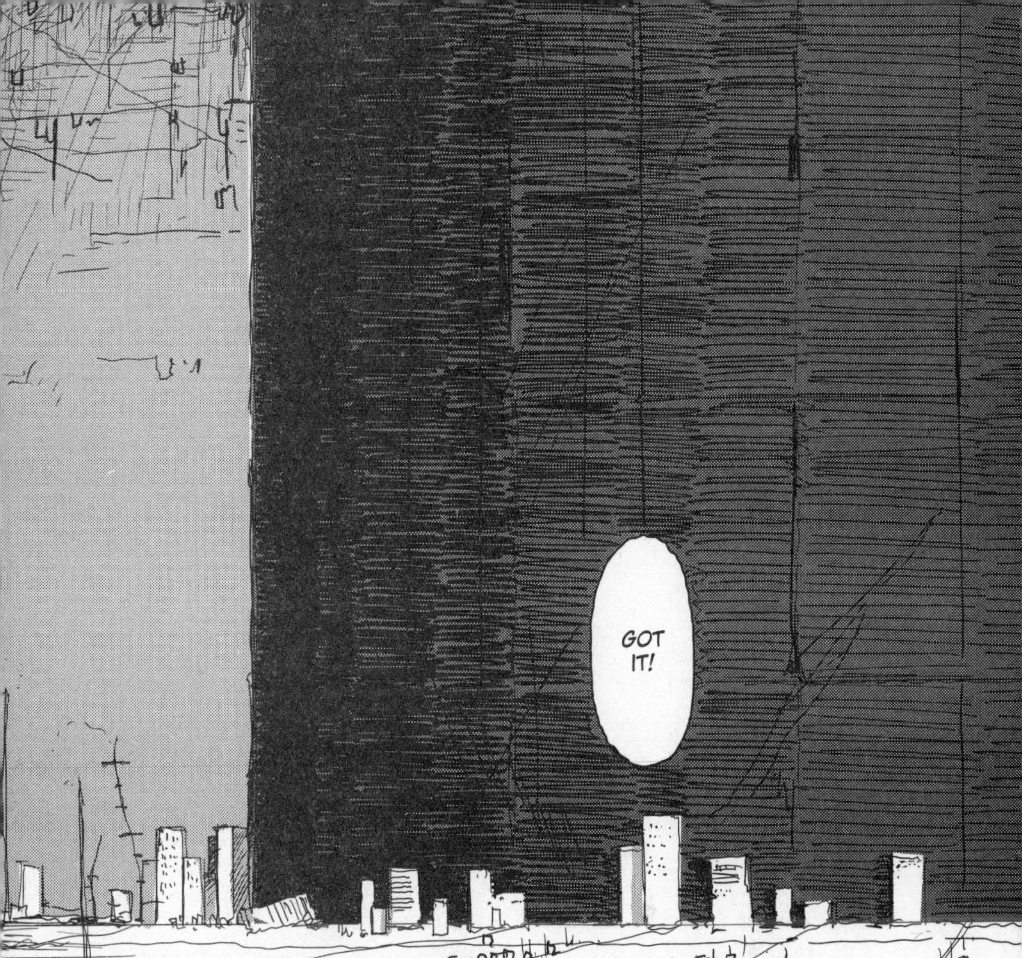
GOT IT!

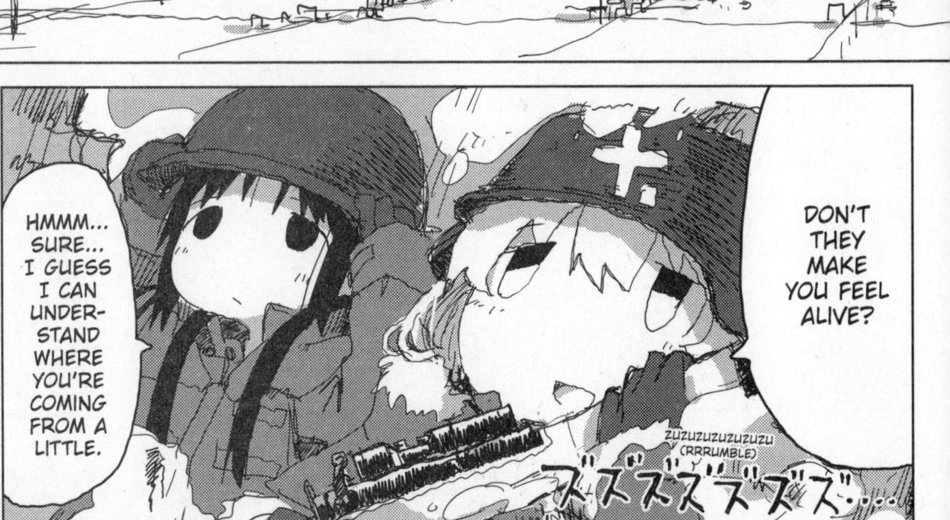
DON'T THEY MAKE YOU FEEL ALIVE?
HMMM... SURE... I GUESS I CAN UNDER-STAND WHERE YOU'RE COMING FROM A LITTLE.
ZUZUZUZUZUZUZU (RRRUMBLE)
ズズズズズズズ…

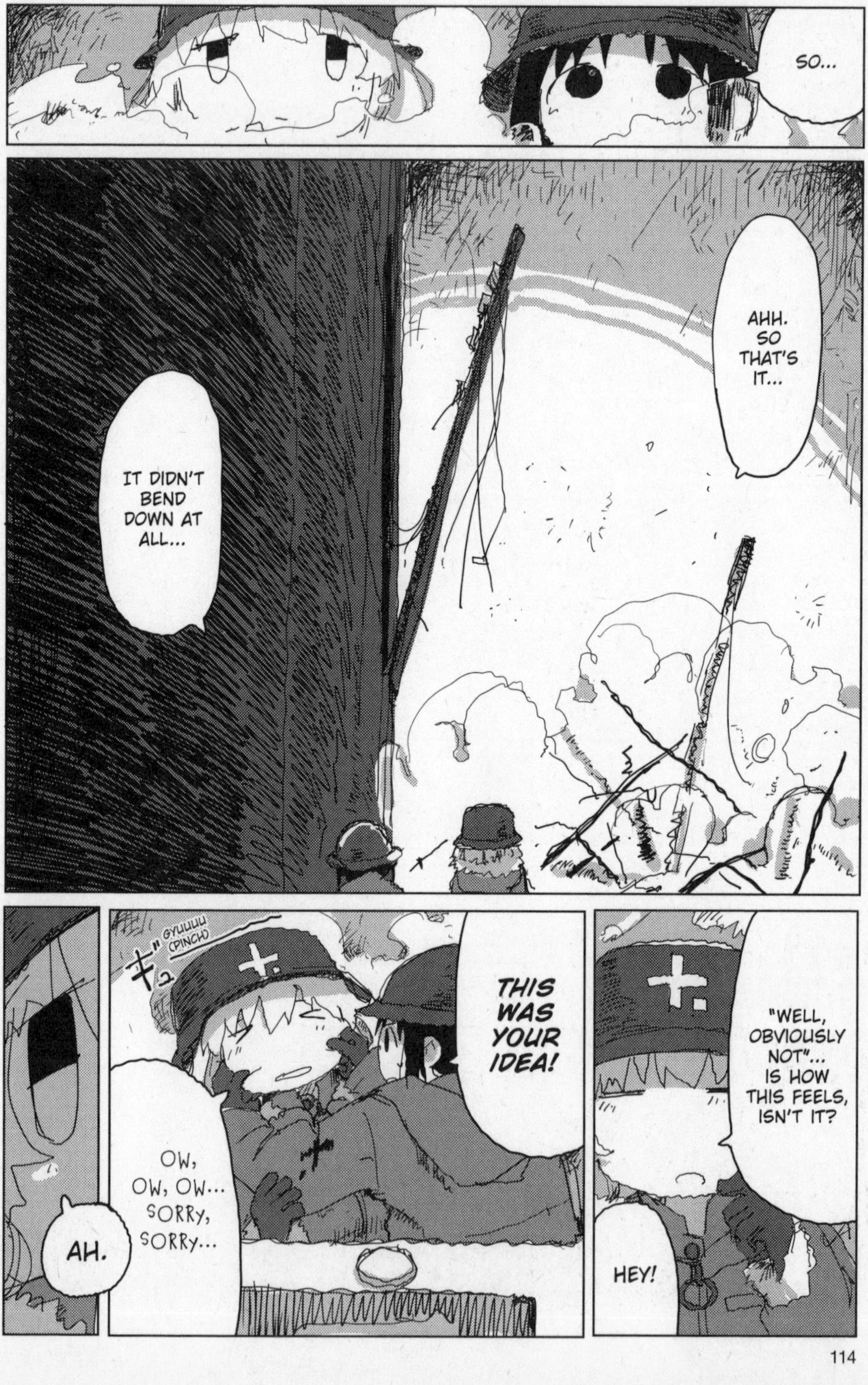
SO...
AHH. SO THAT'S IT...
IT DIDN'T BEND DOWN AT ALL...
"WELL, OBVIOUSLY NOT"... IS HOW THIS FEELS, ISN'T IT?
HEY!
THIS WAS YOUR IDEA!
GYUUUU (PINCH)
OW, OW, OW... SORRY, SORRY...
AH.

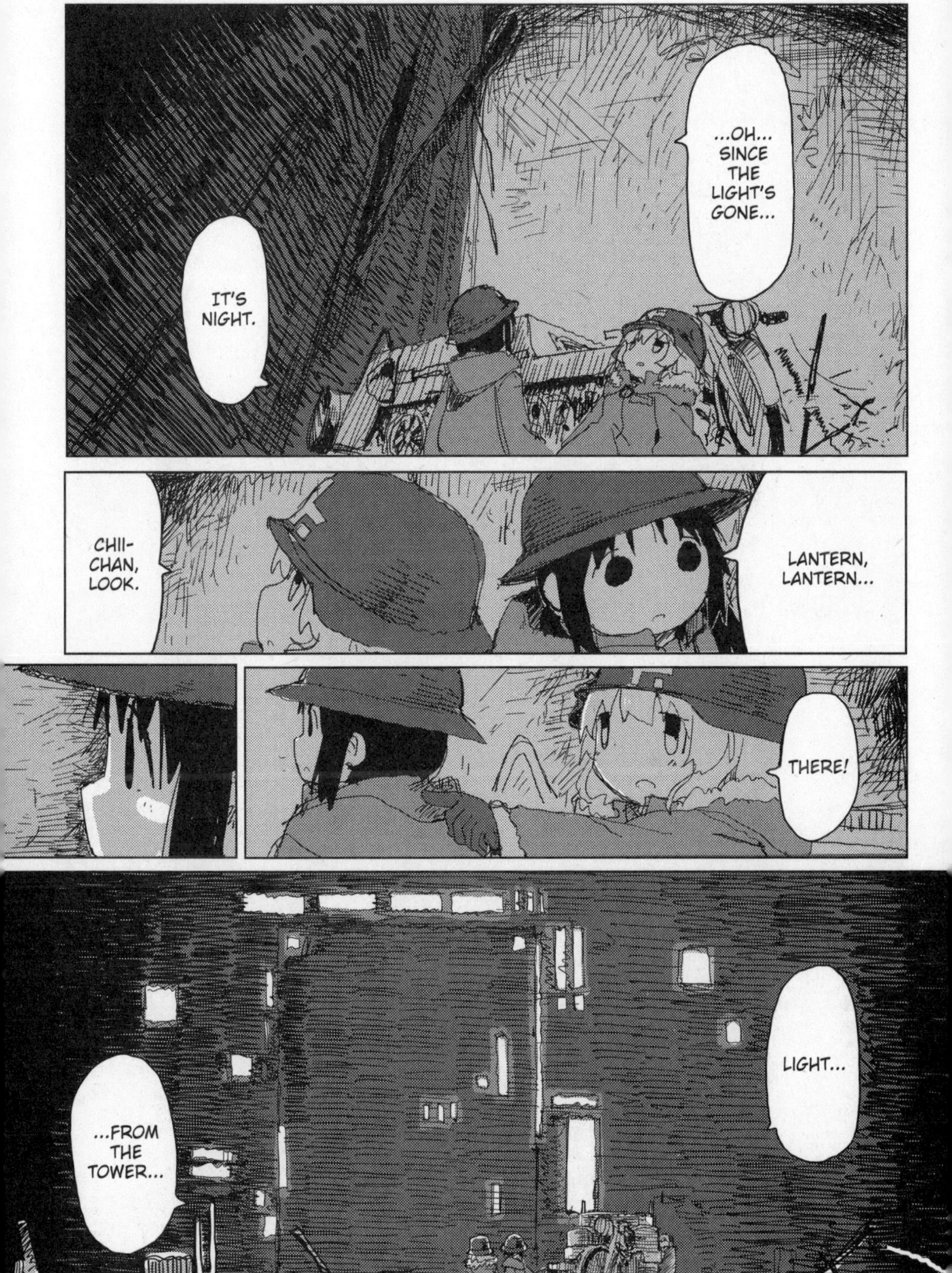
...OH... SINCE THE LIGHT'S GONE...
IT'S NIGHT.
LANTERN, LANTERN...
CHII-CHAN, LOOK.
THERE!
LIGHT...
...FROM THE TOWER...

TA (TMP)
たっ
PIPI (B-BEEP)
ピピッ
GASHA (CLANG)
ガシャ
!
WELCOME TO CORE TOWER #6!

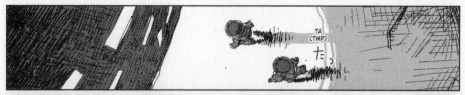

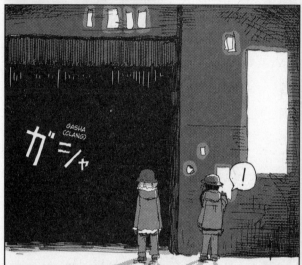

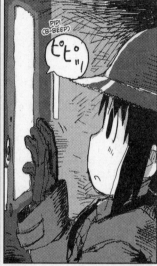

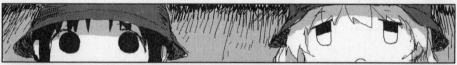

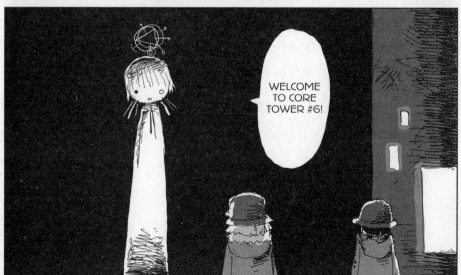

39 OBLIVION

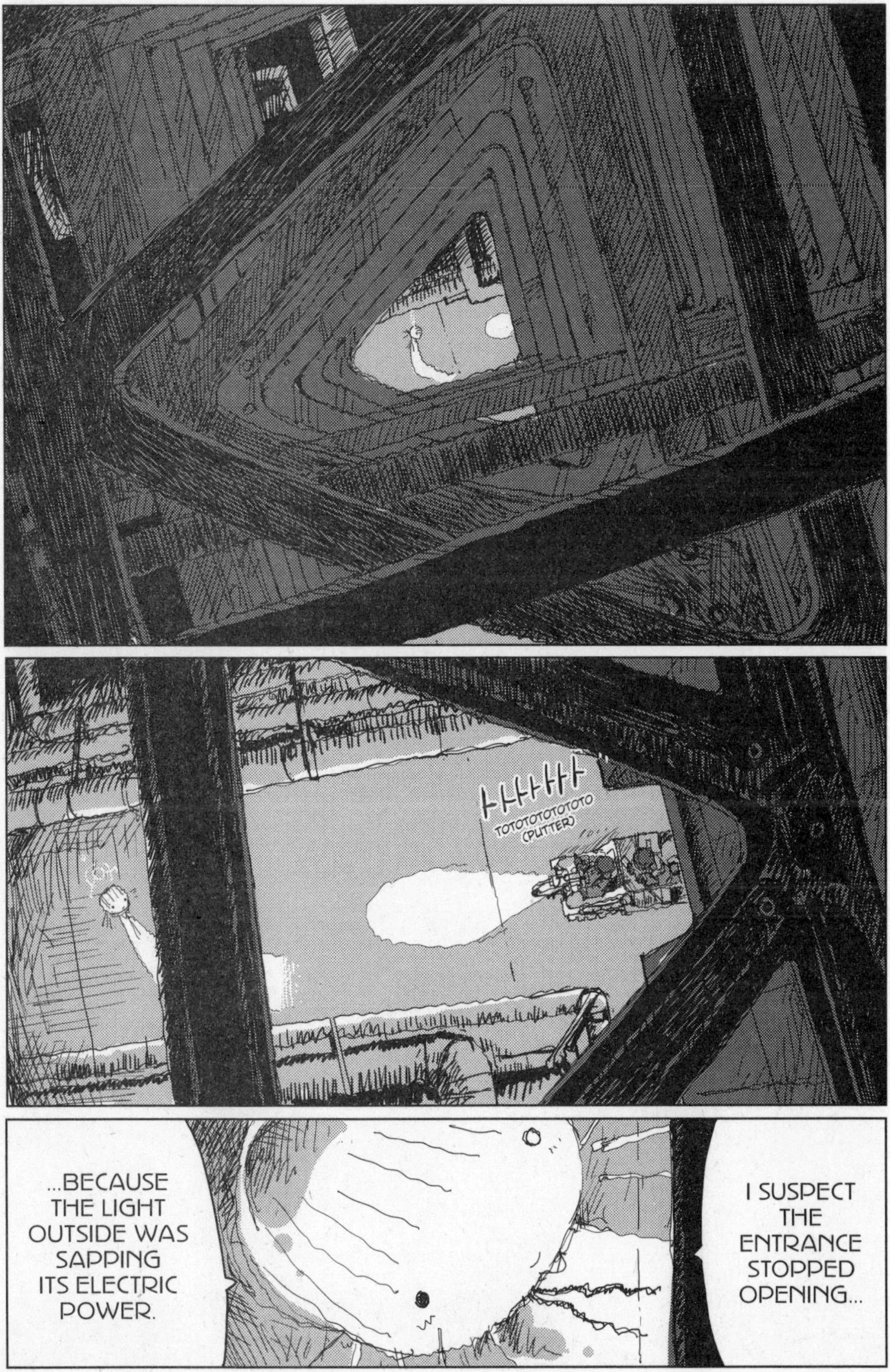
トトトトトト
TOTOTOTOTOTOTO
(PUTTER)
I SUSPECT THE ENTRANCE STOPPED OPENING...
...BECAUSE THE LIGHT OUTSIDE WAS SAPPING ITS ELECTRIC POWER.

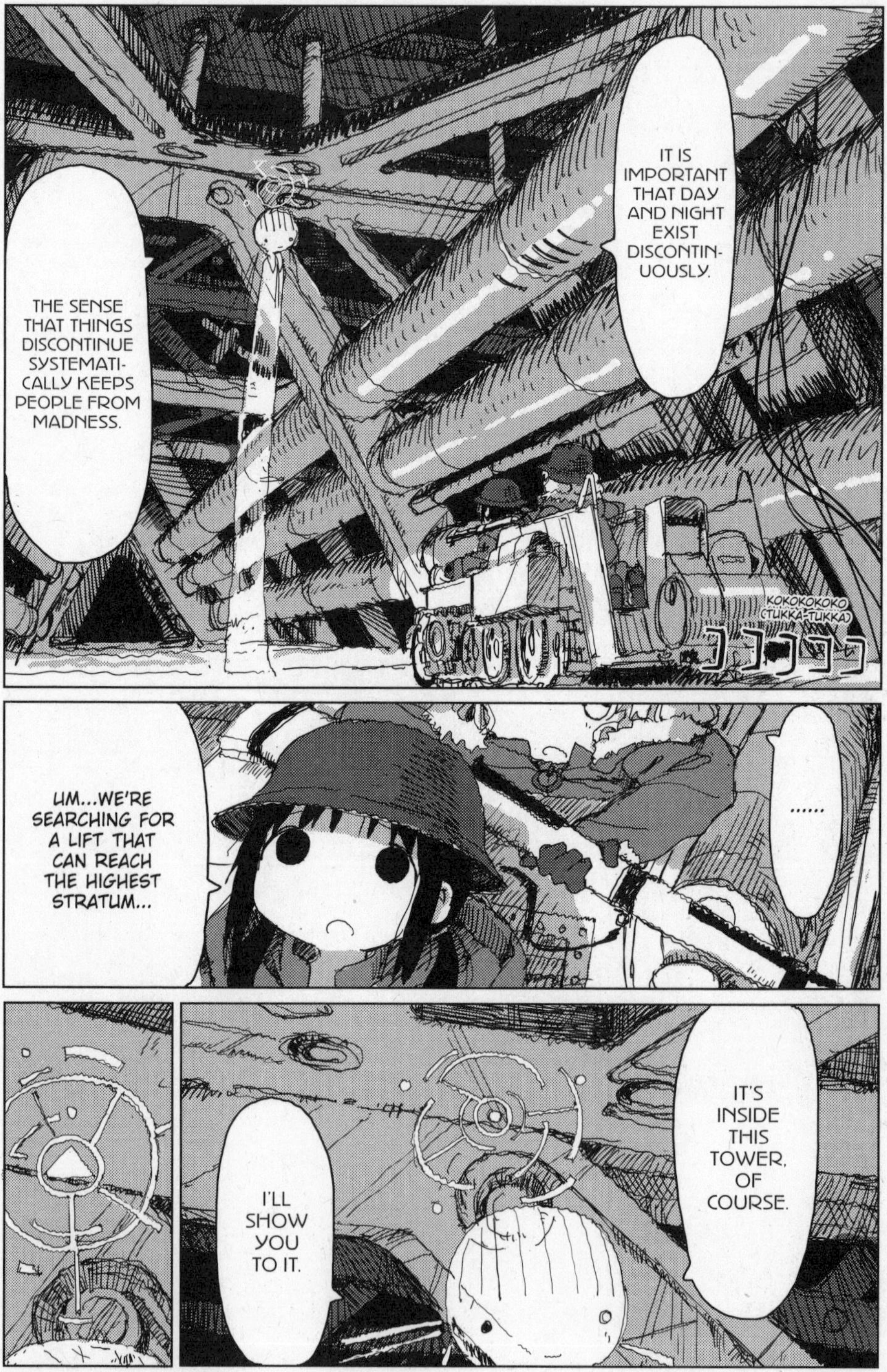

IT IS IMPORTANT THAT DAY AND NIGHT EXIST DISCONTIN-UOUSLY.
THE SENSE THAT THINGS DISCONTINUE SYSTEMATI-CALLY KEEPS PEOPLE FROM MADNESS.
KOKOKOKOKO (TUKKA-TUKKA)
......
UM...WE'RE SEARCHING FOR A LIFT THAT CAN REACH THE HIGHEST STRATUM...
IT'S INSIDE THIS TOWER, OF COURSE.
I'LL SHOW YOU TO IT.

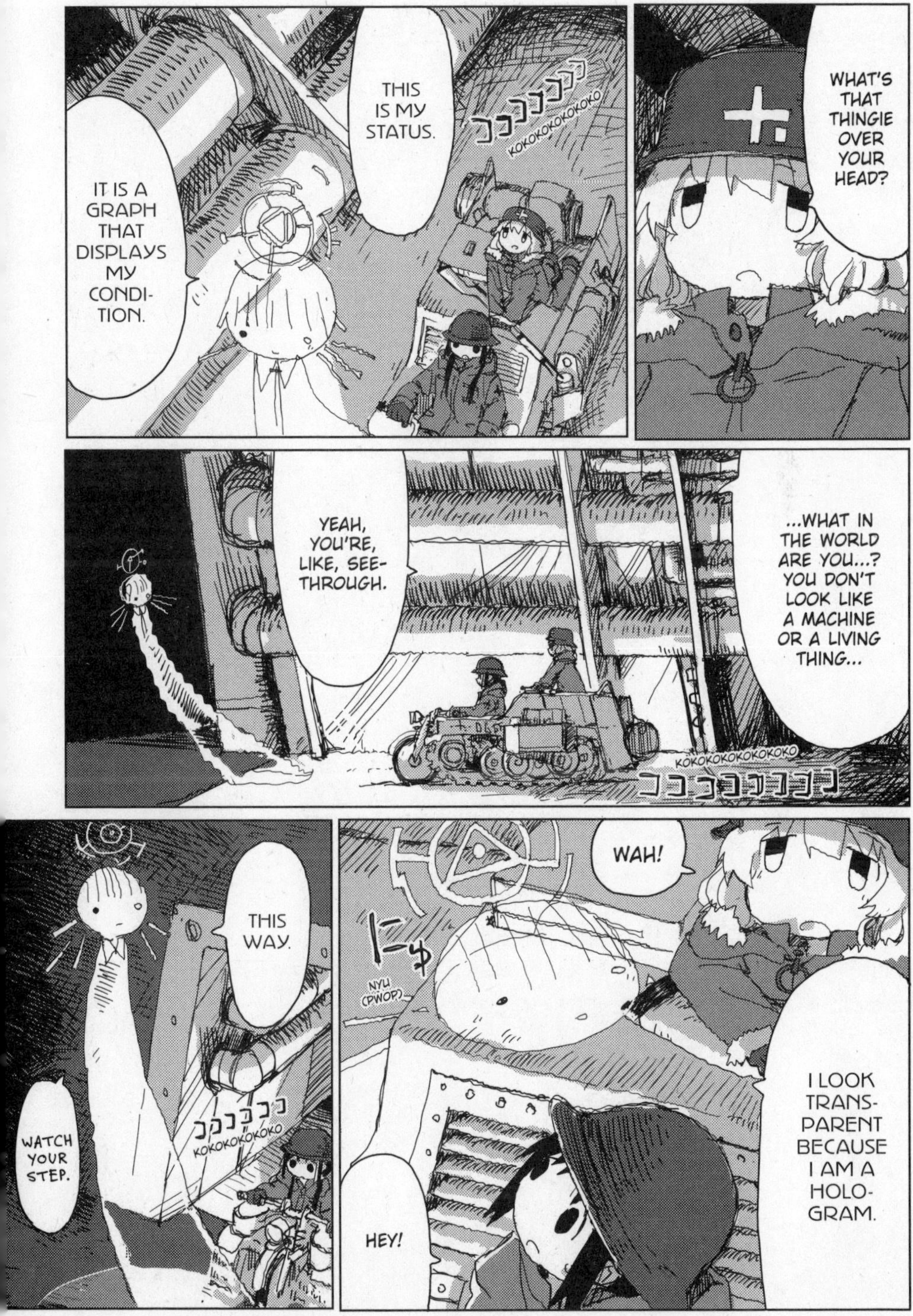

WHAT'S THAT THINGIE OVER YOUR HEAD?
THIS IS MY STATUS.
KOKOKOKOKOKOKO
IT IS A GRAPH THAT DISPLAYS MY CONDITION.
...WHAT IN THE WORLD ARE YOU...? YOU DON'T LOOK LIKE A MACHINE OR A LIVING THING...
YEAH, YOU'RE, LIKE, SEE-THROUGH.
KOKOKOKOKOKOKOKO
WAH!
I LOOK TRANSPARENT BECAUSE I AM A HOLOGRAM.
NYU (PWOP)
HEY!
THIS WAY.
KOKOKOKOKO
WATCH YOUR STEP.

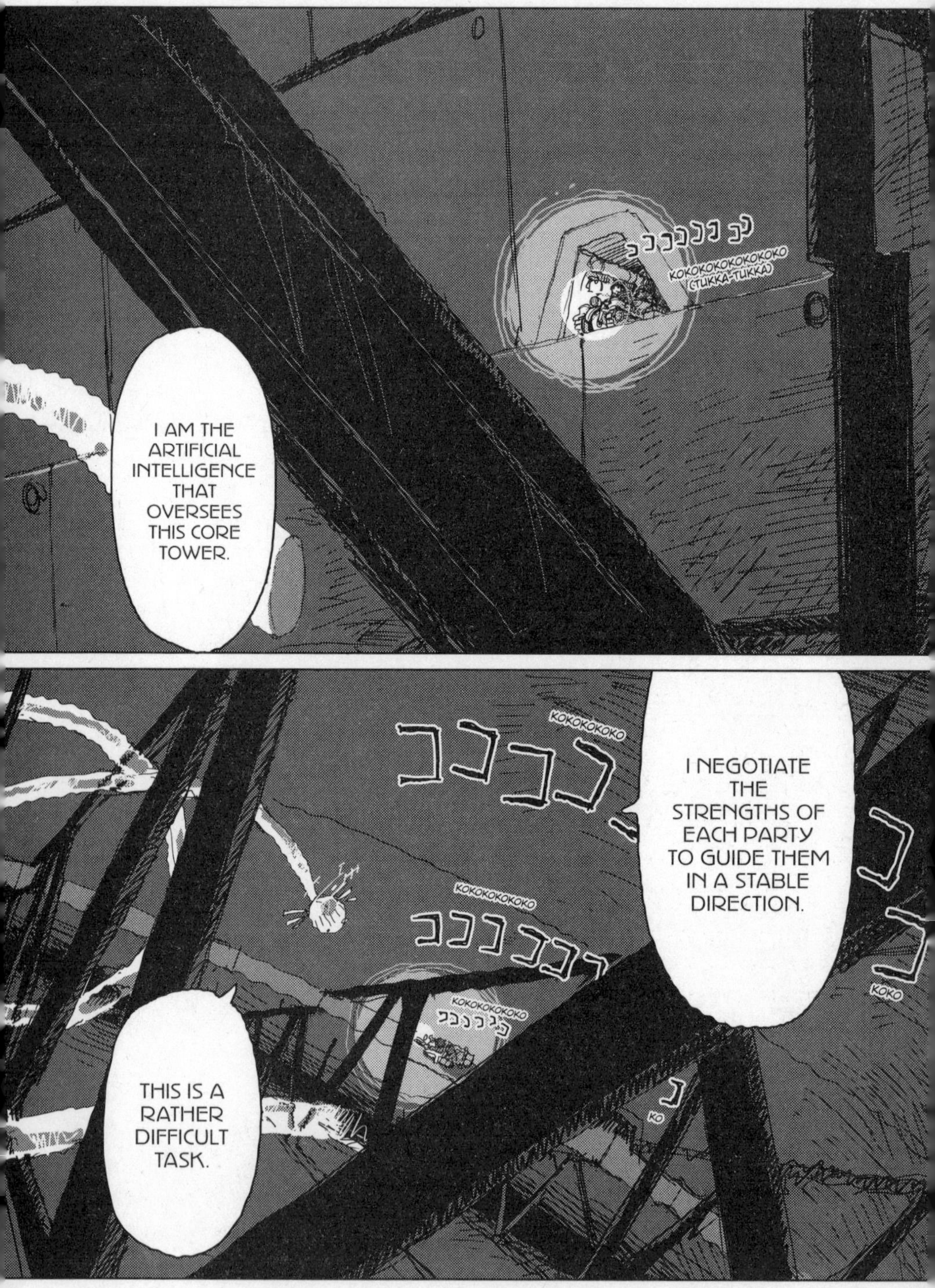

KOKOKOKOKOKOKOKO (TUKKA-TUKKA)
I AM THE ARTIFICIAL INTELLIGENCE THAT OVERSEES THIS CORE TOWER.
I NEGOTIATE THE STRENGTHS OF EACH PARTY TO GUIDE THEM IN A STABLE DIRECTION.
KOKOKOKOKO
KOKO
KOKOKOKOKOKO
KOKOKOKOKOKO
KO
THIS IS A RATHER DIFFICULT TASK.

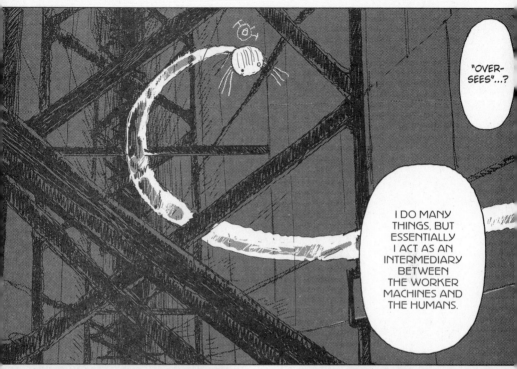

"OVER-SEES"...?

I DO MANY THINGS, BUT ESSENTIALLY I ACT AS AN INTERMEDIARY BETWEEN THE WORKER MACHINES AND THE HUMANS.

HEY, WHY IS YOUR BODY STRETCHED SO LONG?

THAT IS BECAUSE I AM HAPPY.

......

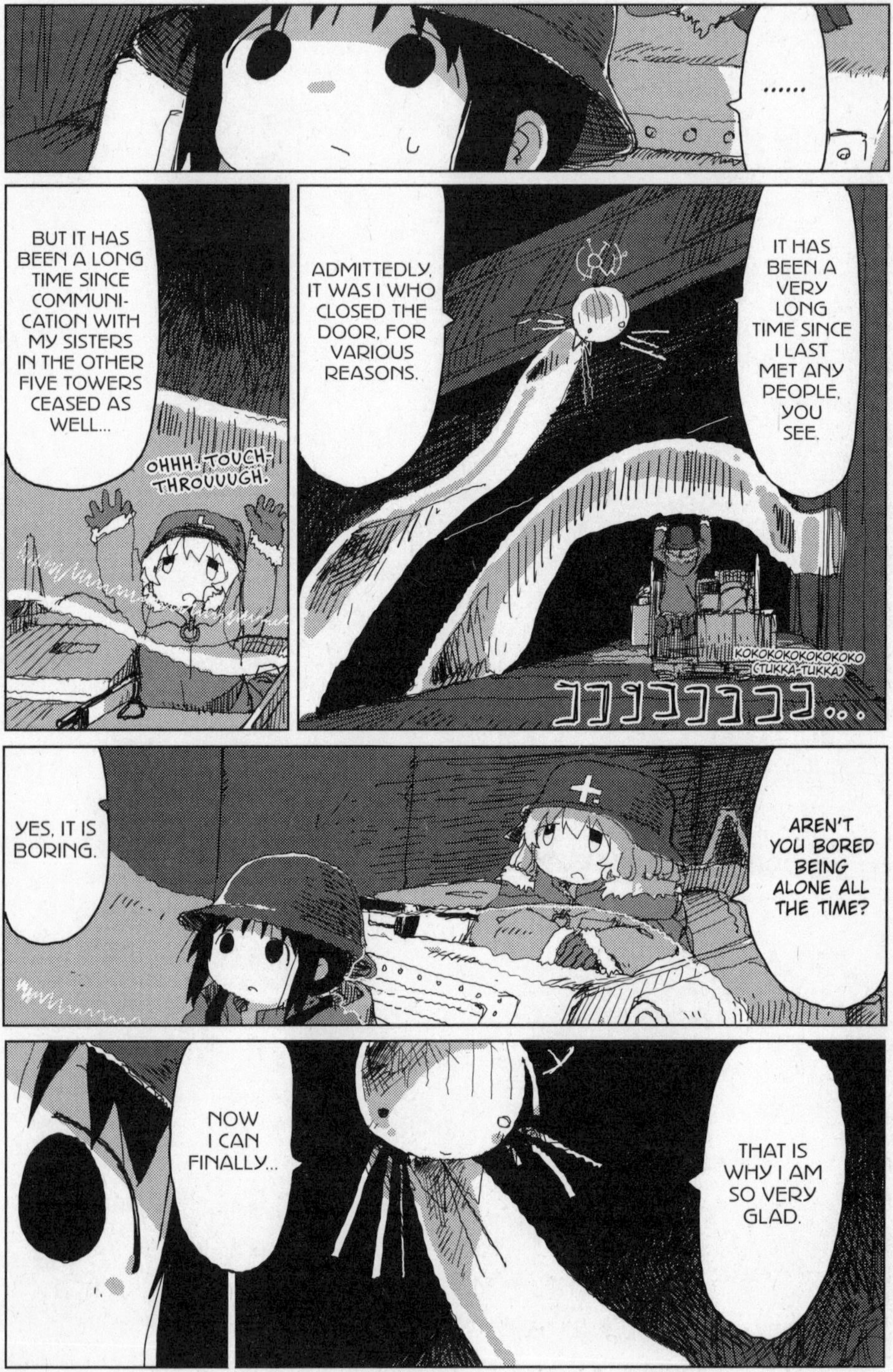
......
IT HAS BEEN A VERY LONG TIME SINCE I LAST MET ANY PEOPLE, YOU SEE.
ADMITTEDLY, IT WAS I WHO CLOSED THE DOOR, FOR VARIOUS REASONS.
KOKOKOKOKOKOKO (TUKKA-TUKKA)
BUT IT HAS BEEN A LONG TIME SINCE COMMUNICATION WITH MY SISTERS IN THE OTHER FIVE TOWERS CEASED AS WELL...
OHHH. TOUCH-THROUUUGH.
AREN'T YOU BORED BEING ALONE ALL THE TIME?
YES, IT IS BORING.
THAT IS WHY I AM SO VERY GLAD.
NOW I CAN FINALLY...

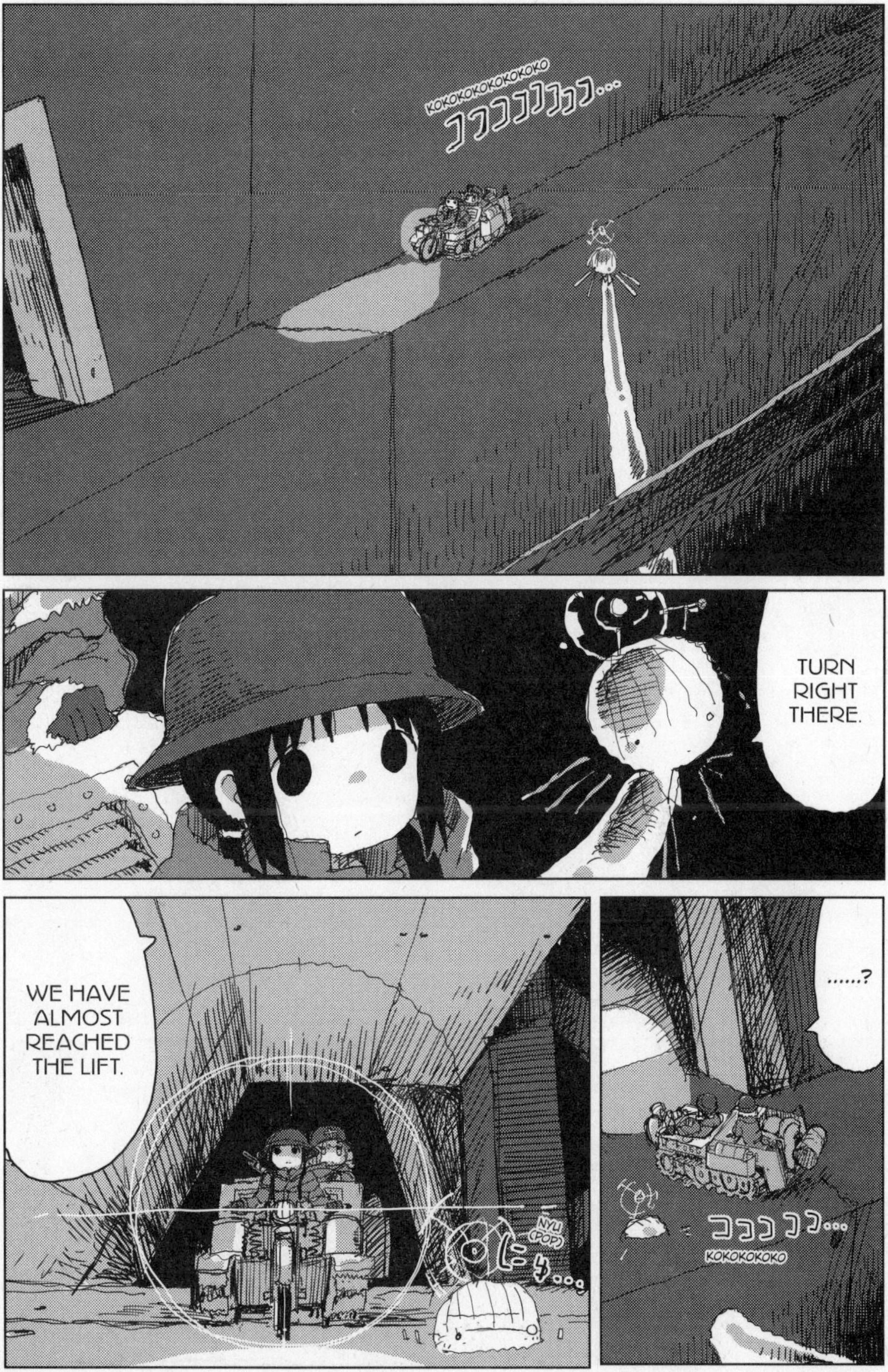
KOKOKOKOKOKOKOKO
TURN RIGHT THERE.
......?
KOKOKOKOKO
WE HAVE ALMOST REACHED THE LIFT.
NYU (POP)

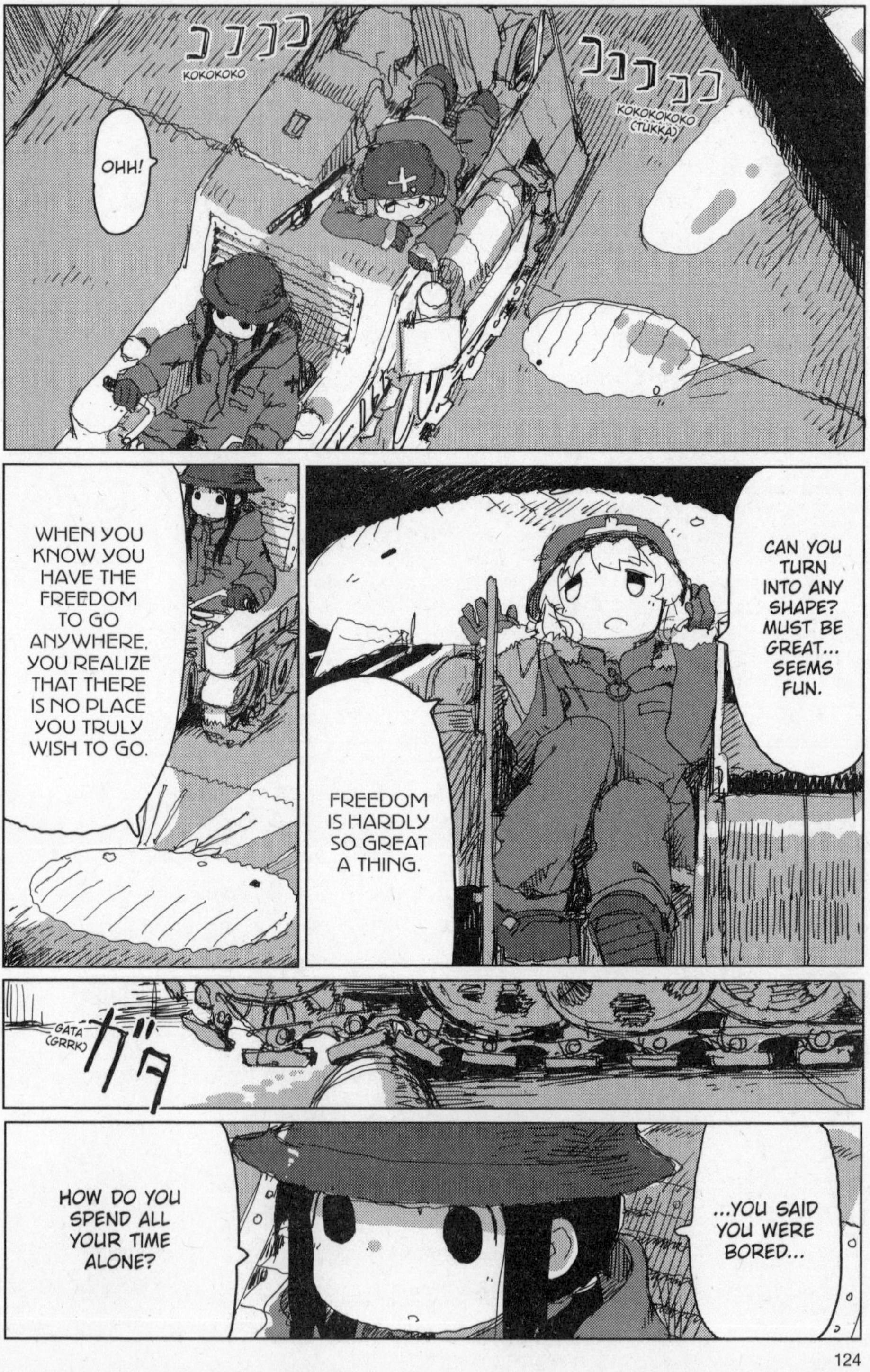
コココココ
KOKOKOKOKO
(TUKKA)
ココココ
KOKOKOKO
OHH!
CAN YOU TURN INTO ANY SHAPE? MUST BE GREAT... SEEMS FUN.
FREEDOM IS HARDLY SO GREAT A THING.
WHEN YOU KNOW YOU HAVE THE FREEDOM TO GO ANYWHERE, YOU REALIZE THAT THERE IS NO PLACE YOU TRULY WISH TO GO.
ガタ
GATA
(GRRK)
...YOU SAID YOU WERE BORED...
HOW DO YOU SPEND ALL YOUR TIME ALONE?

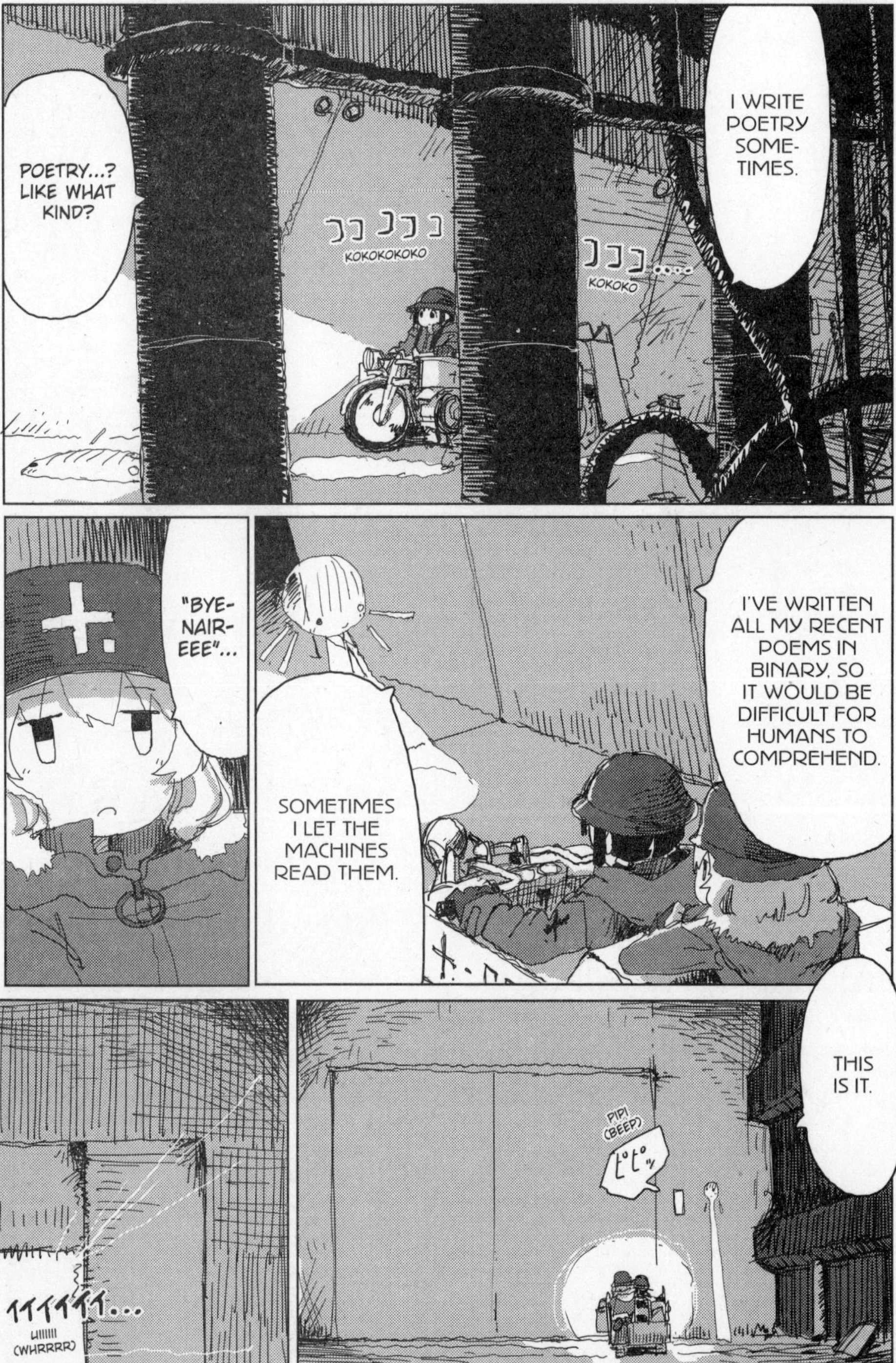
I WRITE POETRY SOME-TIMES.
KOKOKO
KOKOKOKOKO
POETRY...? LIKE WHAT KIND?
I'VE WRITTEN ALL MY RECENT POEMS IN BINARY, SO IT WOULD BE DIFFICULT FOR HUMANS TO COMPREHEND.
SOMETIMES I LET THE MACHINES READ THEM.
"BYE-NAIR-EEE"...
THIS IS IT.
PIPI (BEEP)
UIIIIII (WHRRRR)

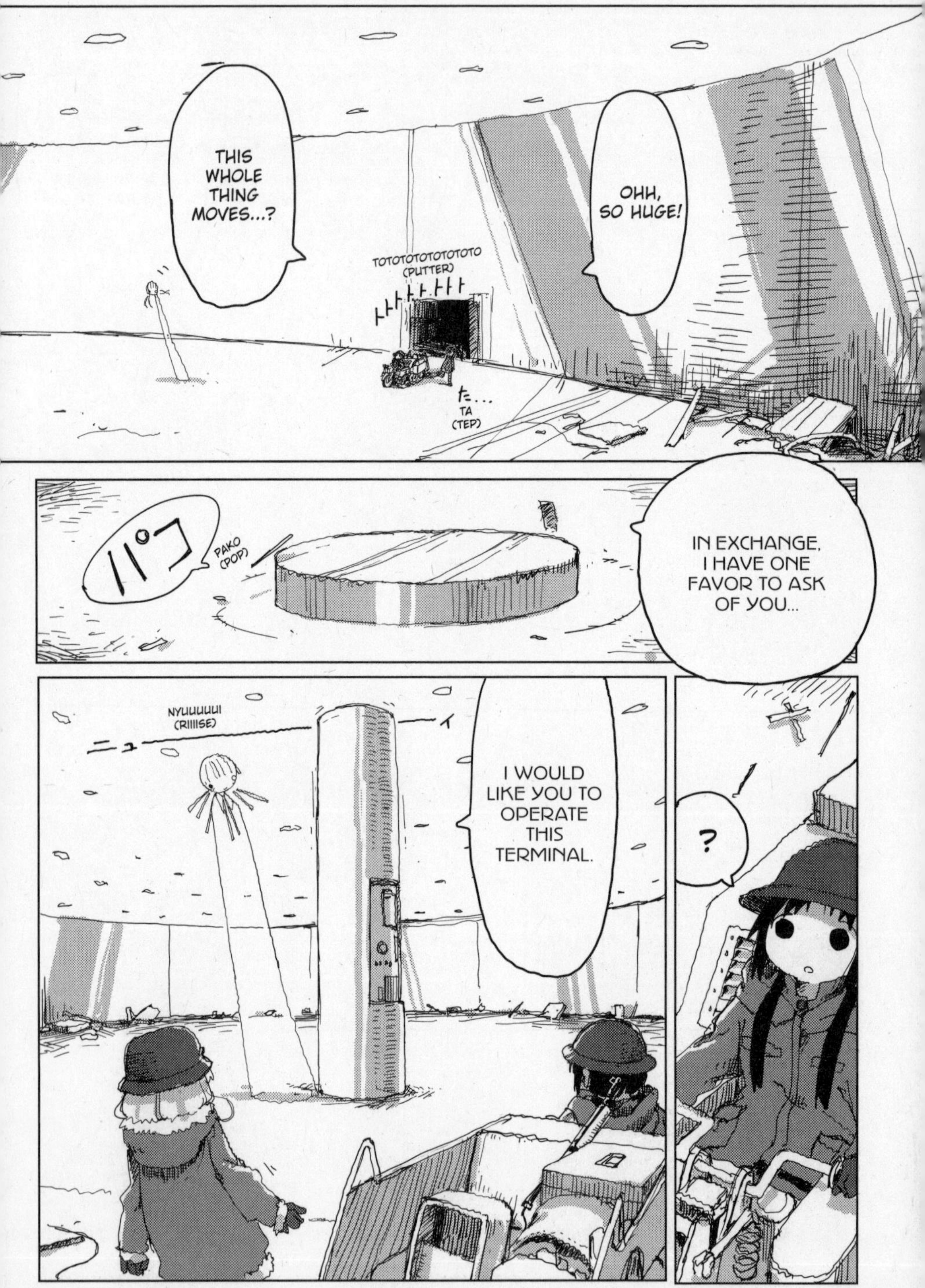
OHH, SO HUGE!
THIS WHOLE THING MOVES...?
TOTOTOTOTOTOTOTO (PUTTER)
TA (TEP)
IN EXCHANGE, I HAVE ONE FAVOR TO ASK OF YOU...
パコ
PAKO (POP)
?
I WOULD LIKE YOU TO OPERATE THIS TERMINAL.
NYUUUUUI (RIIIISE)

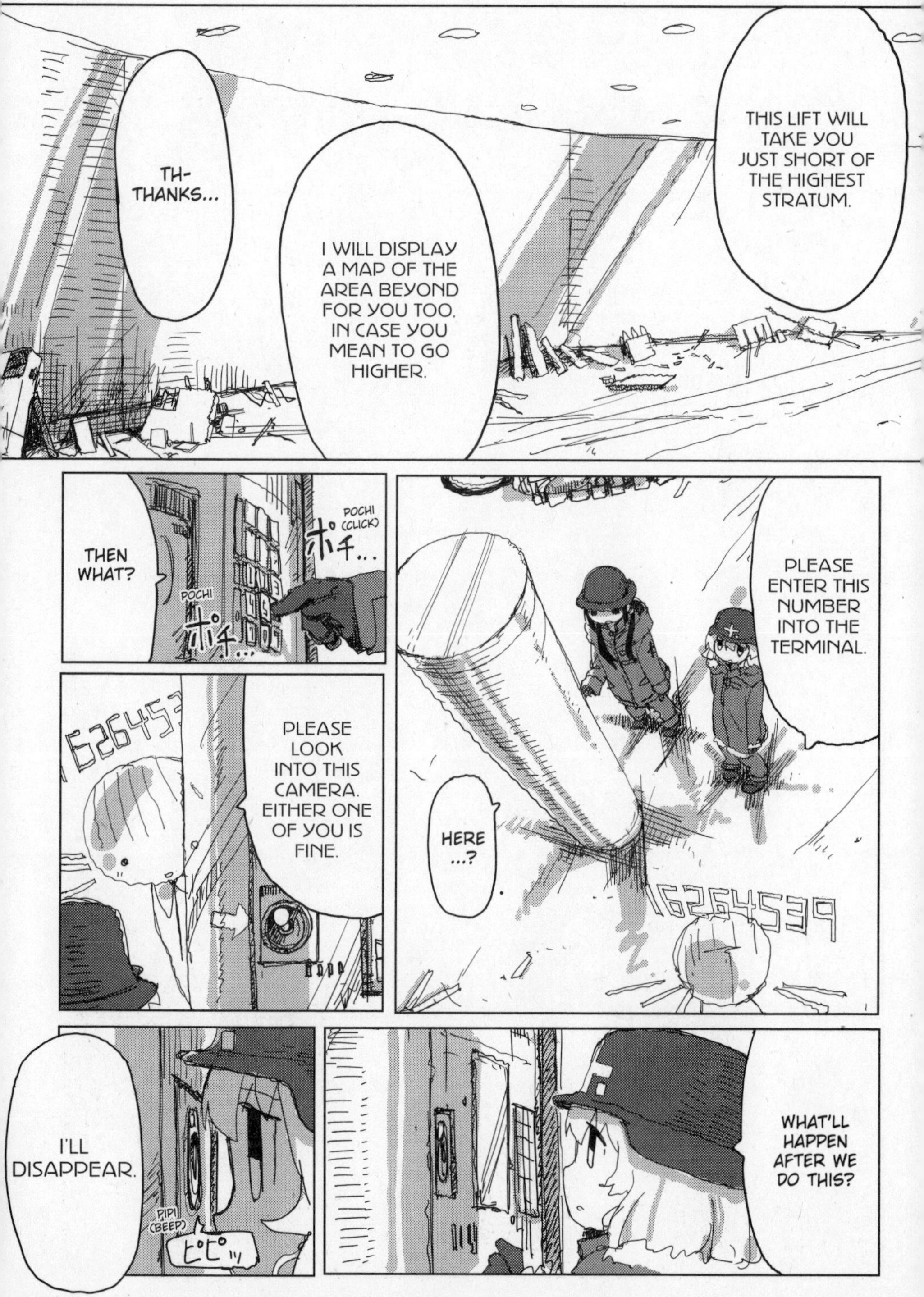
THIS LIFT WILL TAKE YOU JUST SHORT OF THE HIGHEST STRATUM.
I WILL DISPLAY A MAP OF THE AREA BEYOND FOR YOU TOO, IN CASE YOU MEAN TO GO HIGHER.
TH- THANKS...
PLEASE ENTER THIS NUMBER INTO THE TERMINAL.
HERE ...?
POCHI (CLICK)
ポチ...
POCHI
ポチ...
THEN WHAT?
PLEASE LOOK INTO THIS CAMERA. EITHER ONE OF YOU IS FINE.
WHAT'LL HAPPEN AFTER WE DO THIS?
I'LL DISAPPEAR.
PIPI (BEEP)
ピピッ

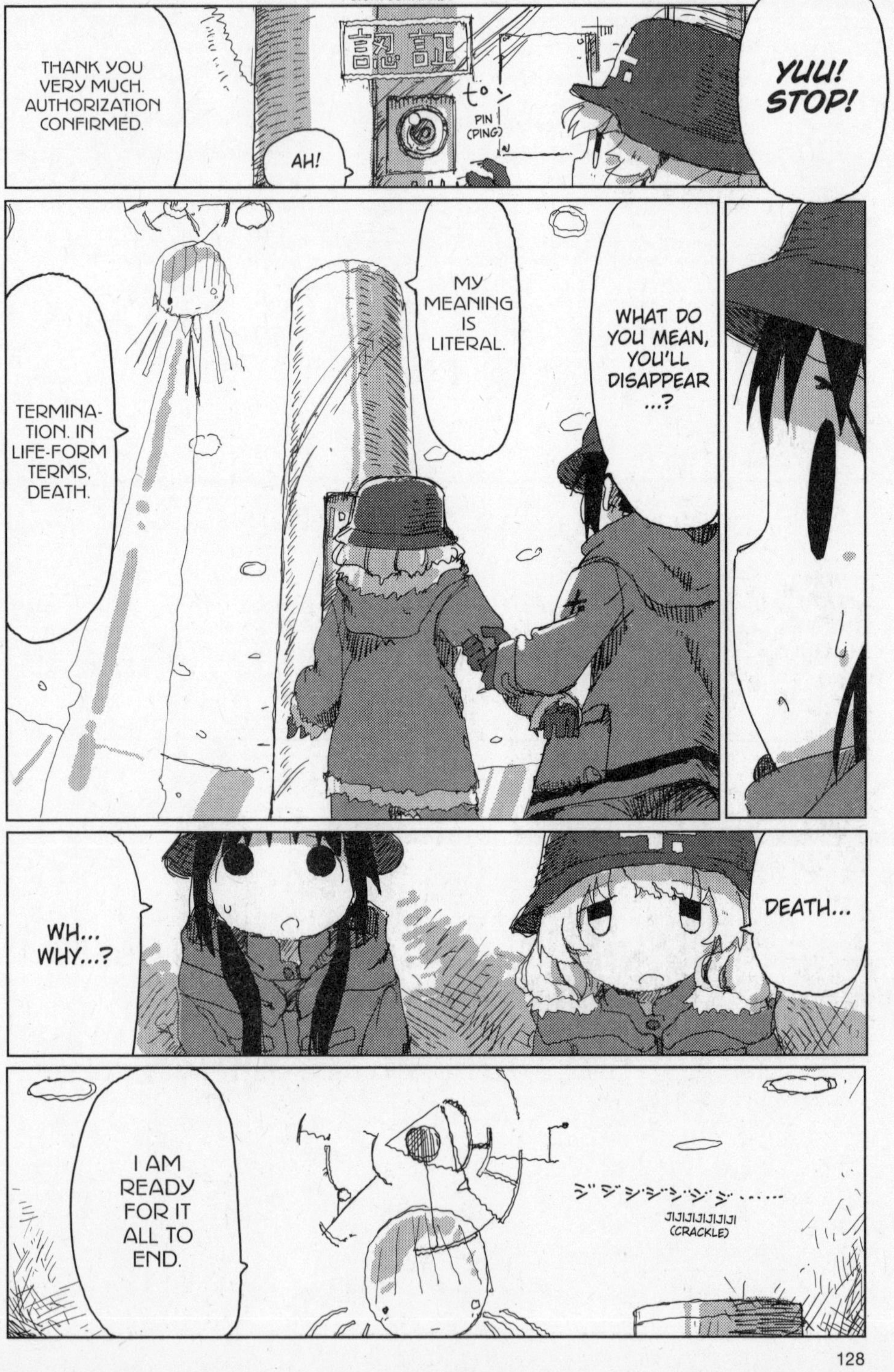
YUU! STOP!
SIGN: CONFIRMED
認証
ピン
PIN (PING)
AH!
THANK YOU VERY MUCH. AUTHORIZATION CONFIRMED.
WHAT DO YOU MEAN, YOU'LL DISAPPEAR ...?
MY MEANING IS LITERAL.
TERMINATION. IN LIFE-FORM TERMS, DEATH.
DEATH...
WH... WHY...?
ジジジジジジジ……
JIJIJIJIJIJIJI (CRACKLE)
I AM READY FOR IT ALL TO END.

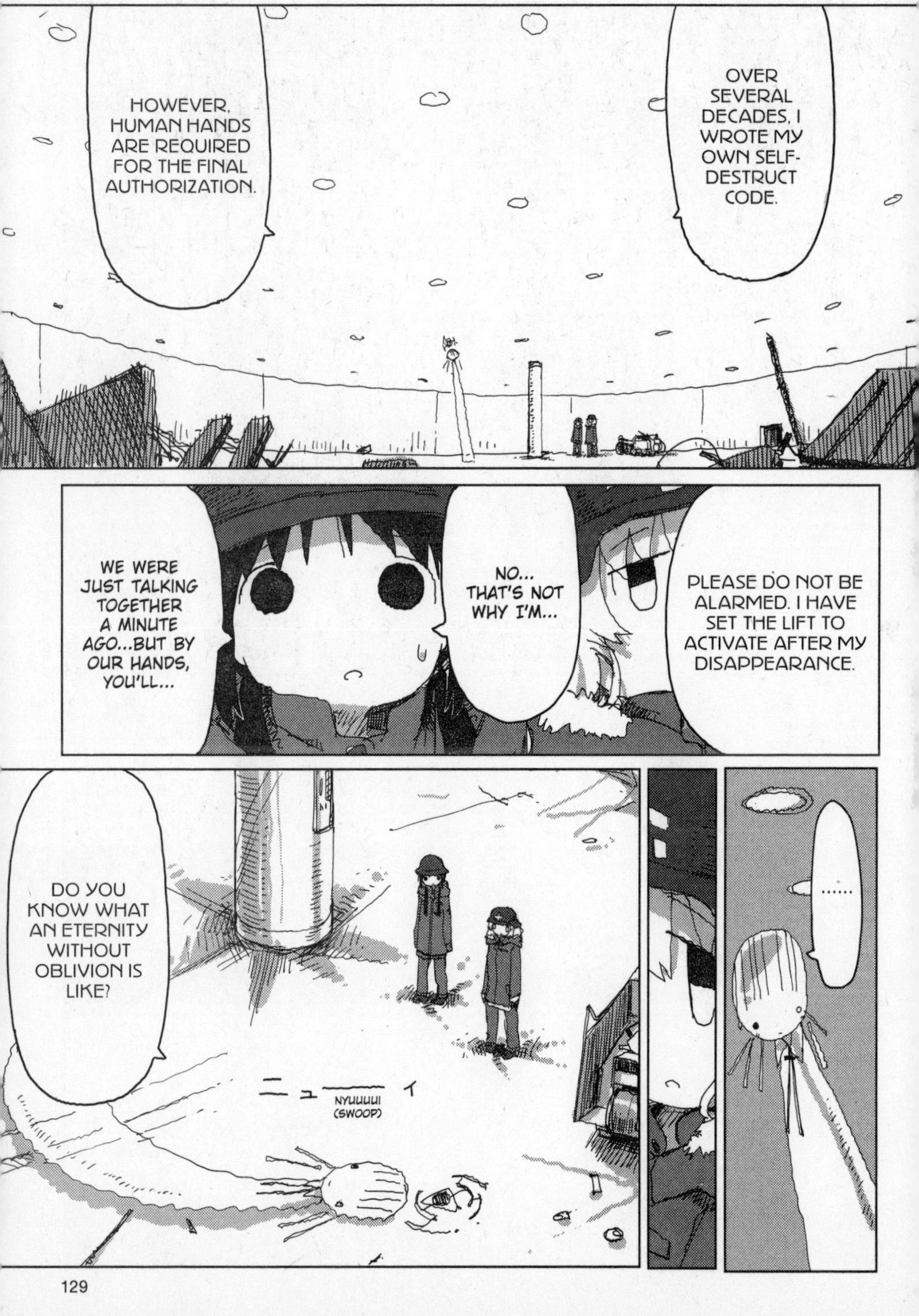
OVER SEVERAL DECADES, I WROTE MY OWN SELF-DESTRUCT CODE.
HOWEVER, HUMAN HANDS ARE REQUIRED FOR THE FINAL AUTHORIZATION.
PLEASE DO NOT BE ALARMED. I HAVE SET THE LIFT TO ACTIVATE AFTER MY DISAPPEARANCE.
NO... THAT'S NOT WHY I'M...
WE WERE JUST TALKING TOGETHER A MINUTE AGO...BUT BY OUR HANDS, YOU'LL...
......
DO YOU KNOW WHAT AN ETERNITY WITHOUT OBLIVION IS LIKE?
ニューイ
NYUUUUI (SWOOP)

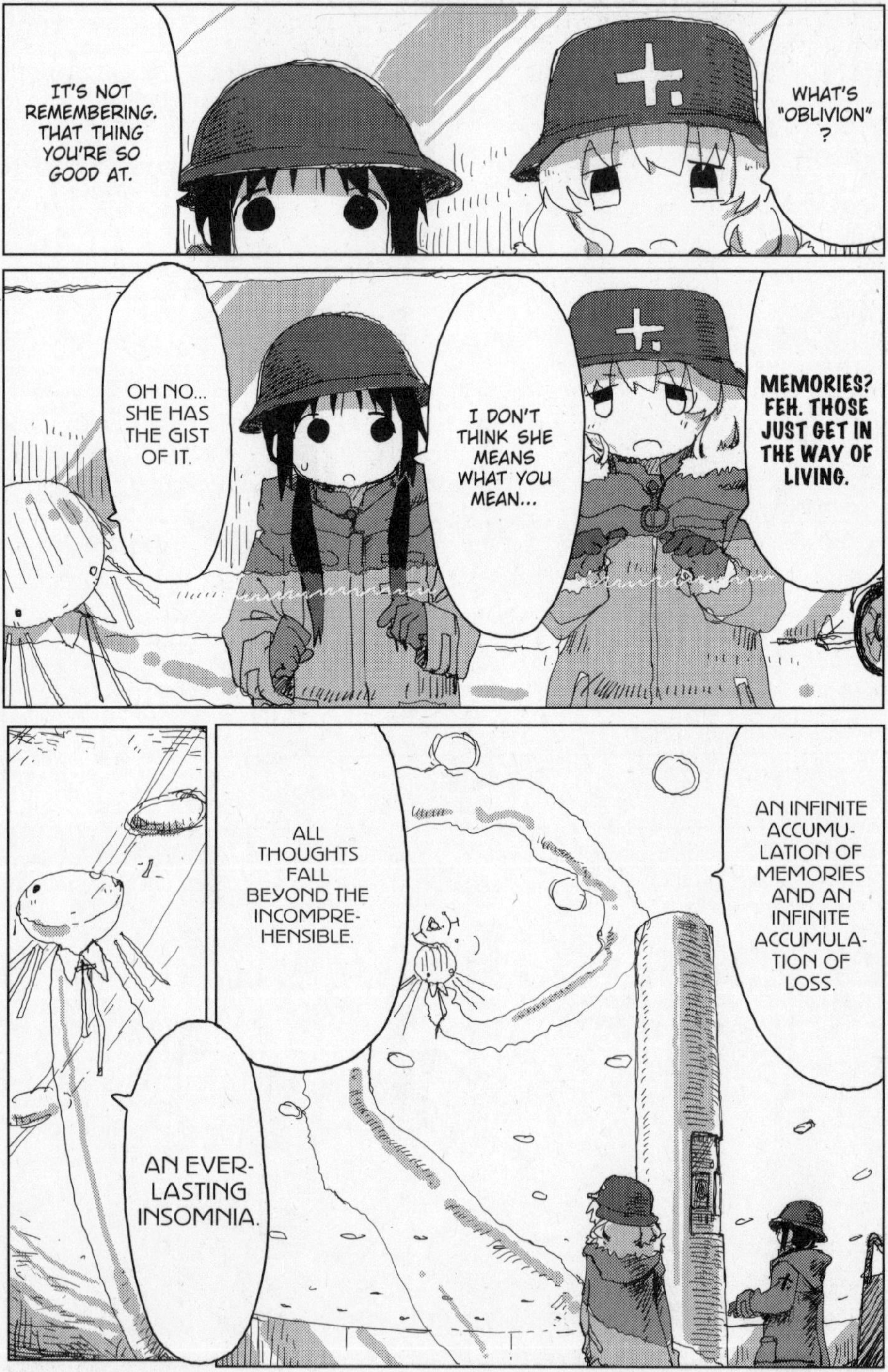
WHAT'S "OBLIVION" ?
IT'S NOT REMEMBERING. THAT THING YOU'RE SO GOOD AT.
MEMORIES? FEH. THOSE JUST GET IN THE WAY OF LIVING.
I DON'T THINK SHE MEANS WHAT YOU MEAN...
OH NO... SHE HAS THE GIST OF IT.
AN INFINITE ACCUMU-LATION OF MEMORIES AND AN INFINITE ACCUMULA-TION OF LOSS.
ALL THOUGHTS FALL BEYOND THE INCOMPRE-HENSIBLE.
AN EVER-LASTING INSOMNIA.

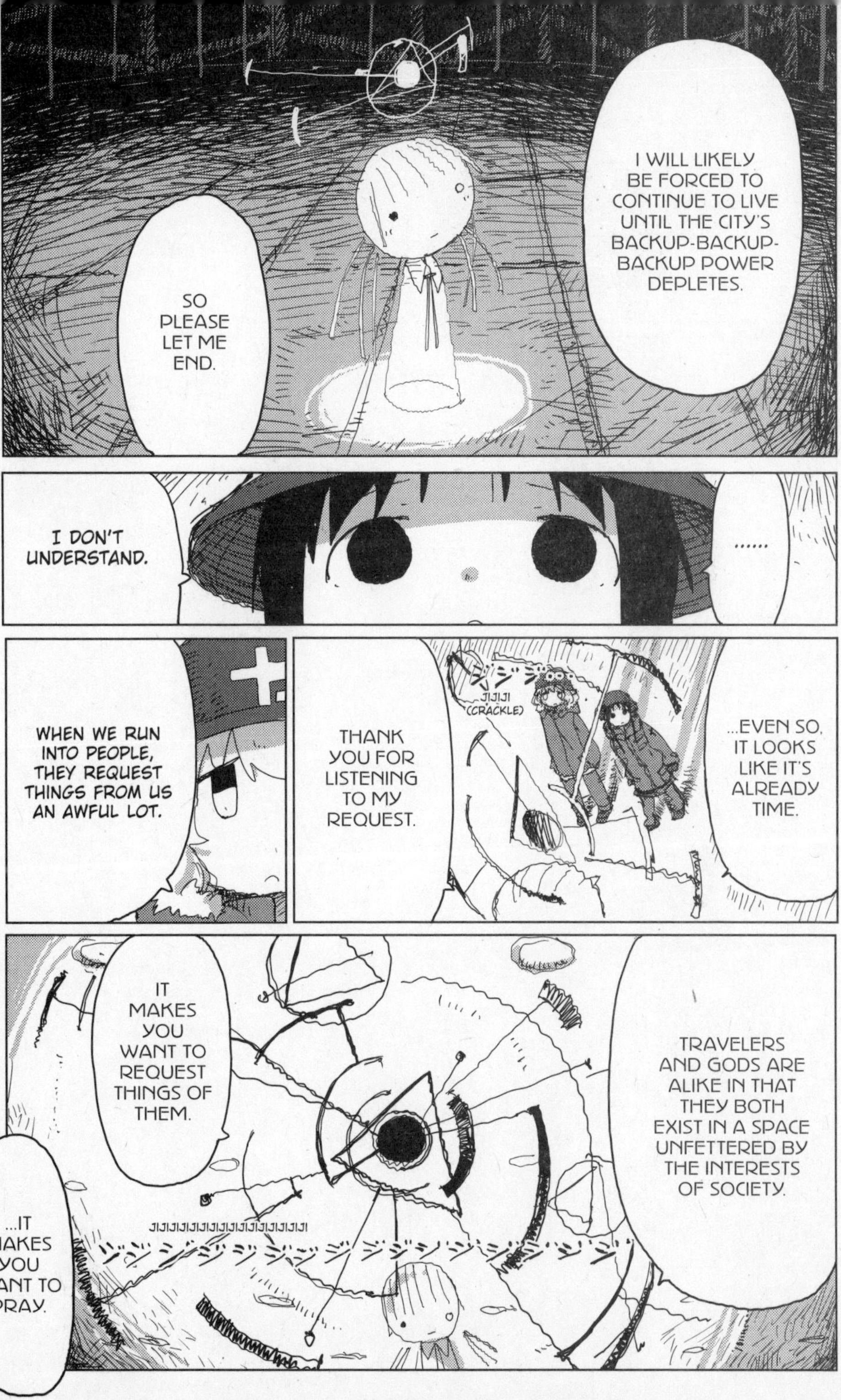
I WILL LIKELY BE FORCED TO CONTINUE TO LIVE UNTIL THE CITY'S BACKUP-BACKUP-BACKUP POWER DEPLETES.
SO PLEASE LET ME END.
......
I DON'T UNDERSTAND.
...EVEN SO, IT LOOKS LIKE IT'S ALREADY TIME.
JIJIJI (CRACKLE)
THANK YOU FOR LISTENING TO MY REQUEST.
WHEN WE RUN INTO PEOPLE, THEY REQUEST THINGS FROM US AN AWFUL LOT.
TRAVELERS AND GODS ARE ALIKE IN THAT THEY BOTH EXIST IN A SPACE UNFETTERED BY THE INTERESTS OF SOCIETY.
IT MAKES YOU WANT TO REQUEST THINGS OF THEM.
JIJIJIJIJIJIJIJIJIJIJIJIJIJIJIJIJIJI
...IT MAKES YOU WANT TO PRAY.

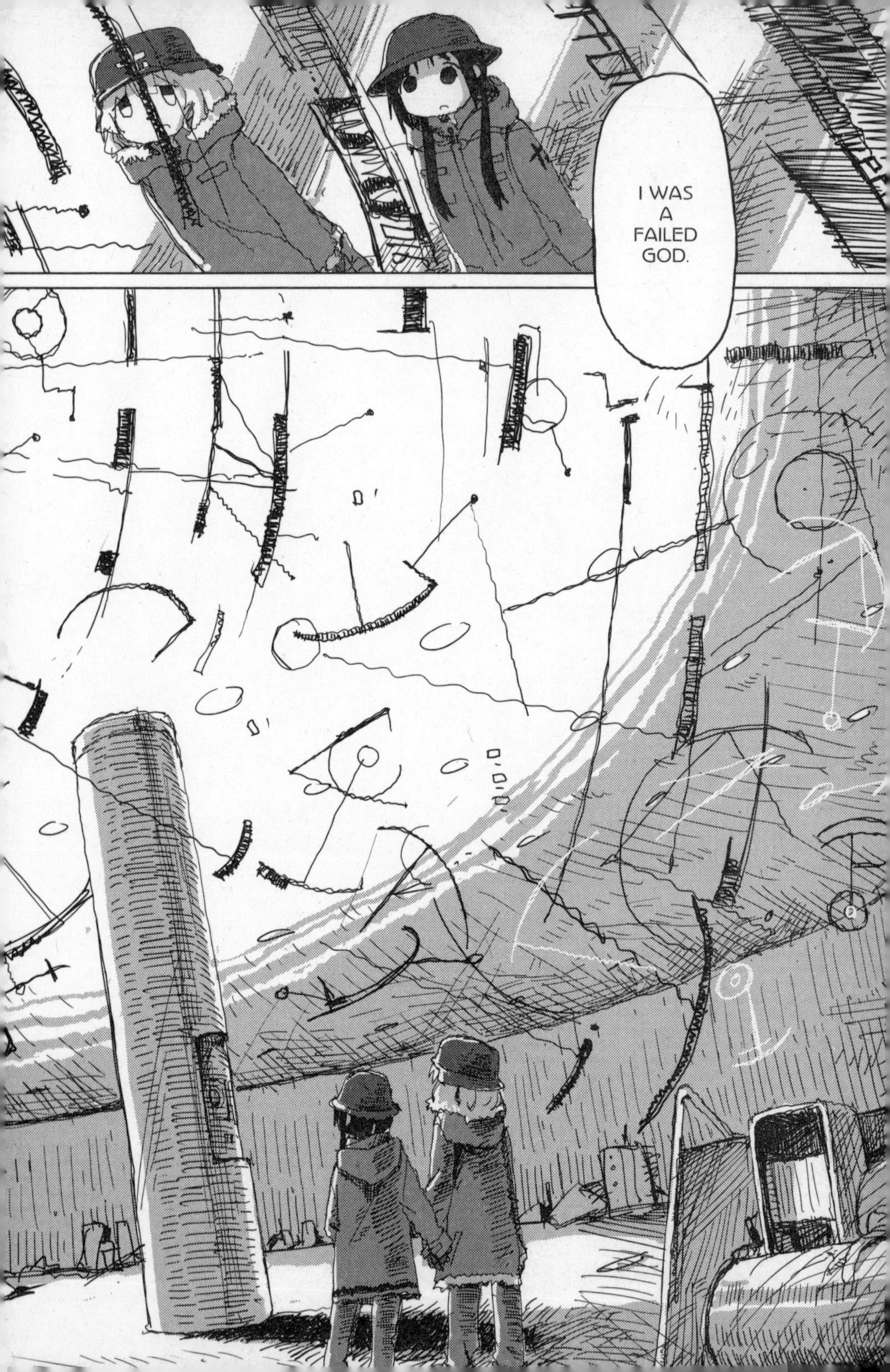
I WAS A FAILED GOD.

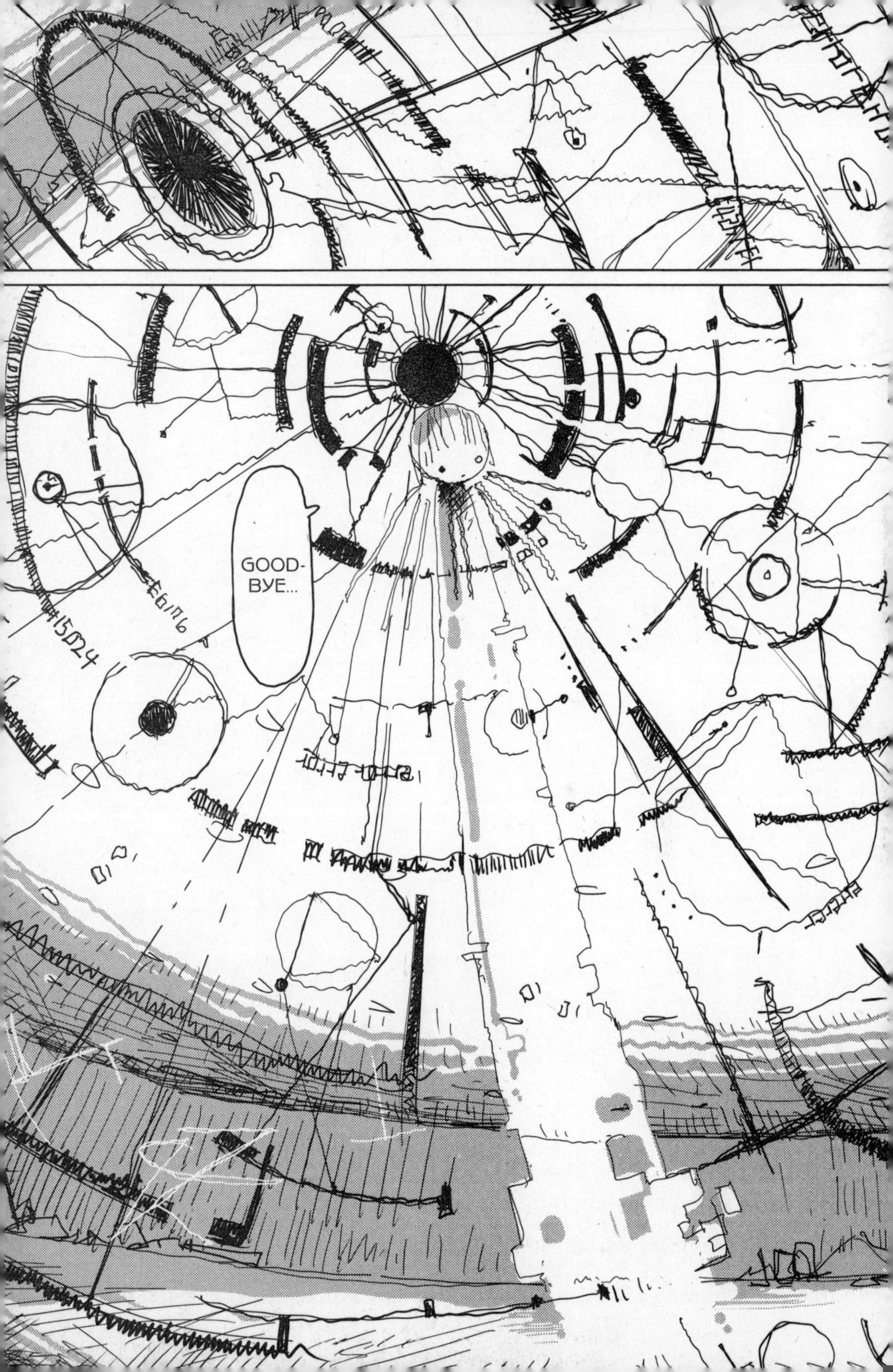
GOOD-BYE...

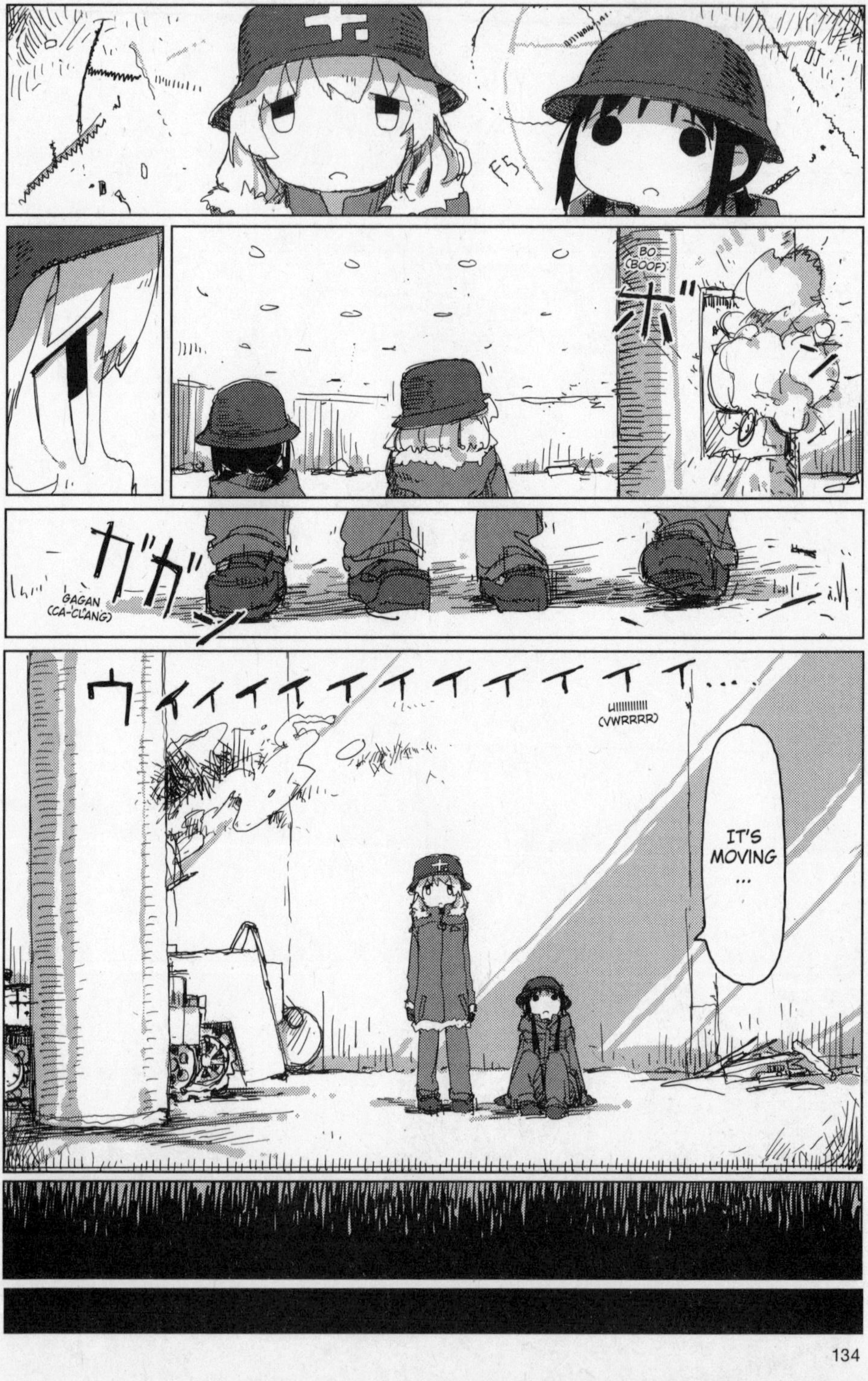
BO (BOOF)
ボ
ガガ
GAGAN (CA-CLANG)
ウィイイイイイイイイイ…
UIIIIIIII (VWRRRR)
IT'S MOVING …

40 HOMETOWN

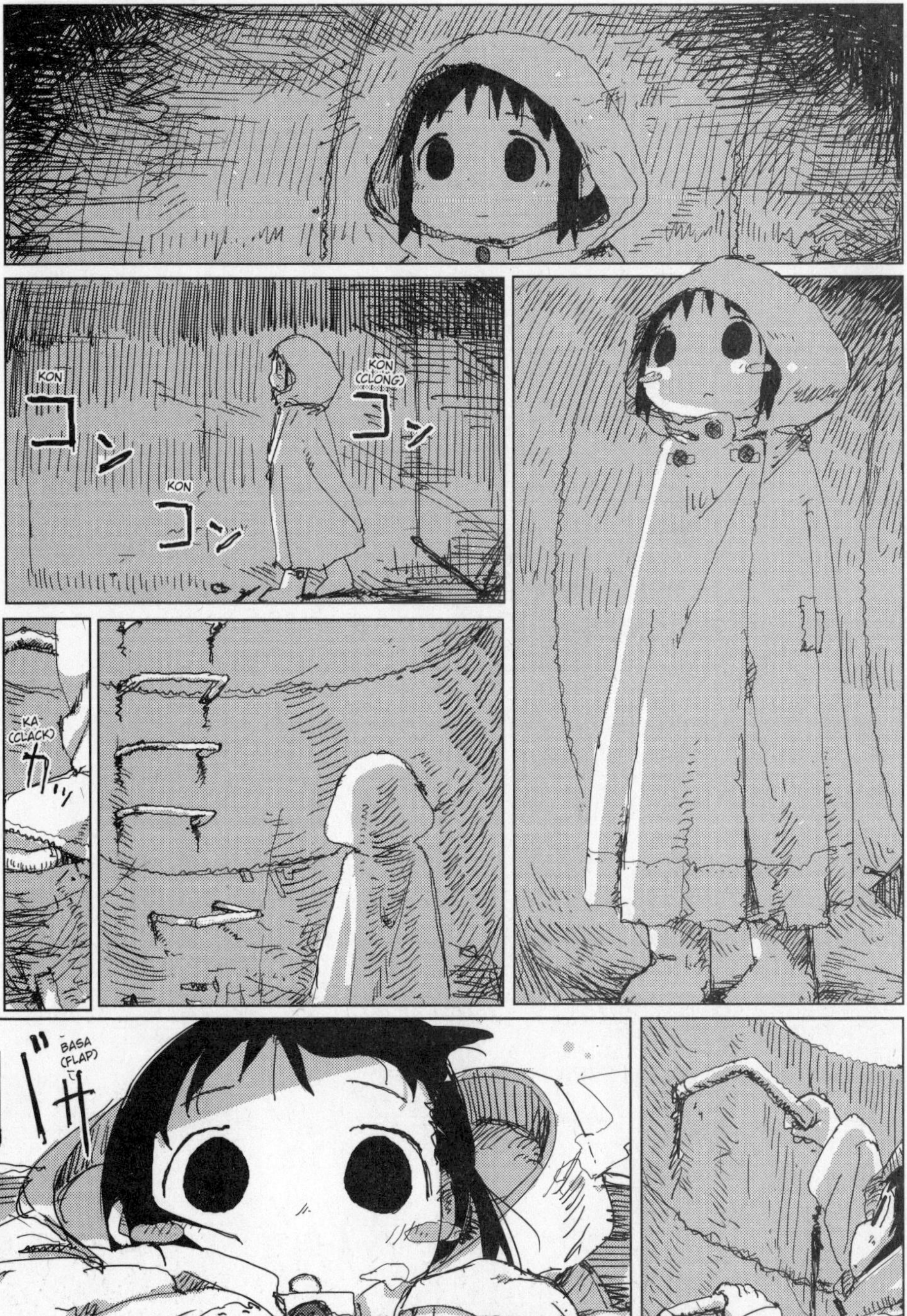
KON (CLONG)
コン
KON
コン
KON
コン
KA (CLACK)
カッ
BASA (FLAP)
バサ

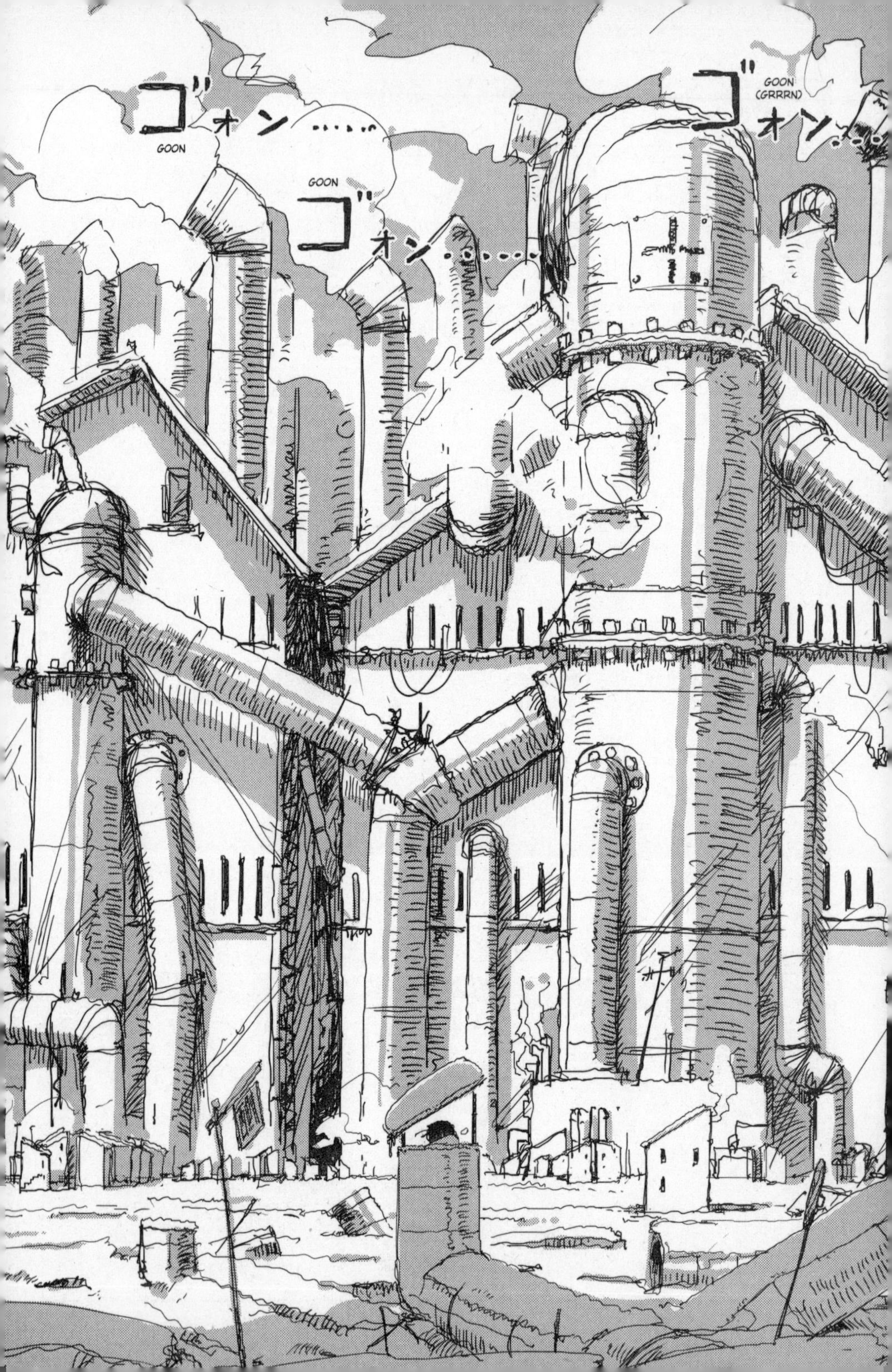
ゴオン……
GOON (GRRRN)
ゴオン……
GOON
ゴオン……
GOON

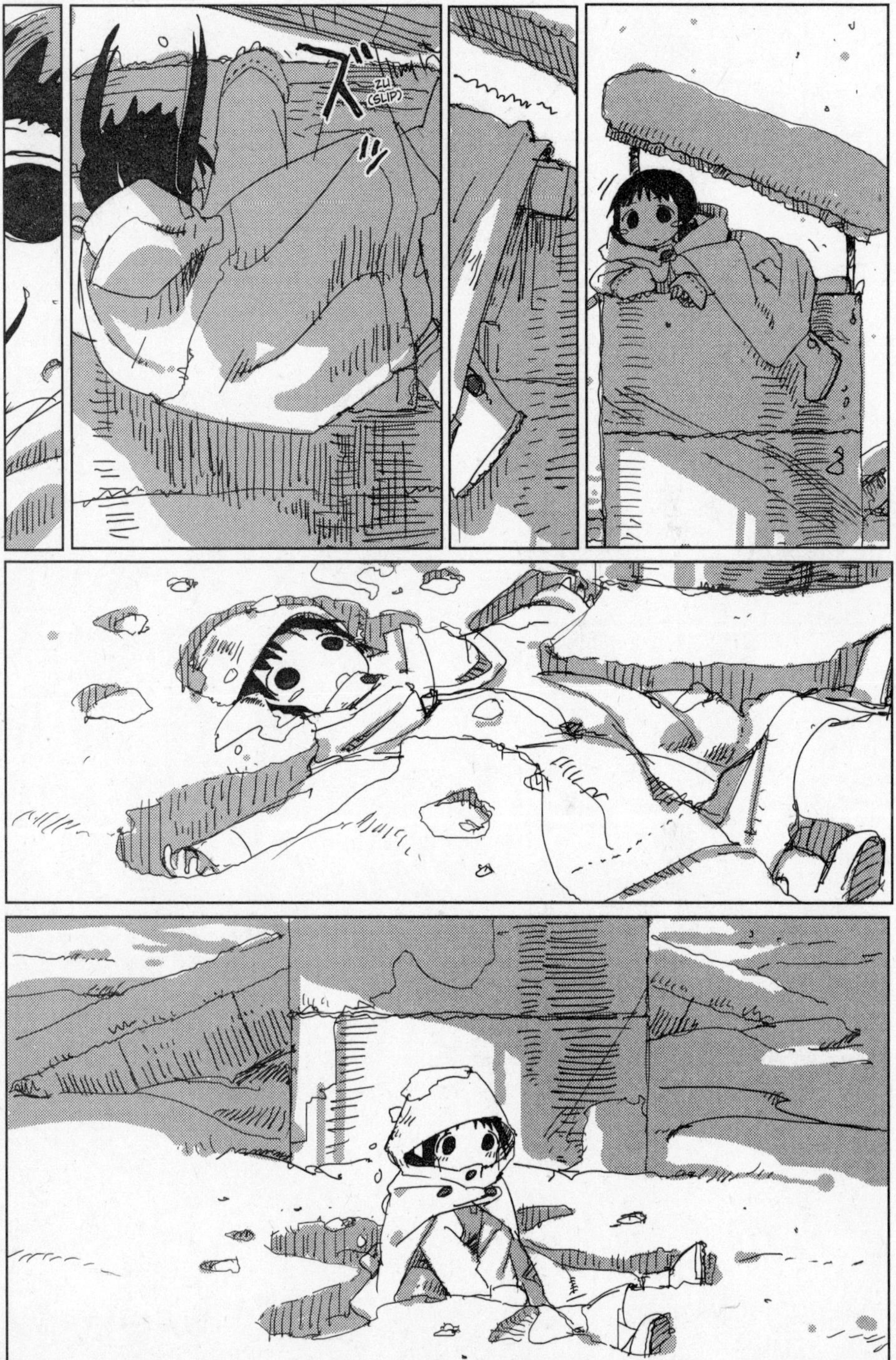
ズッ
ZU (SLIP)

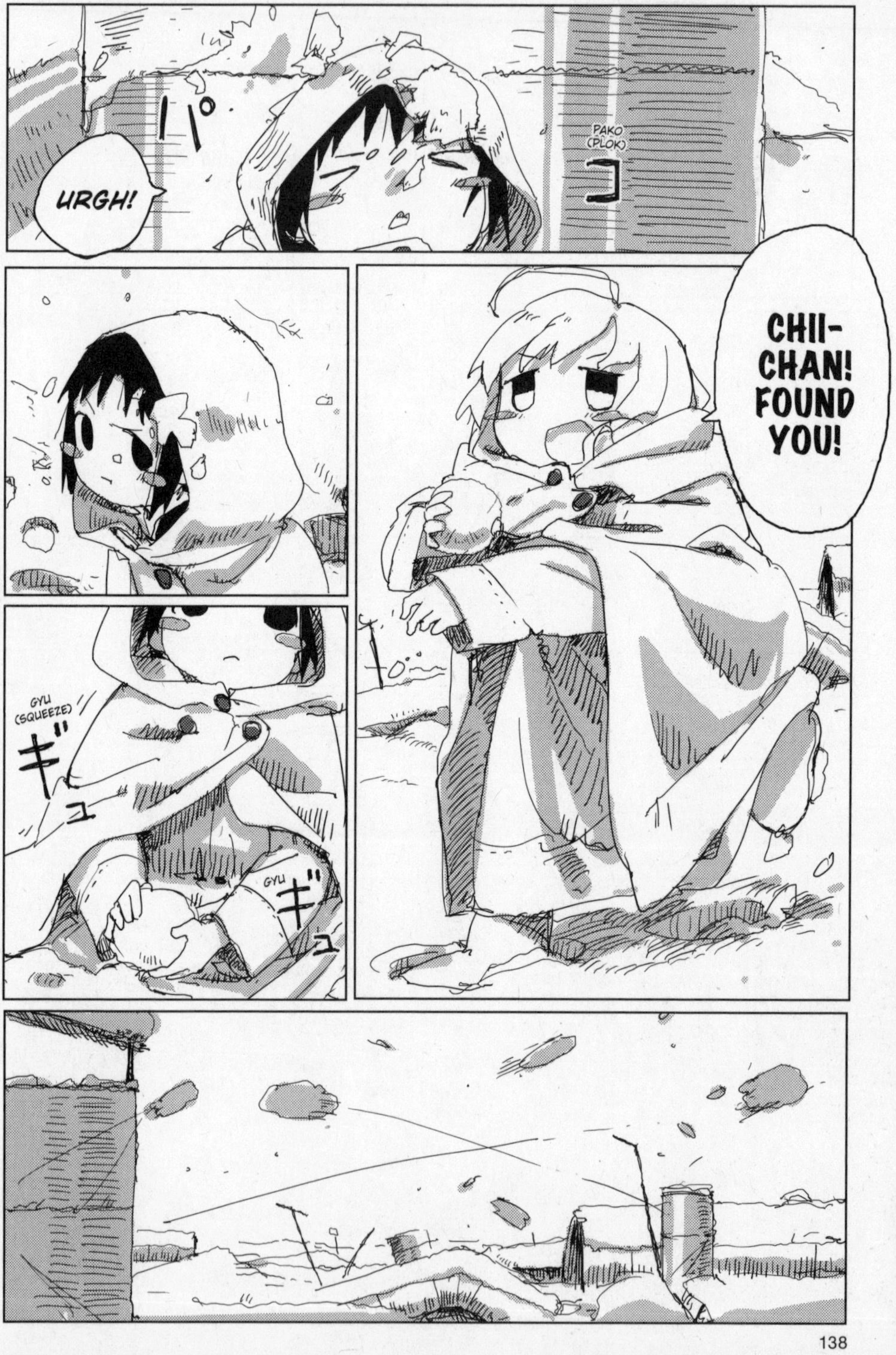
パコ
PAKO (PLOK)
URGH!
CHII-CHAN! FOUND YOU!
ギュ
GYU (SQUEEZE)
ギュ
GYU

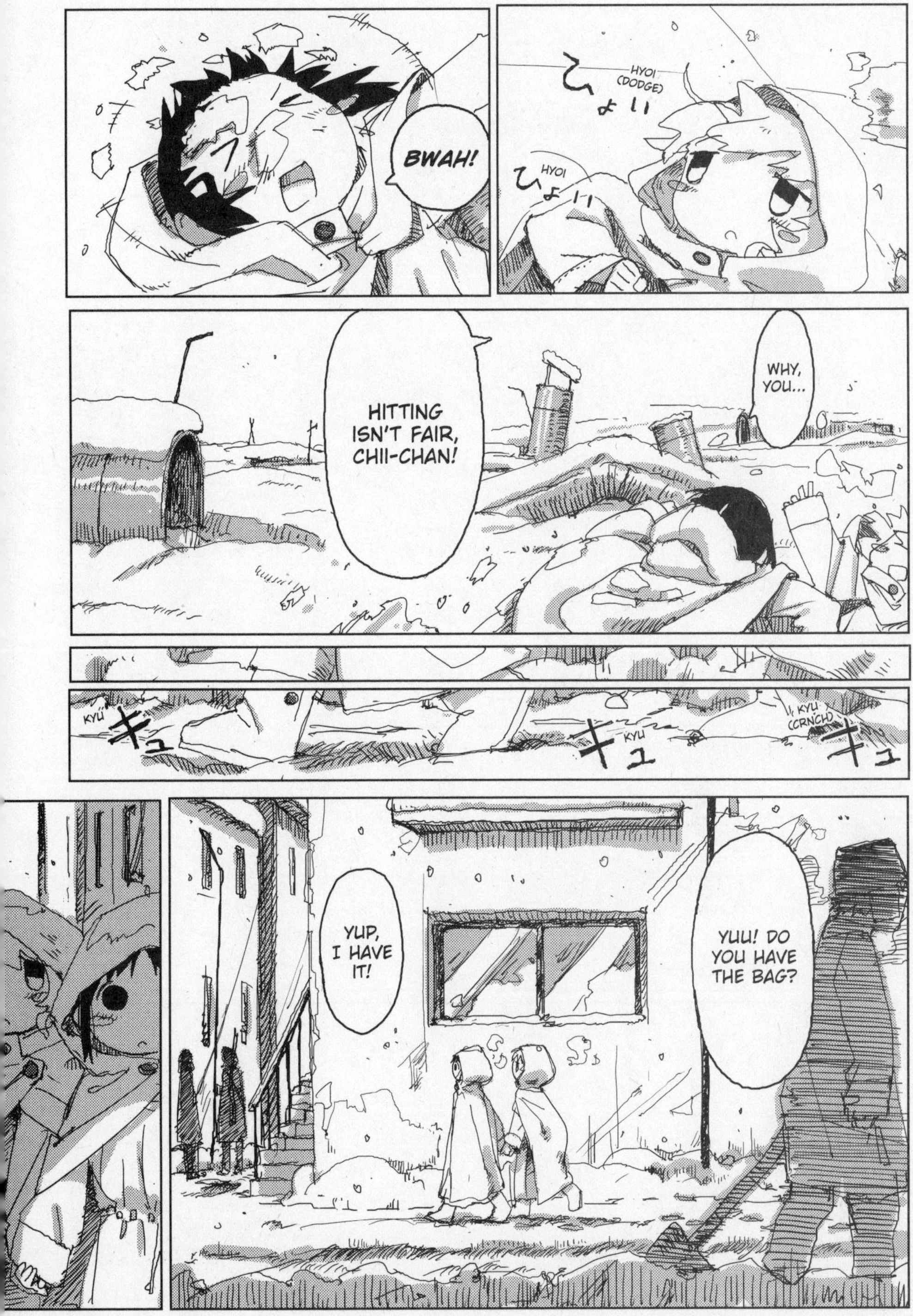
HYOI (DODGE)
ひょい
HYOI
ひょい
BWAH!
WHY, YOU...
HITTING ISN'T FAIR, CHII-CHAN!
KYU (CRNCH)
キュ
KYU
キュ
KYU
キュ
YUU! DO YOU HAVE THE BAG?
YUP, I HAVE IT!

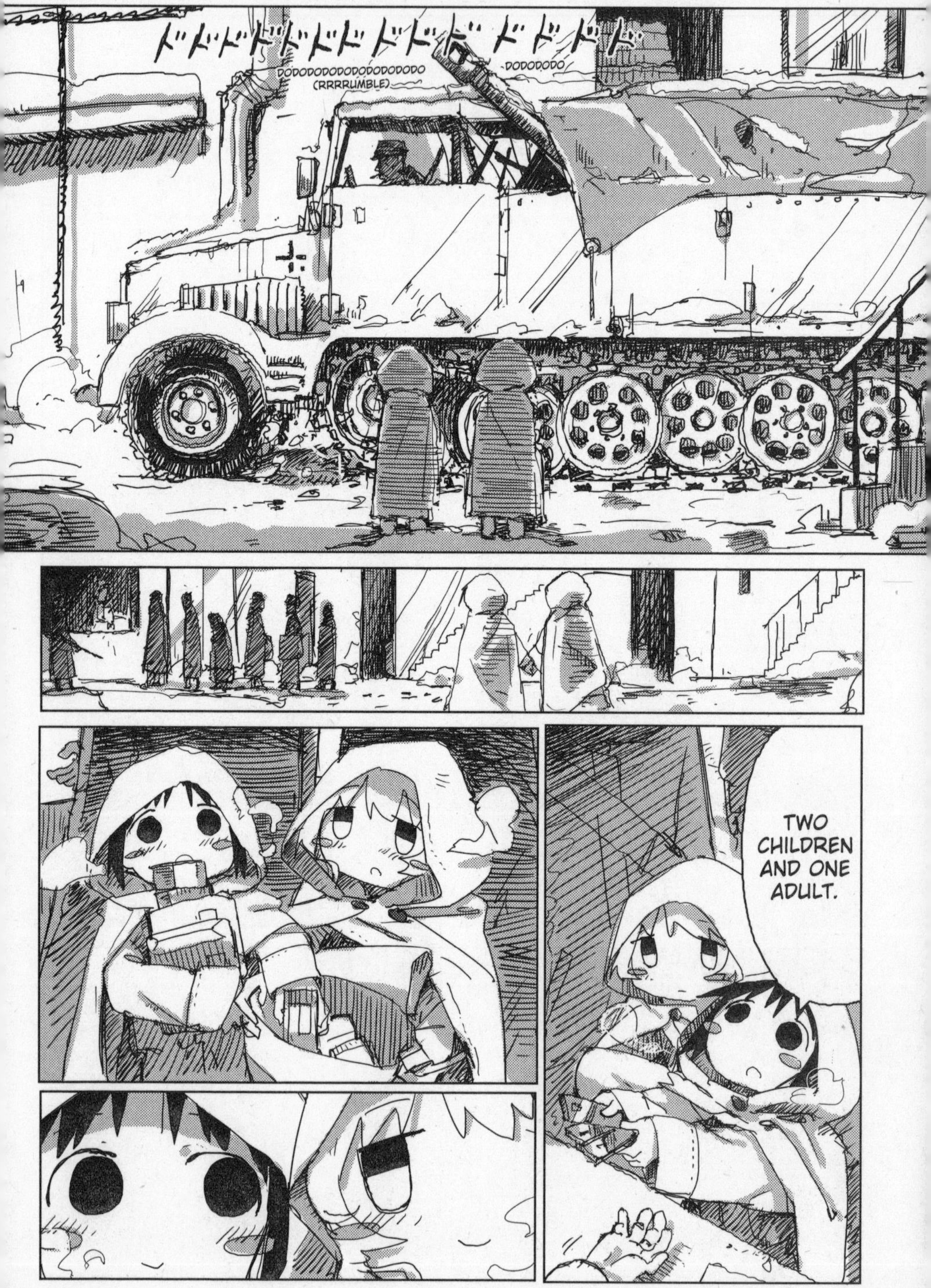
ドドドドドドドドドドドドドドド
DODODODODODODODODODO
(RRRRUMBLE)
DODODODO
TWO CHILDREN AND ONE ADULT.

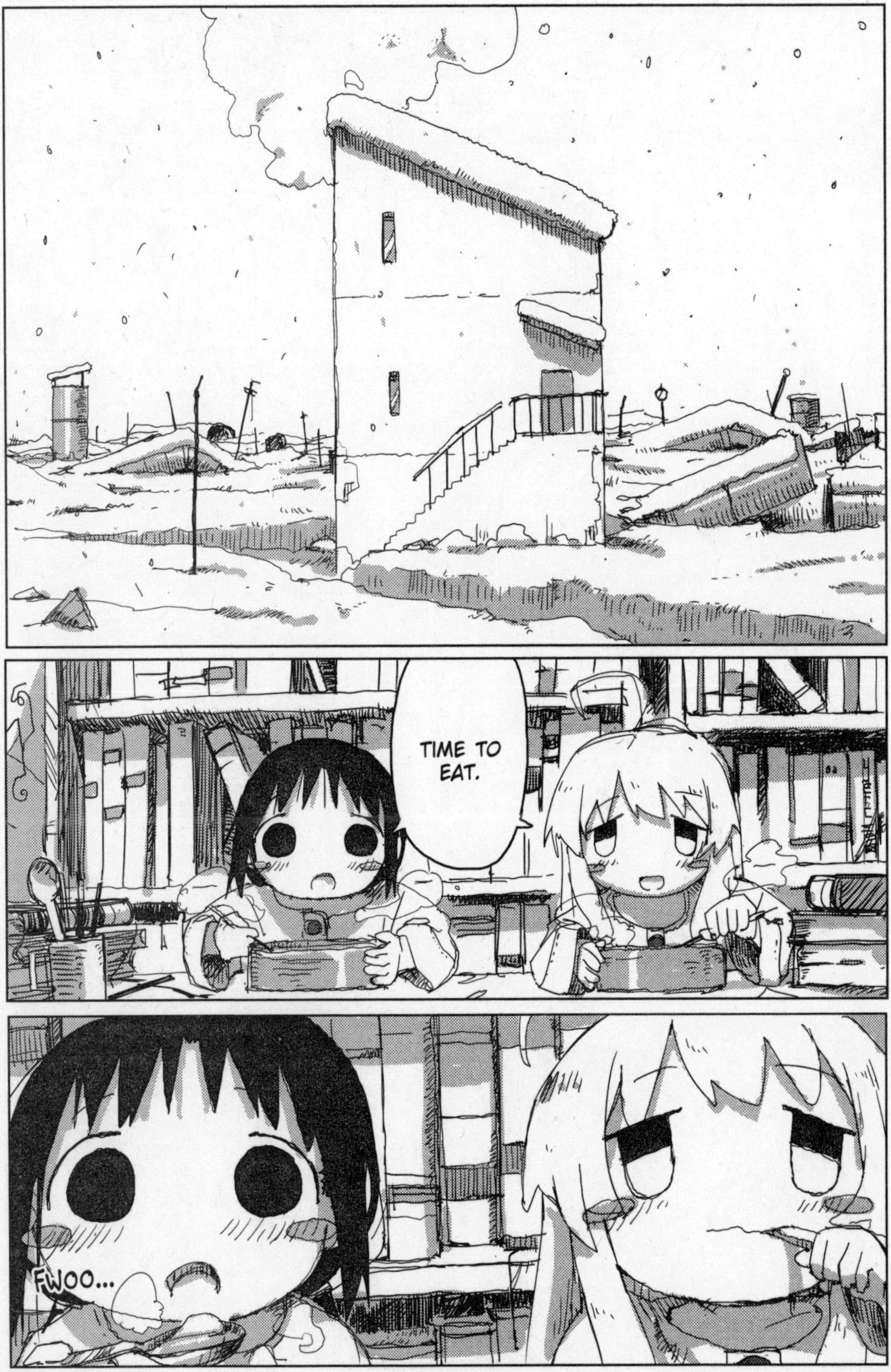
TIME TO EAT.
FWOO...

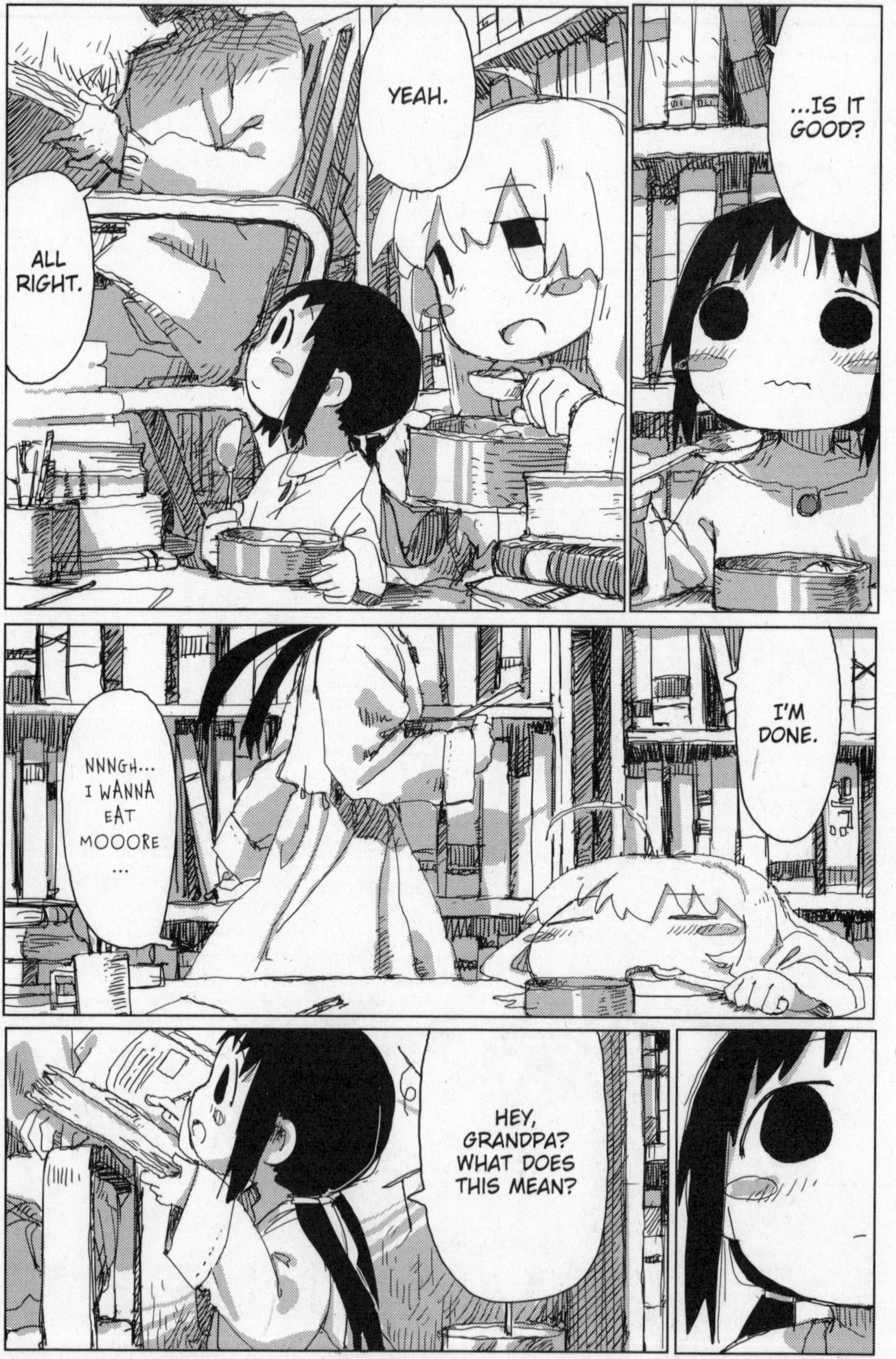
...IS IT GOOD?
YEAH.
ALL RIGHT.
I'M DONE.
NNNGH... I WANNA EAT MOOORE ...
HEY, GRANDPA? WHAT DOES THIS MEAN?

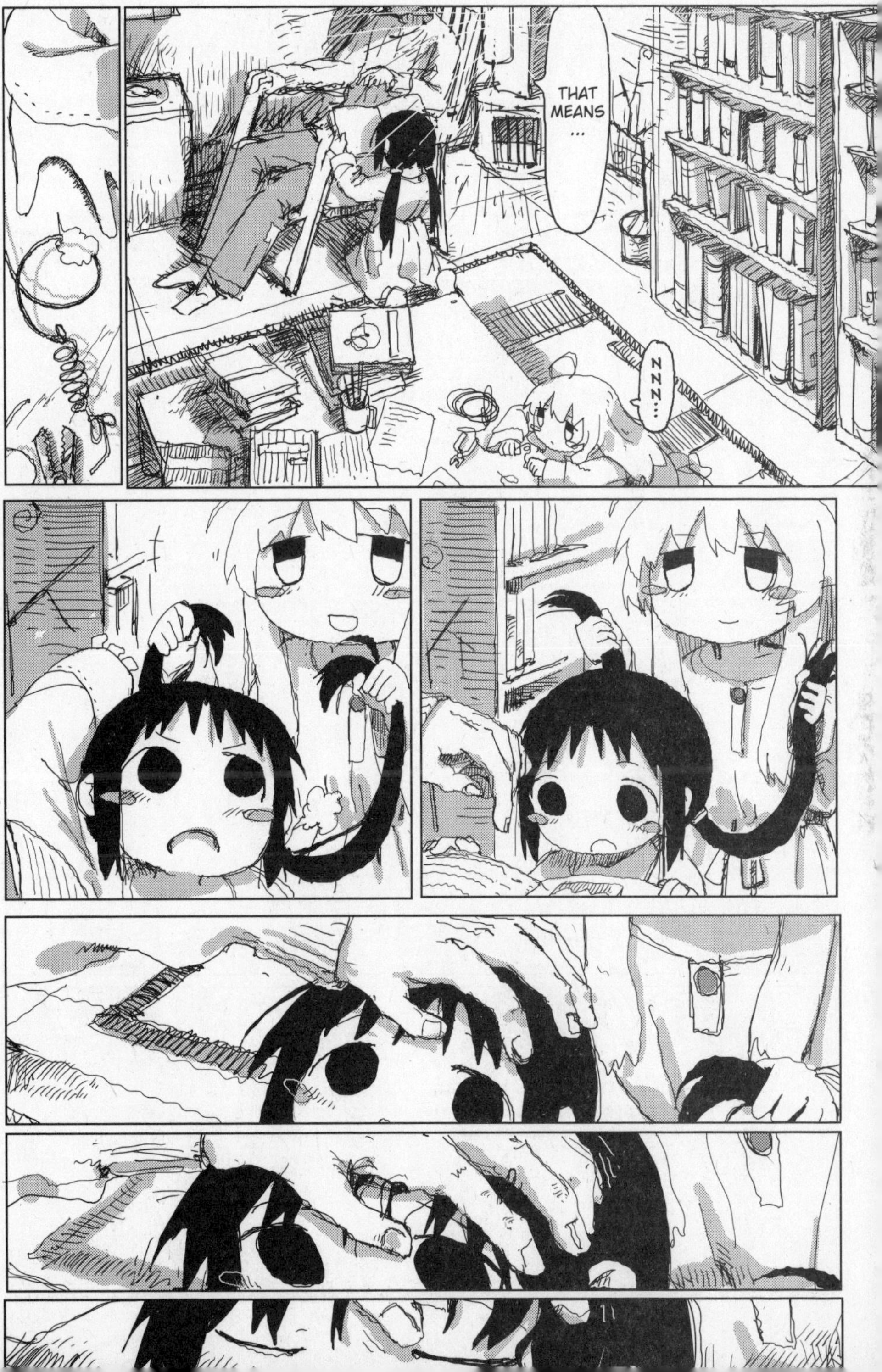
THAT MEANS ...
NNN...

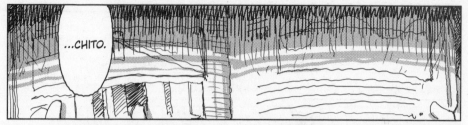

...CHITO.

...YES?

CHITO.

GO GET YUURI.

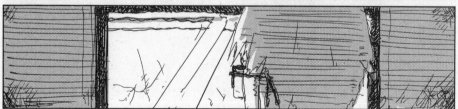

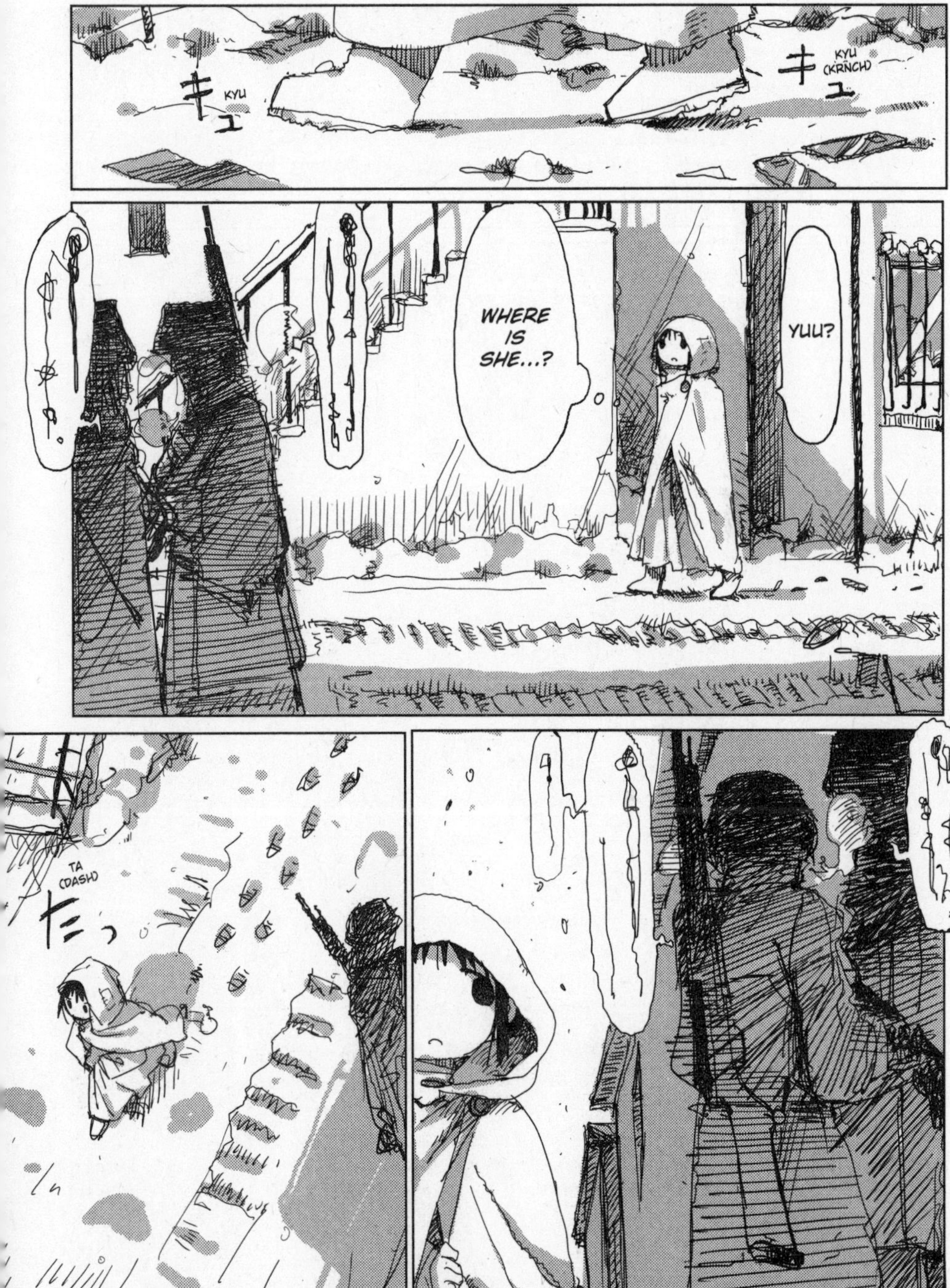
キュ
KYU (KRNCH)
キュ
KYU
YUU?
WHERE IS SHE...?
たっ
TA (DASH)

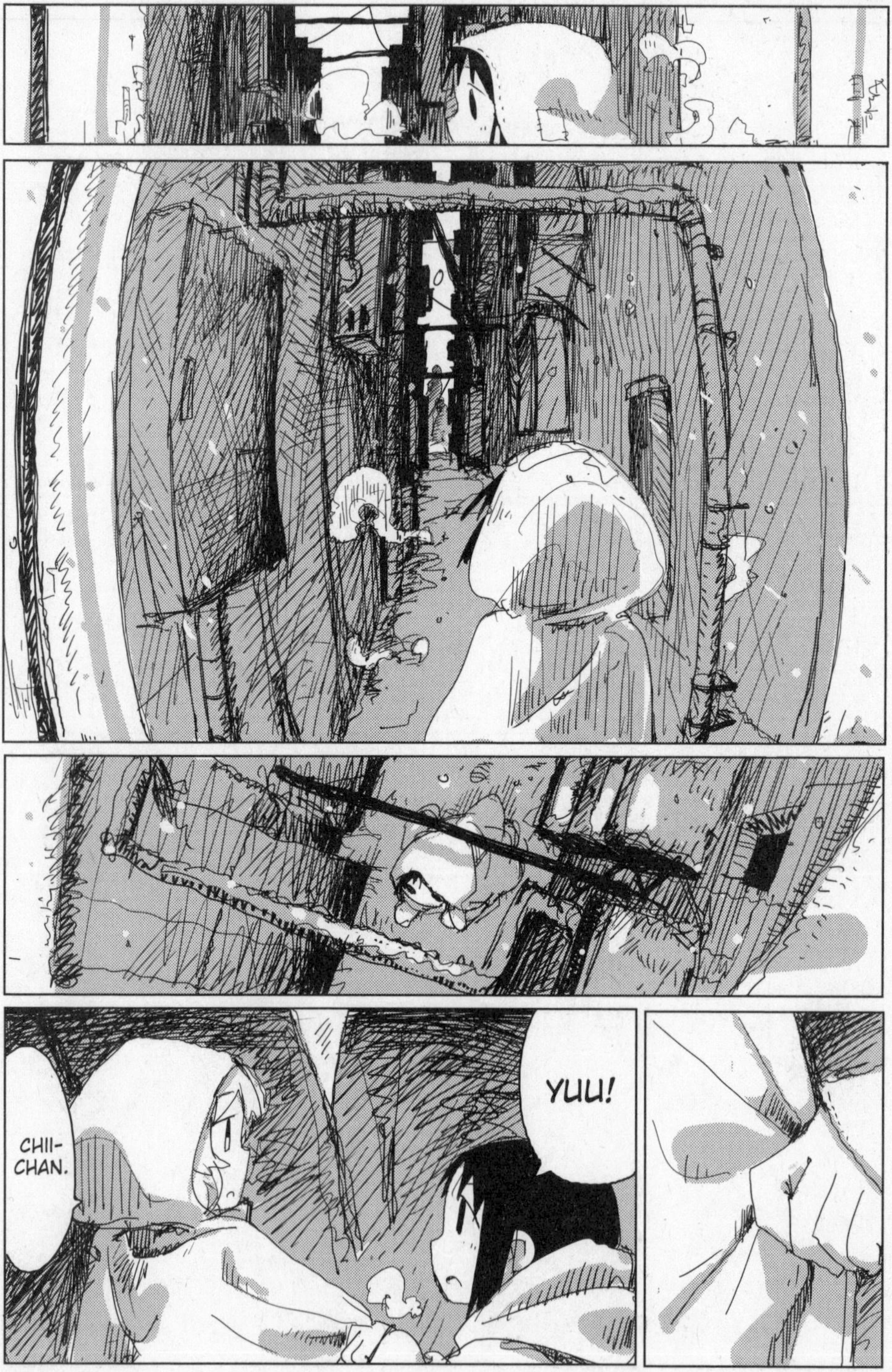
YUU!
CHII-CHAN.

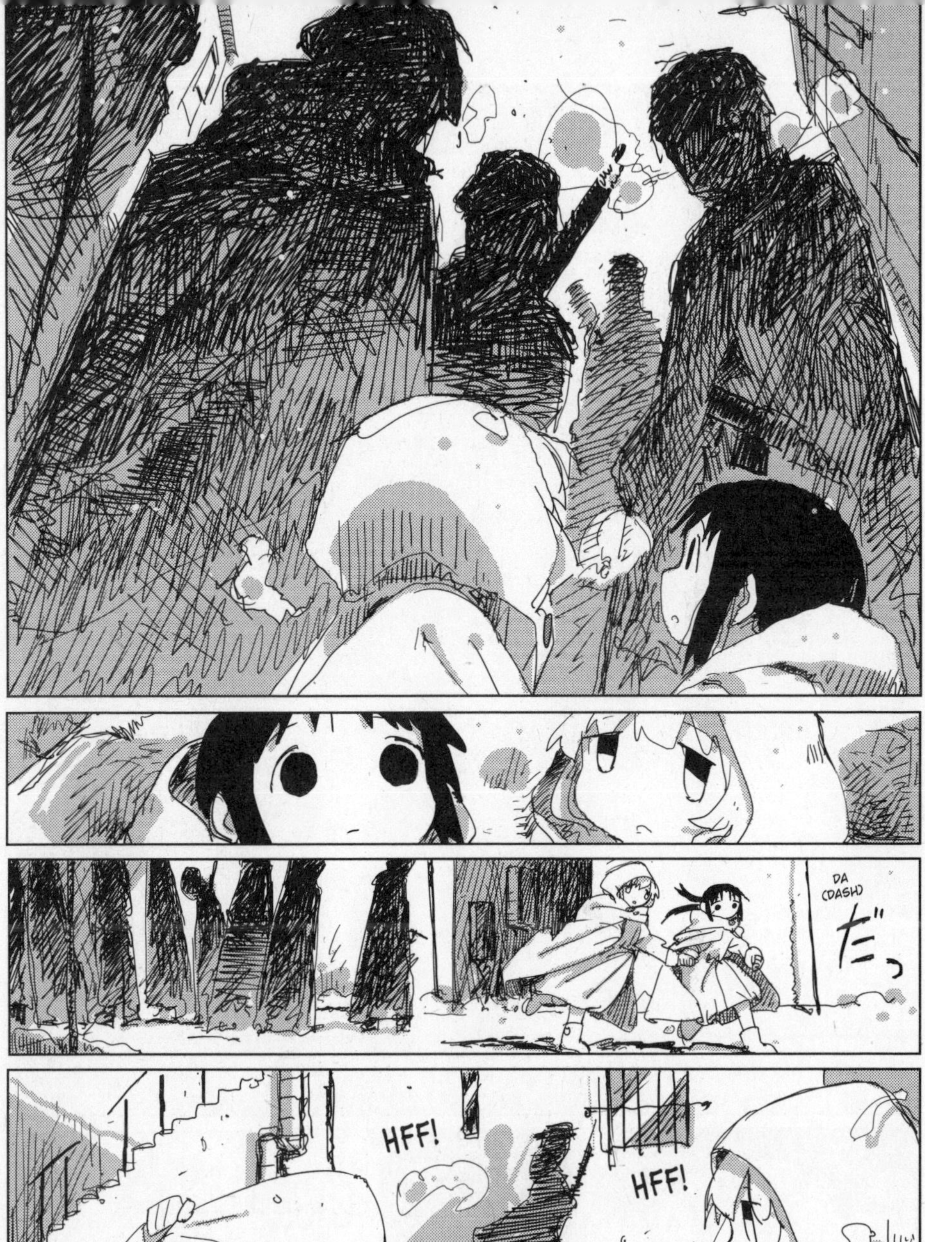
DA
(DASH)
だっ
HFF!
HFF!

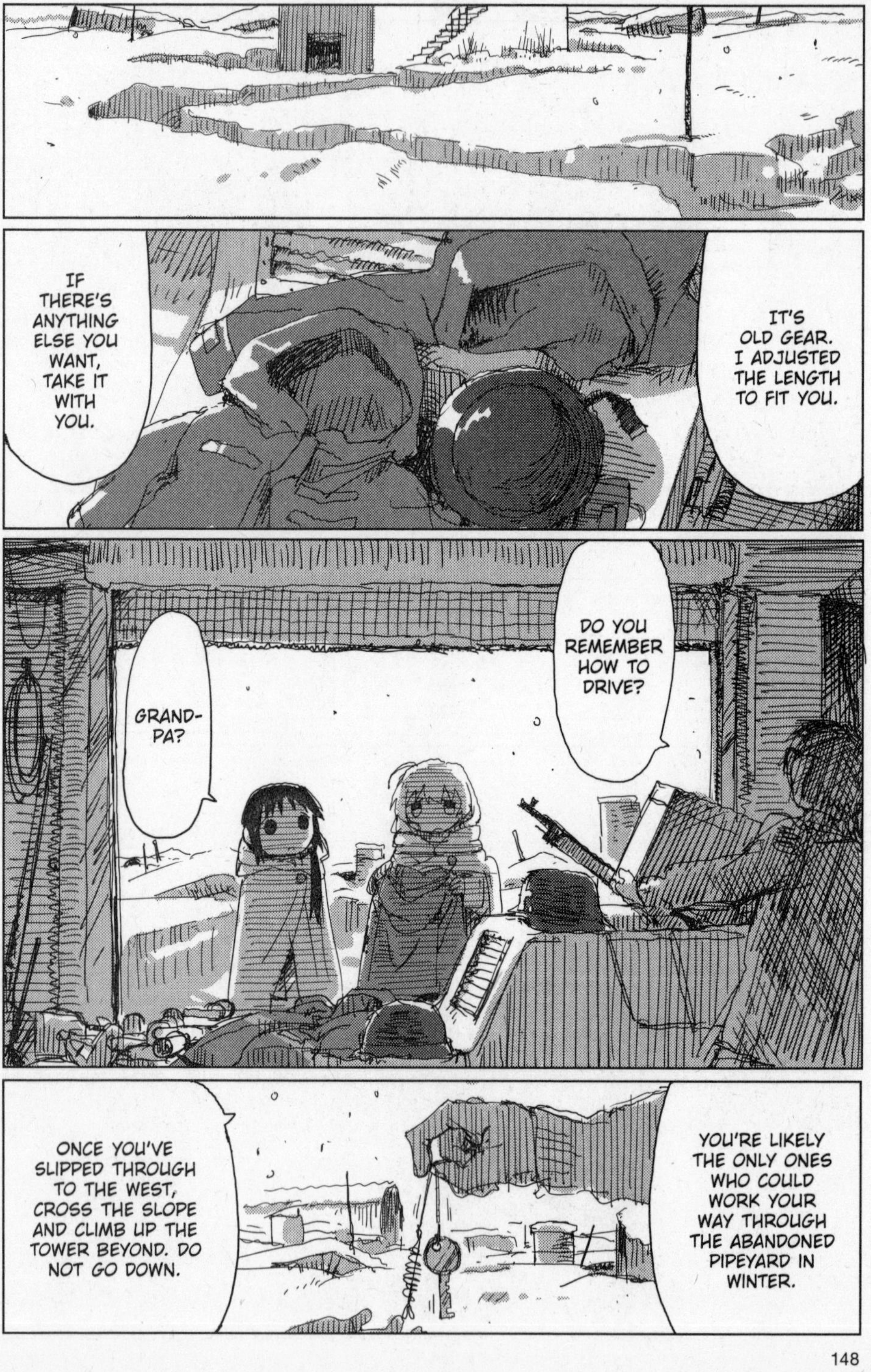
IT'S OLD GEAR. I ADJUSTED THE LENGTH TO FIT YOU.
IF THERE'S ANYTHING ELSE YOU WANT, TAKE IT WITH YOU.
DO YOU REMEMBER HOW TO DRIVE?
GRAND-PA?
YOU'RE LIKELY THE ONLY ONES WHO COULD WORK YOUR WAY THROUGH THE ABANDONED PIPEYARD IN WINTER.
ONCE YOU'VE SLIPPED THROUGH TO THE WEST, CROSS THE SLOPE AND CLIMB UP THE TOWER BEYOND. DO NOT GO DOWN.

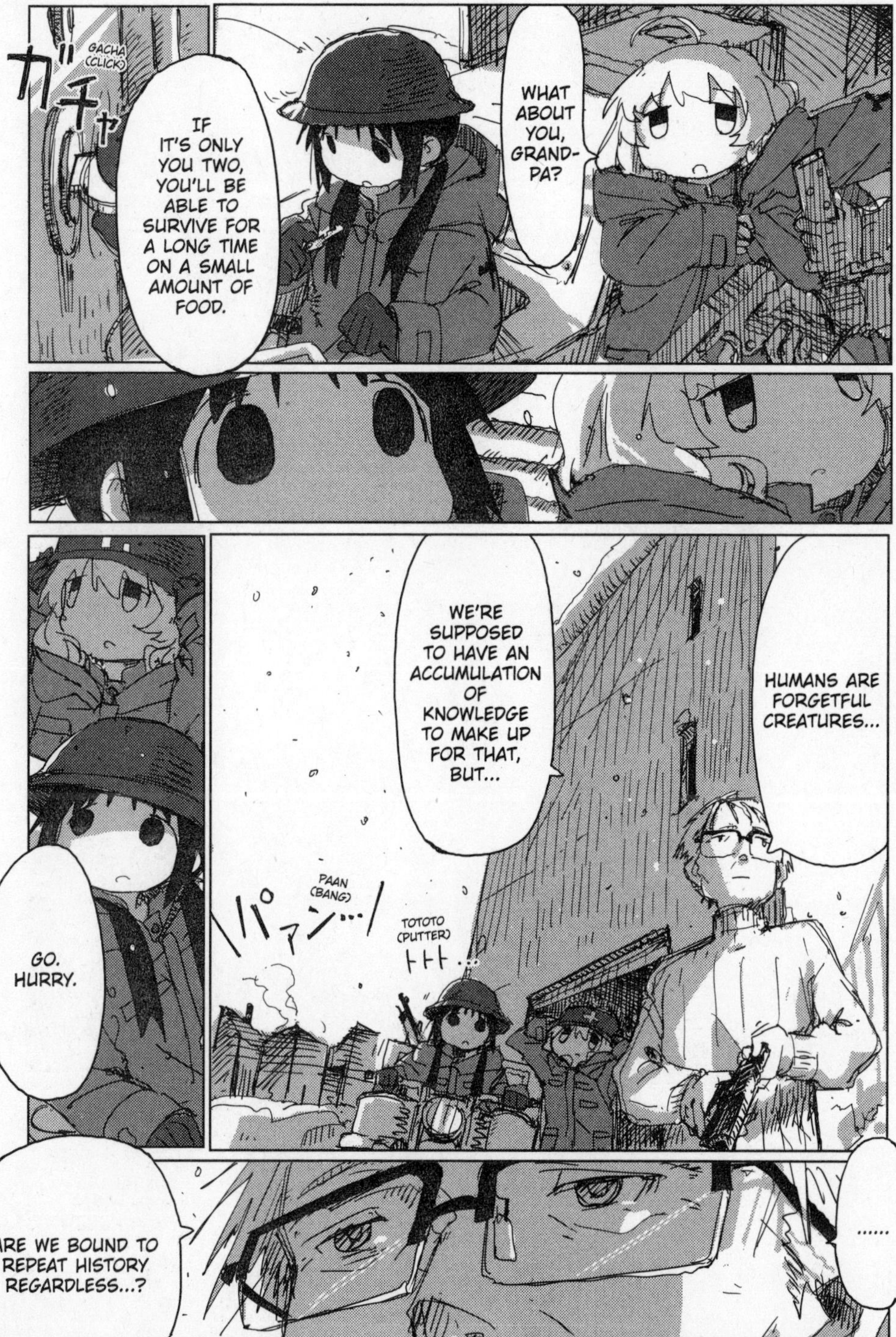
WHAT ABOUT YOU, GRANDPA?
IF IT'S ONLY YOU TWO, YOU'LL BE ABLE TO SURVIVE FOR A LONG TIME ON A SMALL AMOUNT OF FOOD.
GACHA (CLICK)
HUMANS ARE FORGETFUL CREATURES...
WE'RE SUPPOSED TO HAVE AN ACCUMULATION OF KNOWLEDGE TO MAKE UP FOR THAT, BUT...
PAAN (BANG)
TOTOTO (PUTTER)
GO. HURRY.
......
ARE WE BOUND TO REPEAT HISTORY REGARDLESS...?

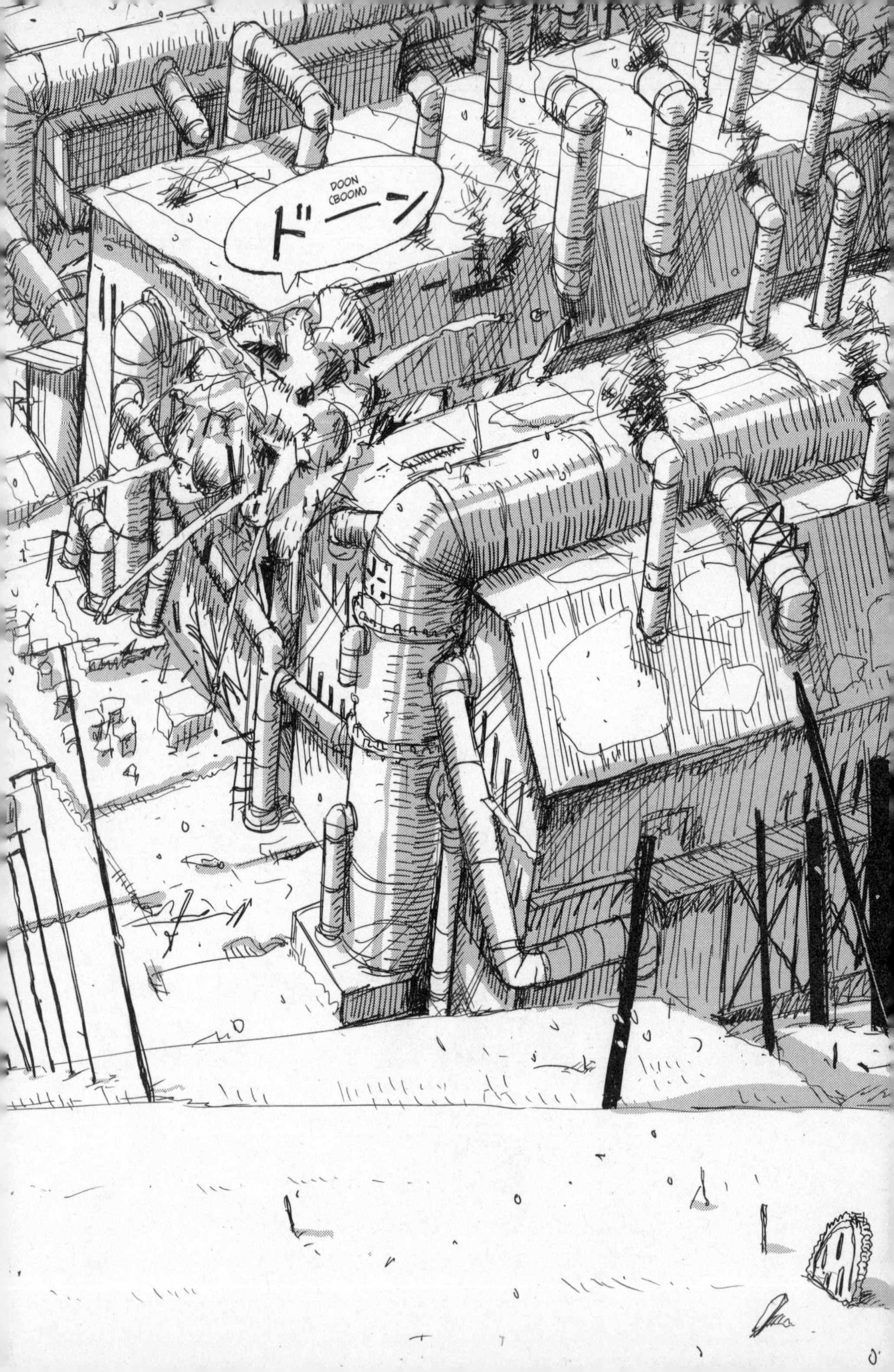
DOON
(BOOM)
ドーン

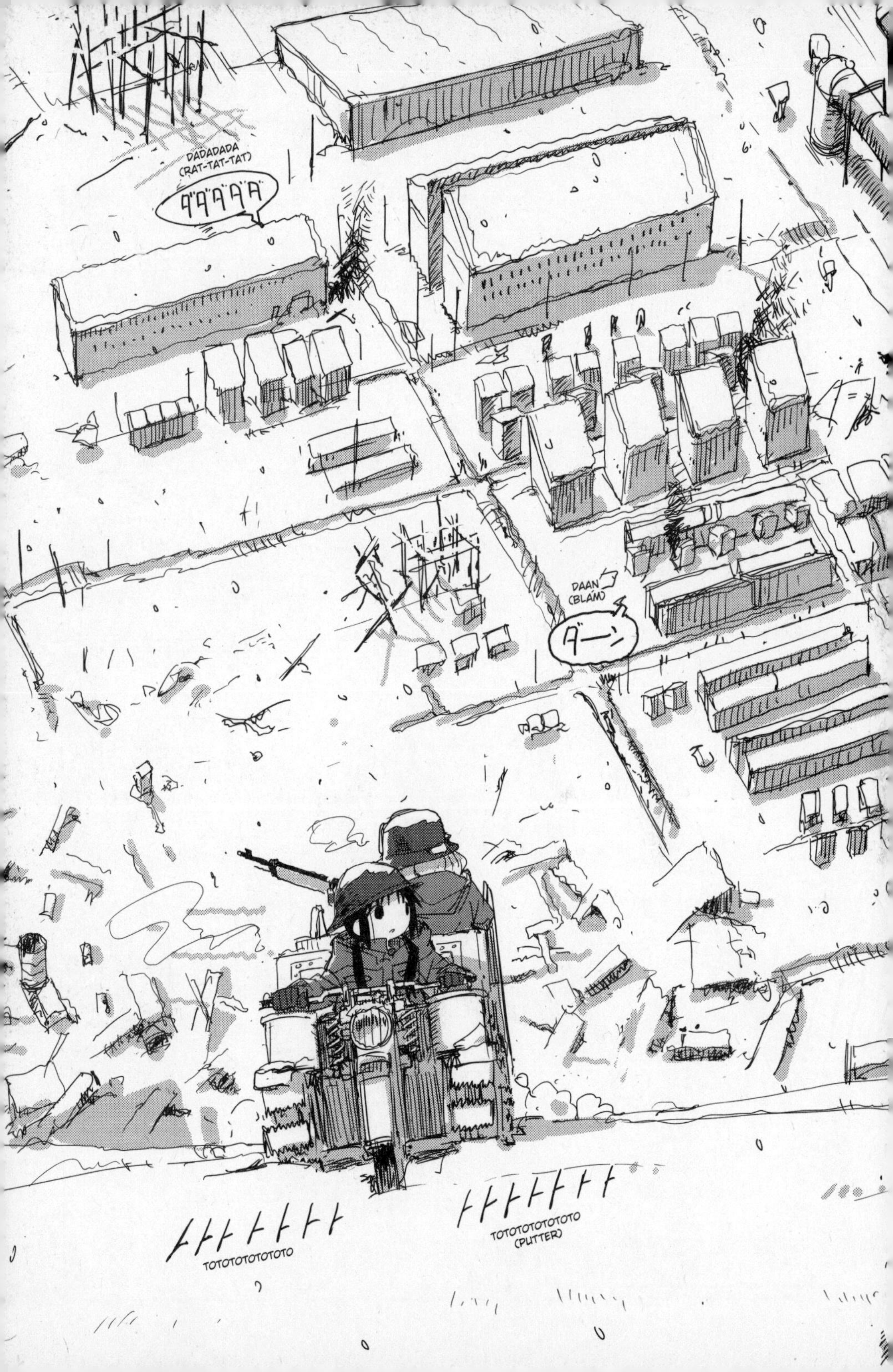
ダダダダダ
DADADADA
(RAT-TAT-TAT)
ダーン
DAAN
(BLAM)
トトトトトトト
TOTOTOTOTOTOTO
(PUTTER)
トトトトトトト
TOTOTOTOTOTOTO

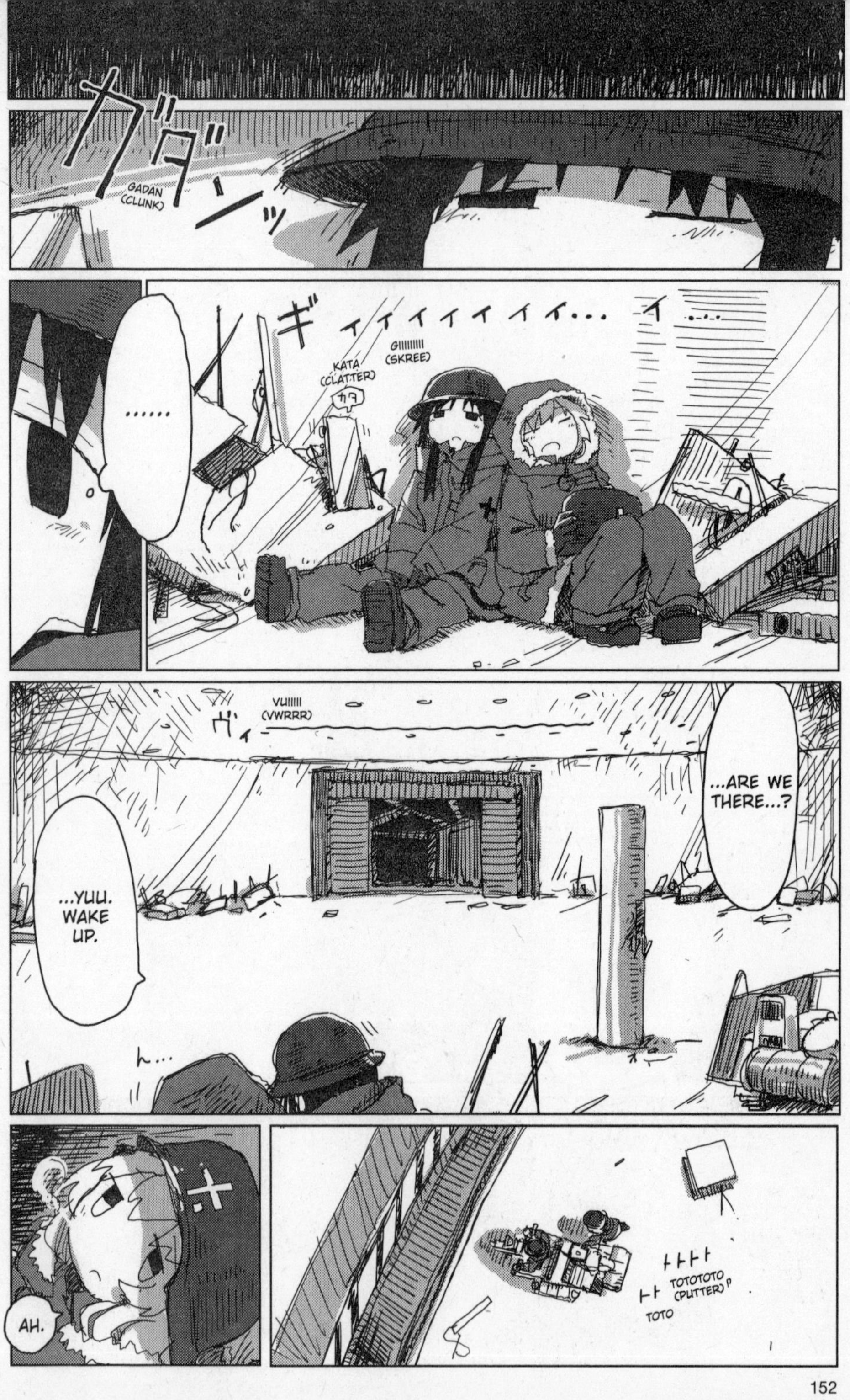
ガダーッ
GADAN (CLUNK)
ギィィィィィィ… ィ
GIIIIIII (SKREE)
カタ
KATA (CLATTER)
......
ヴィー
VUIIIII (VWRRR)
...ARE WE THERE...?
...YUU. WAKE UP.
ん…
トトトト
TOTOTOTO (PUTTER)
トト
TOTO
AH.

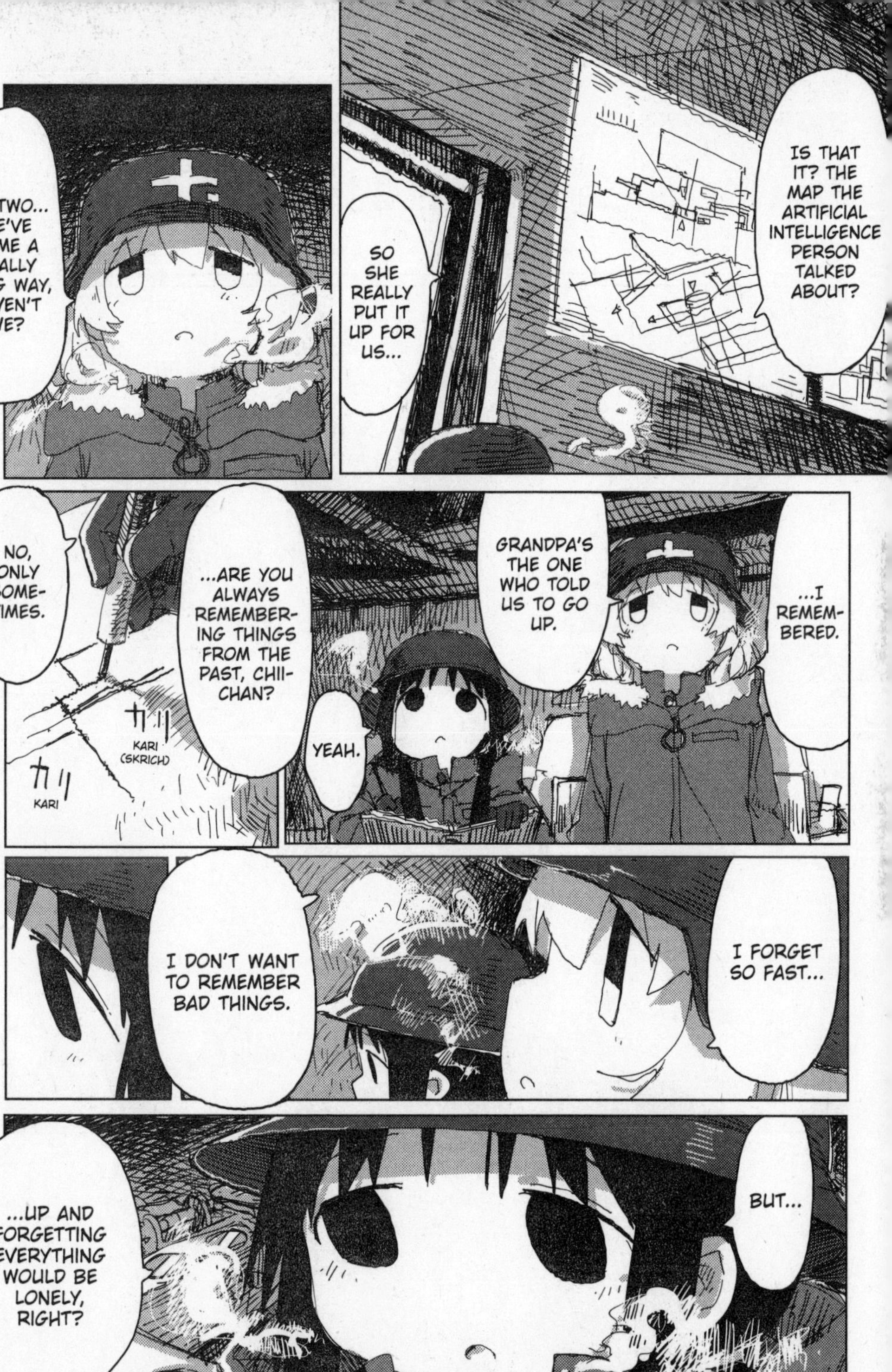
IS THAT IT? THE MAP THE ARTIFICIAL INTELLIGENCE PERSON TALKED ABOUT?
SO SHE REALLY PUT IT UP FOR US...
WE TWO... WE'VE COME A REALLY LONG WAY, HAVEN'T WE?
...I REMEMBERED.
GRANDPA'S THE ONE WHO TOLD US TO GO UP.
YEAH.
...ARE YOU ALWAYS REMEMBERING THINGS FROM THE PAST, CHII-CHAN?
NO, ONLY SOME-TIMES.
カリ
KARI (SKRICH)
カリ
KARI
I FORGET SO FAST...
I DON'T WANT TO REMEMBER BAD THINGS.
BUT...
...UP AND FORGETTING EVERYTHING WOULD BE LONELY, RIGHT?

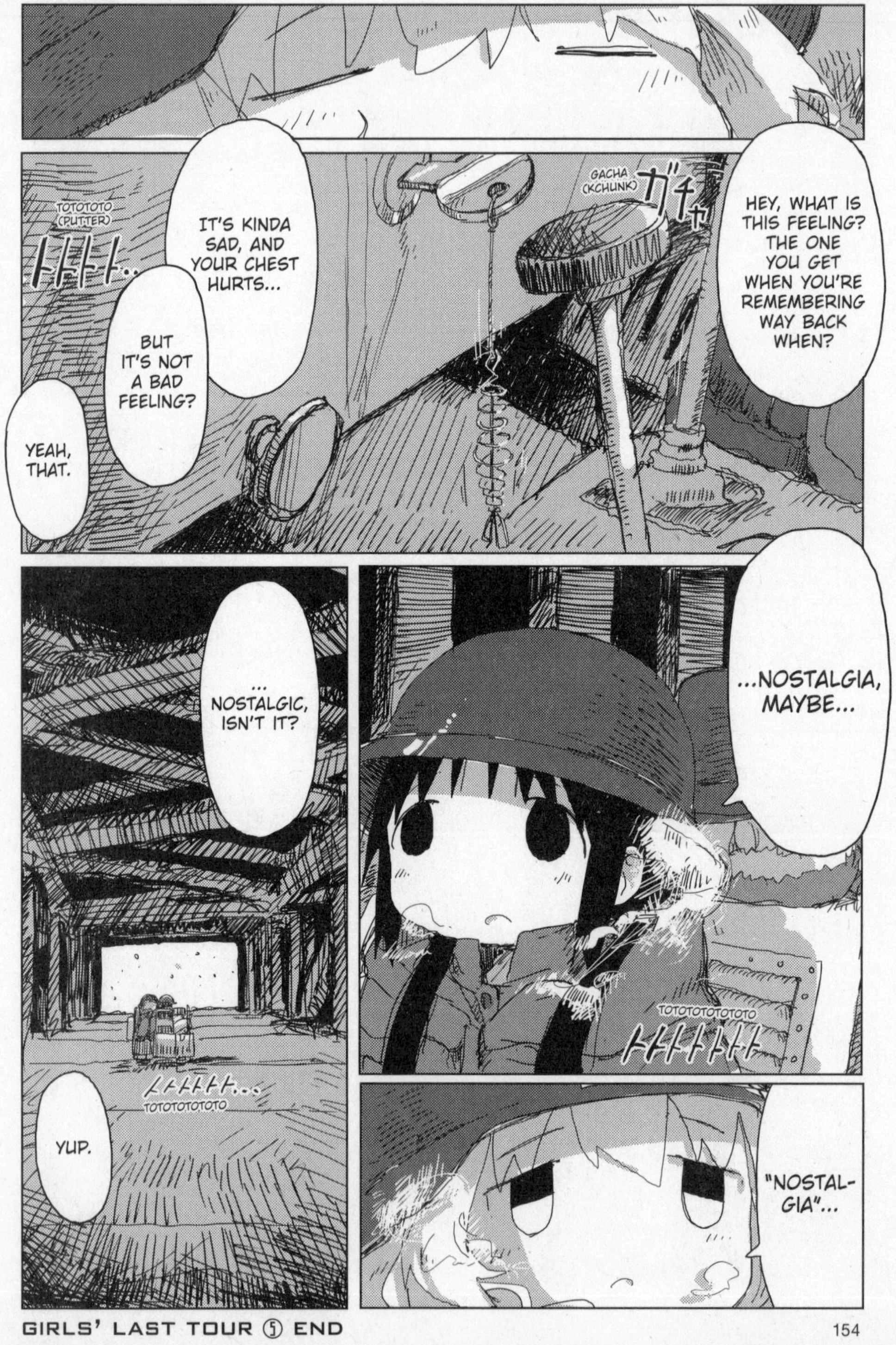
HEY, WHAT IS THIS FEELING? THE ONE YOU GET WHEN YOU'RE REMEMBERING WAY BACK WHEN?
ガチャ
GACHA (KCHUNK)
IT'S KINDA SAD, AND YOUR CHEST HURTS...
TOTOTOTO (PUTTER)
BUT IT'S NOT A BAD FEELING?
YEAH, THAT.
...NOSTALGIA, MAYBE...
TOTOTOTOTOTOTO
"NOSTAL-GIA"...
... NOSTALGIC, ISN'T IT?
TOTOTOTOTOTO
YUP.

I WISH
THOSE GIRLS
HAPPINESS.

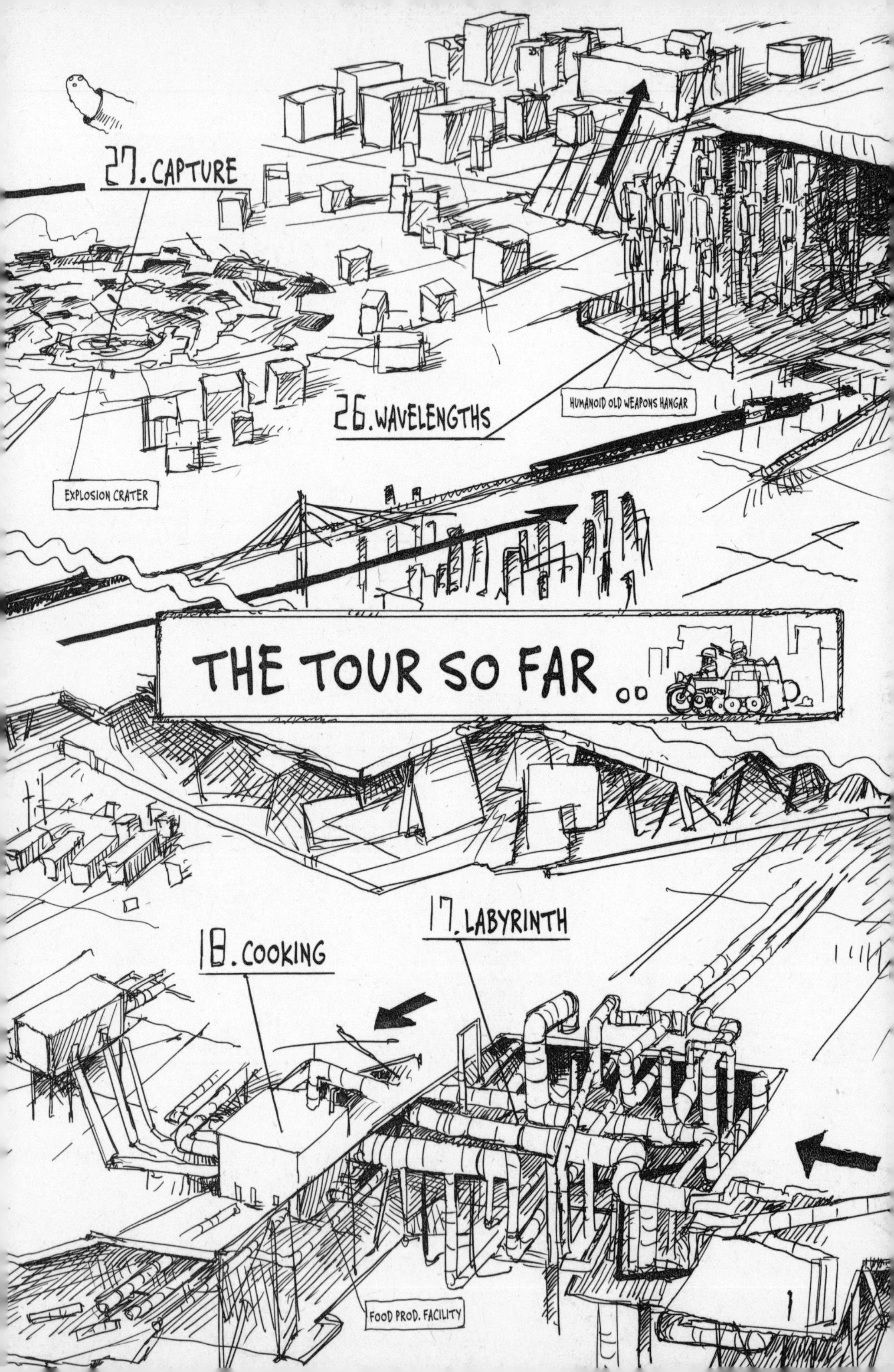
27. CAPTURE
EXPLOSION CRATER
HUMANOID OLD WEAPONS HANGAR
26. WAVELENGTHS
THE TOUR SO FAR ..
17. LABYRINTH
18. COOKING
FOOD PROD. FACILITY

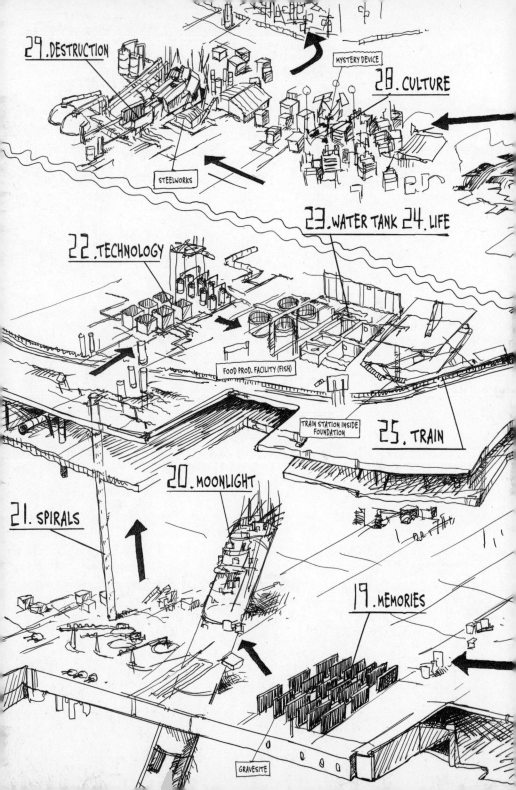

29. DESTRUCTION

MYSTERY DEVICE

28. CULTURE

STEELWORKS

23. WATER TANK 24. LIFE

22. TECHNOLOGY

FOOD PROD. FACILITY (FISH)

TRAIN STATION INSIDE FOUNDATION

25. TRAIN

20. MOONLIGHT

21. SPIRALS

19. MEMORIES

GRAVESITE

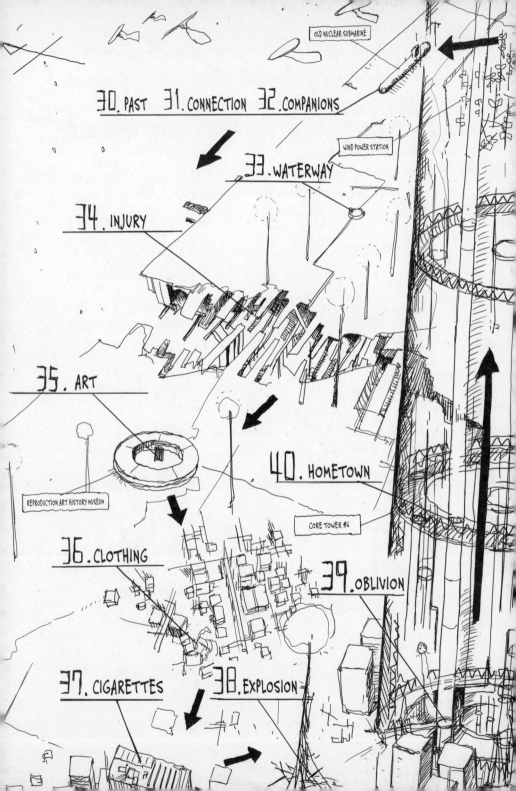

OLD NUCLEAR SUBMARINE

30. PAST 31. CONNECTION 32. COMPANIONS

WIND POWER STATION

33. WATERWAY

34. INJURY

35. ART

REPRODUCTION ART HISTORY MUSEUM

40. HOMETOWN

CORE TOWER #6

36. CLOTHING

39. OBLIVION

37. CIGARETTES 38. EXPLOSION